Contents

Acknowledgements

We would like to acknowledge the Economic and Social Research Council for funding the study on which this book is based, 'Parenting and step-parenting after divorce/separation: issues and negotiations', under grant number R000236288. There are also a number of colleagues whom we would like to thank for their support, advice, discussion and debate over the course of the empirical research and the writing of this book. In particular, we are grateful for the input of our advisory group: Linda Bell, Julia Brannen, Dorit Braun and David Morgan. Other people who have been important in developing our ideas include: Margareta Bäck-Wiklund, Maren Bak, Graham Crow, Catherine Donovan, Simon Duncan, Brian Heaphy, Janet Holland, Ann-Magrit Jensen and Jeffrey Weeks. We would also like to acknowledge Sue Kirkpatrick's contribution, supporting us in further analytic work in the early stages of writing this book. Any deficiencies in our ideas or arguments, however, should be laid at our door. Finally, we are grateful to the parents, step-parents and children who took part in our research, for sharing their lives and feelings with us. We hope that we have presented these 'fairly', in all senses of the word.

Chapter 1
Constructing (step-)families: continuity or difference?

> 'It's a word,' Josie said to the still children. 'Family is a word. So is step-family. Step-family is a word in the dictionary too whether you like it or not. And it's not just a word, it's a fact and it's a fact that we all are now, whether you like that or not, either.'
> (Joanna Trollope, *Other People's Children*, 1998: 84)

Families are widely discussed in Western societies as breaking down or as radically changing, with both policy-makers and people generally struggling to make sense of these shifts. How we chart a map of these changes, however, is highly contestable. Josie, the step-mother in Joanna Trollope's novel quoted above, indicates one of the contours that may be drawn on these new (or maybe not so new) maps: that between 'ordinary' nuclear families and step-families.

So, is step-family a word that represents relationships and preoccupations that are inherently distinct from those of 'ordinary' family life, and that people have to deal with whether they like it or not? This book addresses these issues, beginning from the stance that looking at step-families can tell us something significant about family life and parenting generally. We regard step-families as a form of critical case study. On the one hand, they can be seen as representing the forefront of family and lifestyle change. From this point of view, their potential placement outside of the 'conventional' can reveal the typical itself through contrast, as well as providing knowledge about differences. On the other hand, diversity of family forms may not necessarily mean diversity of family lifestyles: people in step-families may be drawing on images and meanings of 'ordinary' family in how they create and understand their lives together. Either way, as Jacqueline Burgoyne (1987) observed, step-families throw light on broader assumptions and values concerning families. They highlight fundamental issues in family life and parenting that people may want to re/create and/or dis/continue under changing circumstances, as well as those that they may feel their situation precludes.

Literature addressing step-families, however, can often focus around, or take for granted, differences from 'normal' family life, rather than exploring similarities or overlaps. In this introductory chapter we will look at how step-families are constructed in various commentaries on contemporary family life, legal discourses and literature on step-families and parenting, raising key tensions around continuity and difference that run throughout this book.

Works of fiction may also treat step-families as a fundamentally different kind of environment in which to bring up children. Joanna Trollope's *Other People's Children*, an acclaimed novel about middle-class step-family life, paints a picture of inherent tensions and resentments. The members of the step-family at the centre of the book experience complex and tumultuous emotions as Josie and Matthew begin married life together, each with children from a previous marriage, in one household. Initially the adults involved do not want, cannot love, and cannot find a way to establish a relationship with 'other people's children'. Sometimes they are too self-absorbed in problems even to notice the suffering inflicted on their own children, who are made miserable and angry as their lives are disrupted by new schools, new homes and new parents. While Josie's ex-husband keeps his distance, Matthew's ex-wife is bitter and determined to undermine her children's relationship with their father and prevent one developing with their step-mother. Adults and children quickly reach breaking point, and step-family life becomes a fraught and bleak existence. At the height of crisis, however, people pull back from the brink. Allegiances and loyalties begin to form. Connections are being made, they are beginning to 'fit together' and find a common purpose:

> 'Maybe,' [Josie] said, 'we've got a sort of chance now. Maybe we could start, well, mending things after all that breaking. If – if we stopped being afraid of being a step-family, that is.' She folded her right hand over her wedding ring. 'I know I'm not your mother. I never will be. You've got a mother. But I could be your friend, I could be your supporter, your sponsor. Couldn't I? Sometimes hard things turn out better because you've had to make an effort to overcome them.' She stopped. 'Sorry,' she said. 'I don't want to lecture you.' She took her hands off the table and put them in her lap. 'I really just want to say that we may be a different kind of family, but we don't have to be worse. Do we?'
> (Trollope, 1998: 277)

Trollope's story raises a number of pertinent questions. What does it mean to 'be a family'? Do people in step-families see themselves as making a different kind of family? Is individual happiness in a couple relationship prioritised at the expense of responsibilities towards children? Can a step-parent ever be regarded as the same as a biological mother or father? What do people in step-families do to try to make step-family life work? It is these and similar issues that this book seeks to explore. It is concerned with how biological and step-parents themselves make sense of parenting, both within and between households, and within the wider social context. It looks at how people create, understand and experience their parenting and family lives. It reveals how these understandings are rooted in a strong moral sense of responsibility, but that what such responsibility constitutes varies according to gender and social class. In this focus, then, the book goes to the heart of academic, political and popular debates, and professional concerns, about the nature of contemporary family life and parenting.

Making families: forms, norms and guidelines

Somewhat surprisingly, given the concerns we discuss below regarding children involved in family breakdown and re-partnering, this book is one of the first British in-depth sociological research studies that focuses on parents' and step-parents' own understandings and experiences of their parenting in step-families since Jacqueline Burgoyne and David Clark's (1984) classic study.[1] Conducting their fieldwork in the late 1970s, Burgoyne and Clark found that most of their interviewees drew on and were committed to nuclear family norms. Some thought of themselves as just an 'ordinary' family, especially where they and the children in the step-family were young and/or they had been together for some time. Others consciously attempted to create an 'ordinary' family life for children, by adopting as fully as possible a 'normal' mother or father 'role', and with step-fathers partly or wholly transferring their allegiances from any non-resident biological children. Some of their interviewees' attempts to create an 'ordinary' family life were undermined and the autonomy of their family routines disrupted, especially by continuing contact and conflict with the non-resident parent. In other cases, when children were nearly adult and parents themselves were older, the parent and step-parent focused on their couple relationship, because they saw attempting to create an 'ordinary' family as problematic.

According to this aspect of Burgoyne and Clark's findings, it would seem that a generation or so ago parents and step-parents largely did not see themselves as attempting to create a different kind of family, but just family. Indeed, a self-help book for step-parents published around the same time (Atkinson, 1986) advises that joining a family unit is like a skin graft that has to 'take', eventually becoming indistinguishable from a 'normal' family. There is little indication in Burgoyne and Clark's discussion that parents or step-parents could not or did not regard step-mothers or step-fathers as acting or feeling the same as a biological mother or father. Indeed, the step-parent was often regarded as providing children with the 'second' parent that they needed in their day-to-day life within the step-family household. Whether or not they had the ability to do so, most of their interviewees felt that the best thing to do was to 'reconstitute' (to use Burgoyne and Clark's term) an 'ordinary' family life, because this was regarded as a 'good, natural and wholesome' environment in which to bring up children. For some, this was also driven by a concern for the respectability, reputation and good-standing of their (step-)family, a view particularly held by working-class interviewees.

There was another, minority, group of Burgoyne and Clark's interviewees, however: the 'progressive' step-families as they term them. Here, parent and step-parent did not articulate images of conventional family in their accounts. Rather, the image they drew on was one of diversity of patterns in family and domestic life, with people concerned with 'personal growth', depicting themselves as making choices and asserting a positive value to their difference from 'ordinary' families. Such parents sometimes posed having a new, joint, child within their family as important because they saw blood ties as significant. Burgoyne and Clark argued that it was couples who were assured in their social position and material circumstances who could afford to ignore pervasive public moralities stressing the normality and desirability of conventional family, and indicated that most of the couples drawing on 'progressive' step-family images were middle class.

Burgoyne and Clark (1984: 204) seem to point towards the 'progressive' version of step-family life as the way forward, when they conclude overall that:

> *'Making a go of it' involves recognising the 'historical changes' and, on occasion, challenging the institutional contradictions which bear most heavily upon remarried parents and their children.*

Indeed, there are arguments that the 'progressive' acknowledgement of diversity in family forms and lifestyles has itself become the contemporary norm (e.g. Boh, 1989), as reflected in statistical trends.[2]

Diversity or continuity?

The statistical presentation of trends in family forms and household types can be emphasised in different ways to construct particular arguments about the state of contemporary family life (for reviews and analyses of some of the evidence see Fox Harding, 1996; Robertson Elliot, 1996; McRae, 1999). Administrative boundaries are drawn around, and definitions constructed for, categories of family and household. These categories are regarded as socially significant, and understood as 'different' from, and contrasted with, each other. Such constructions then have important consequences for how we perceive the state of family life in contemporary society, and for the social policies that are developed in order to deal with this administratively defined situation.

Between the early 1970s and the late 1990s, the number of first marriages in the UK fell by two-fifths, while remarriages accounted for over one third of all marriages. During the same period the number of divorces more than doubled, lone motherhood almost doubled and births outside marriage trebled. Cohabitation has become a routine mode of partnership for many, and of parenting, but cohabiting parents are twice as likely to separate than married parents (Office of National Statistics, 1998; Haskey, 1999; Ermisch and Francesconi, 2000). There has also been a significant increase in step-families, although definitional problems around whether the statistical framework should be 'household-' or 'family-' based mean that data on this is not comprehensive (for example, a child might be defined as living in a lone-mother household, but still have experience of involvement in a step-family through the non-resident father's re-partnering). Nevertheless it has been estimated that around one in eight children live in a household with a step-parent for at least some period of time (Haskey, 1994). While there are no figures for non-heterosexual partnerships, some of which will involve children living in gay or lesbian step-families, awareness of and openness about their existence increased during this period (Weeks et al., 2001). Further complicating matters is the fact that some of these trends in the diversity of family forms and structures are more evident in some ethnic groups than in others (Heath and Dale, 1994).

Yet the other side of the coin of these figures about trends towards discontinuity in family forms is that there is also considerable continuity. In the late 1990s, just under three-quarters of households were still composed of a heterosexual couple. Forty per cent of people lived in a family comprising a couple with dependent children, with two-thirds of these couples being married (Office of National Statistics, 1998). Over three-quarters of dependent children in their mid-teens were living together with their biological parents (Haskey, 1997). If one in eight children have been estimated to live in a household with a step-parent for at least some period of time, even if this is a conservative estimate, the majority of children still do not.

Social theorists and commentators often highlight the discontinuity that can be discerned in statistical trends, emphasising family forms and household structures as a facet of the growing impact of the processes of individualisation and democratisation on family life in the UK and elsewhere in the last quarter of the twentieth century (see Allan and Crow, 2001; Crow, 2002b). They point to the way that marriage, sex, childbearing and childrearing have become unhooked. While some commentators regard these changing trends in family forms as a 'breakdown' of the family and see them as bringing social and moral disorder in their wake (e.g. Murray, 1990; Davies, 1993; Dennis and Erdos, 1993; Phillips, 1999), others argue that they have gone too far for a return to the traditional one-marriage nuclear family pattern to be possible, and are more positive about the implications of this:

> *If this diagnosis* [that the nuclear family is falling apart] *is right, what will take over from the family, that haven of domestic bliss? The family, of course! Only different, more, better: the negotiated family, the alternating family, the multiple family, new arrangements after divorce, remarriage, divorce again, new assortments from your, my, our children, our past and present families.*
> (Beck and Beck-Gernsheim, 1995: 2)

Indeed, sociologists and other writers increasingly refer to 'families' rather than 'the family' in discussing the topic (e.g. Berger and Berger, 1983; Denzin, 1987; Cheal, 1993).

Individualisation and democratisation?

For ill or good, though, there is some consensus about the root of structural family change: individualisation. Ideas about individualisation highlight the way that people have been freed from traditional moral obligations and standard pathways, and have greater choices in family form and lifestyle. Previously taken-for-granted ideas about forms of family life and shared norms have fragmented and been replaced by more individualistic responses to lifestyle construction (Cheal, 1991), leaving contemporary family relationships as 'undecided' (Stacey, 1990), 'unclear' rather than 'nuclear' (Simpson, 1998), more 'fluid' and less 'solid' (Bauman, 2000). People are now reflexive authors of their own biographies, rather than following structurally predetermined pathways (Giddens, 1992). They are able to create their own identities, social networks, commitments and moral values (Weeks *et al.*, 2001).

Ulrich Beck and Elisabeth Beck-Gernsheim (1995) claim that romantic love is being accorded an overwhelming significance as the moral guideline for relationships and new family ties, and Beck-Gernsheim (1998) has elaborated on this to argue that a 'post-familial' family is emerging. Traditional family relationships were built around a 'community of need', comprising unquestioned ties of obligation and permanence. In contrast, contemporary everyday family relationships are increasingly characterised by 'elective affinities', whereby people are charting and negotiating their own personally chosen togetherness. Similarly, Anthony Giddens (1992) has argued that people are pursuing 'pure relationships' based on contingent 'confluent love'.

'Elective affinities' and 'pure relationships' are not necessarily founded on notions of long-term and absolute commitment, but are continued only in so far as both parties feel that the relationship delivers enough emotional and intrinsic satisfaction for each individual to stay within it. As women are increasingly entering the labour market, and no longer materially dependent on husbands, so the structural framing of heterosexual partnership has changed. Furthermore, kin obligations are no longer completely normatively determined, but are negotiated in a variety of ways, emerging over time within changing networks of family relationships and moral responsibilities (Finch and Mason, 1993; Smart and Neale, 1999). Thus the moral parameters of family life are said to have changed radically, focusing more around individual choices and rewards rather than predefined familial obligation. Under these circumstances, people in families have to search for and create their own 'meaningful realities', rather than having these provided for them by tradition and convention – they are part of what Judith Stacey (1990) terms 'brave new families', entering a relational world of experiment and invention.

The emphasis on individualisation as an experimental and growing feature of family relationships has been challenged as ethnocentric, however. In particular, Harry Goulbourne and Mary Chamberlain (1998) have argued that individualisation has long been a feature of African-Caribbean traditions of family and community. Affinal relationships are seen as subject to choice, negotiation and re-evaluation of belongingness and obligations, although blood lineage relations are not (see also Beishon et al., 1998). From this perspective, it may be that contemporary White family life is following long-standing Black family norms, rather than carving out a new path.

Linked to ideas about the impact of individualisation on family life is the notion that it has become 'democratised' (Beck, 1997). Giddens, (1992, 1998) in particular, argues that contemporary family life is – and indeed has to be if it is to work – becoming characterised by values of communication, autonomy, equality and mutual respect. Within democratised family life there is a requirement for flexibility, adaptability and negotiation. For Giddens, this applies not just to adults but also to children, who also should be part of the democratic management of family life. They should be treated as 'the putative equal of the adult' (Giddens, 1992: 191) based on how 'the child' would legitimate parental authority if she or he had access to adult knowledge. Within a context of family change and diversity, Giddens sees co-parenting of children after divorce or separation as the way forward because (biological) parents have lifetime responsibilities that do not end when the relationship that begat them does (Giddens, 1998). Children need to be shielded from the full effects of increasing individualisation, when parents focus on themselves and contingent pure relationships.

Graham Crow (2002b: 60) suggests that 'Step-family relationships occupy a pivotal position in the debates generated by theorists of individualisation, and as such deserve exploration in some detail.' Indeed, ideas about individualisation and democratisation lead us to expect that people in contemporary step-families will be drawing on and working towards rather different and more diverse images of family life than the majority of those in Burgoyne and Clark's sample in the late 1970s. Their attempts at making families will not be shaped by trying to become *the* 'ordinary' family within the household unit, because this is no longer the dominant norm and, indeed, is not regarded as desirable for the children involved. Nor will they be adhering to a unitary notion of 'the step-family'. They will be a loose-knit assemblage of individuals creating their own moral guidelines for relationships of responsibility and care, in which they will be considering some people to be some sort of 'family' relations, and there will be complex negotiations around family and across household boundaries. Indeed, it is perhaps this sort of perspective on family life that led to the National Stepfamily Association, which was set up around the time Burgoyne and Clark's study was published and focused on one distinct family form, to be incorporated into the diversity-encompassing Parentline Plus UK organisation in the late 1990s.

Views of individualisation and democratisation as fundamentally shaping contemporary family lifestyles have been challenged, however. For example, Graham Crow (2002b) has argued that there was far more fluidity and diversity in people's family understandings and behaviours historically than is often recognised, and there is still adherence to longstanding family values and norms in contemporary society. Furthermore, he also points to more structural constraints, linked to social class, gender, age, ethnicity and so on, as still important in shaping people's family lives. Indeed, ideas about individualisation in family life have been criticised because they obscure key social aspects of mothers' and children's experiences, and only address a particular version of individuality (Ribbens McCarthy and Edwards, 2002).

In the course of a wide-ranging survey of literature on the topic, Lynn Jamieson (1998) concludes that individualisation and democratisation arguments are difficult to sustain as a depiction of either the current state of family relationships or the direction in which such relationships are moving. Adult couple relationships are about other things than confluent love, and parent–child relationships encompass a greater span of activities, experiences and images than democratic intimacy (see also Smart, 1997; Sevenhuijsen, 1998, 2000). Studies of young people's views of their family lives also point to a continuing sense of responsibility and obligation towards, and connection with, other family members (Holland et al., 1999). Other empirical work shows that the moral commitment to 'putting the family first' and foregoing individual self-interest still has a strong hold (e.g. Jordan et al., 1994). Arguments that individualisation is central to African-Caribbean traditions of family life (noted earlier) have also been questioned (Reynolds, 2002).

Some social theorists who argue that contemporary families have to create their own lifestyles acknowledge such critiques to some extent when they note that individualisation processes can prompt longings for a return to the security of apparently stable family norms (Beck and Beck-Gernsheim, 1995; Beck-Gernsheim, 1998; Stacey, 1990). In particular Beck and Beck-Gernsheim point to the significance of children in this:

> [The child] *promises a tie which is more elemental, profound and durable than any other in this society. The more other relationships become interchangeable and revocable, the more a child can become the focus of new hopes – it is the ultimate guarantee of permanence, providing an anchor for one's life.*
> (Beck and Beck-Gernsheim, 1995: 73)

Furthermore, Jeffrey Weeks and colleagues' depiction of non-heterosexual 'families of choice' (Weeks *et al.*, 2001) is tempered by the 'major exception' of their interviewees' acceptance of an absolute commitment to any children involved. There seems to be, then, an intertwining of continuity and diversity in contemporary family life (McRae, 1999; Silva and Smart, 1999).

These critiques and caveats mean that it does not necessarily follow that diversity of family forms means diversity in family lifestyles and moral guidelines. People in step-families may still be making families drawing on similar images on the cusp of the twenty-first century as they did in the late 1970s, and class, gender and other social divisions may well still be important in how they create and understand their parenting and step-family life.

Whether step-family members are working towards creating a nuclear family norm or negotiating amongst a diversity of images, they will be 'making' some set of relationships. Jon Bernardes (1997) has argued that family lives – of whatever form – are the product of everyday lived realities rather than a structure: families are 'made' or 'constructed'. Jaber Gubrium and James Holstein (1990) have focused on the ways in which family is as much a way of thinking and talking about relationships as it is a concrete set of social ties and sentiments, because family derives its meaningful reality through the process of dialogue and interaction. These notions resonate with the explicit concept of 'family practices' developed by David Morgan (1996, 1999). This term captures the idea that families are not structures or forms but 'practices'; that is, they are created through the process of individuals actually 'doing' everyday material, verbal and emotional activities, both positive and oppressive, and which may overlap with other practices, such as gendered practices, class practices and age practices. The concept conveys the importance of the perspectives of both the person carrying out the practice and those 'observing' (such as family members and friends, or politicians and professionals), as well as the location in culture, history and personal biography. It also carries a sense of ongoing and fluid routine action:

> If we compare the terms 'family structures' and 'family practices' ... [t]he former is static and carries a sense of something thing-like and concrete. Even if the idea of social structure need not have these characteristics there does appear to be a built-in tendency to conceive of it in this way. The latter carries with it a sense of doing and action.
> (Morgan, 1996: 189)

This book is concerned with these issues, with the (step-)family practices of parents and step-parents themselves in the context of the wider political, legal, professional and moral discourses around families and family life. In part, it is an assessment of the ways that these 'public' discourses may be drawn on, reframed or ignored in place of quite different 'private' understandings and projects by people involved in step-family life (see Ribbens McCarthy and Edwards, 2001, for broader discussion).

Legal discourses on family life

One of the most obvious ways in which public discourses affect step-family life is through family policy and law. In contrast with discussions about the trend towards diversity of family forms and lifestyles outlined above, Government policy statements promulgate the view that a married (and thus heterosexual) couple, who are the child's biological parents, is the best family form for bringing up children (see Home Office, 1998). Nevertheless, the law still has to deal with the consequences of divorce and separation. As we have discussed in detail elsewhere (Edwards *et al.*, 1999a), recent legislation in the UK, in the form of the Children Act 1989, the Child Support Act 1991, and the Family Law Act 1996, reflects the view that bringing up children is primarily a job for biological parents, and is a proactive attempt to redefine personal understandings of parenting and reshape boundaries around families. While marriage has become more freely interchangeable, terminable at will and non-exclusive, biological parenthood is being increasingly emphasised as an unchangeable, continuing relationship that is not generally terminable at will. In contrast, the legal position of step-parents is largely one of invisibility.[3] This is a position that Lynn Wardle (1993) refers to as 'legal schizophrenia'.

The State classifies and represents households through the collection and presentation of household statistics (noted earlier), and through the law. Social policy constructs administratively defined family boundaries that maintain a particular view of family relationships – what is involved in them, and how they should be conducted. The 1989 Children Act places a legislative boundary around parents and children from a first marriage, and militates against 'clean break' divorce. A central principle of the Act (reaffirmed under the Family Law Act 1996) concerns the continuing parental responsibility of married biological parents after divorce or separation, diffusing 'family' across households. There is now wide adherence to the view that the best interests of children are served by maintaining their relationship with both their parents after separation or divorce (Richards, 1999), unhooking family from household and prioritising biological parenting relationships over social ones in step-family situations. (This is despite the fact that reviews can conclude that the research evidence is equivocal about the need and benefit for children of continuing contact with their non-resident parent – see Maclean and Eekelaar, 1997; Gorell Barnes *et al.*, 1998.)

Other people in 'actual care' of a child, including step-parents, may be able to acquire parental responsibility through applying to the court for a residence order, but this responsibility only applies for the duration of the order and does not affect the rights or responsibilities of the non-resident parent. The fact that a court order that was created to settle disputes about where a child lives is central to step-parents' legal standing reflects the prevailing status of step-families as a legal non-entity. Step-parent adoption represents the only clear way of legally cordoning off a step-family household, and there is concern about excluding the non-resident biological parent through these means (Adoption Law Review, 1992).

The 1991 Child Support Act also actively attempted to reshape views concerning family responsibility, primarily by stressing the financial accountability of 'absent' fathers. It attempted to draw a tight boundary around biological parents and their children by forcing non-resident parents to contribute towards their child's upbringing. Generally creating much dissent, the actual practice of the Act was later (summer 2000) changed to take account of any new financial responsibilities a non-resident parent has towards step-children, as well as any subsequent children they may father (see Clarke and Roberts, 2002).

This shift in the operation of the child support legislation signals a partial return to at least some acknowledgement of social parenthood. As Mavis Maclean and John Eekelaar (1997) discuss, family law can be viewed as a field of interaction between legal and social rules. While policy has vacillated between grounding parental obligations on the social fact of the household and the biological fact of parenthood, prior to the Child Support Act 1991, magistrates' courts largely saw a father's obligations in terms of the children he lived with (i.e. household fact). The Child Support Act overrode this, and ignored social parenthood obligations in step-families. Maclean and Eekelaar's study showed, however, that fathers, rather than adhering to legal rules, related their obligations more to the status of social parenthood than to biology alone. This was in contrast to mothers, for whom social and biological parenthood are most likely to coincide. These considerations around the law's promotion of biological or social parenthood obligations have some resonance with our discussion below of the nature of fatherhood as ascribed or achieved – albeit the family law focus is on financial obligations through (biological or social) status rather than on the relationships through practice that are stressed in the fatherhood debate.

Legislation and policy provide an important administrative context for parents' and step-parents' experiences and step-family practices, largely cutting across any desire by such families to see themselves as 'ordinary' families. The findings of research into step-family life provide another potential shaping context, as these may filter into or reflect everyday popular understandings, including through informing 'self-help' literature.[4] As several authors point out, negative stereotypical images of step-parents' relationship to their step-children can be drawn on by parents, step-parents and step-children themselves (for example, Hughes, 1991; Nemenyi, 1992).

Children, parenting and step-parenting

Most of the literature on step-families stresses the complexity of the family forms and family life involved. As Graham Allan and Graham Crow (2001: 151) remark, 'typically, step-families are more complex organisations than natural [sic] families'. The complexities are posed both in terms of their demographic characteristics and relational dynamics. Demographically, within the generic term 'step-family', more detailed categorisations have been constructed based on criteria such as biological and/or step- parents' marital status and children's residence and access patterns. A total of 16 forms of step-family have been identified, derived from a classification of who in the step-family couple has birth children and which of these children reside with them (Batchelor *et al.*, 1994), and if pathways into step-family formation are also taken into account, there can be 72 permutations (Aleksander, 1995). This further resonates with arguments about increasing diversity of family forms generally, which suggest that, just as we need to speak of 'families' rather than 'the family', there are 'step-families' rather than 'the step-family'. What step-families do tend to have in common, though, is that the overwhelming majority – over eighty per cent – of children in step-families live with their mother and a step-father (Haskey, 1994). Within family diversity then, it would seem that gender divisions endure, in that mothers retain the main responsibility for the everyday care of children after divorce or separation, and this is reflected in step-family forms.

The complex relational dynamics of step-family life are said to derive from the demographic characteristics noted above. Morgan (1996) suggests that re-partnering and step-families may mean that self-identity becomes more unstable, as multiple identities may be needed for each and every family that one is involved in at any one time. Different individuals within step-families are posed as likely to have different loyalties and different notions of who constitutes 'their' family (Smith, 1990; Robinson and Smith, 1993). This can extend beyond the household boundaries to encompass not only non-resident parents (discussed below) and any partner they may have, but also (step-)grandparents and other kin. This latter issue has not received sustained attention, but see discussion in Allan *et al.*(1999), Bornat *et al.* (1999b), as well as Clarke and Roberts (2002). Within the family household, the relationship between step-parent and step-child is seen as a difficult one to manage because it is primarily built on, and mediated through, a third person, i.e. the step-parent's partner and the step-child's parent (Hodder, 1989; Coleman and Ganong, 1995). This is said to result in resentment and jealousy on both the step-parent's part – about the time and attention children require impinging on their own time and relationship with their partner – and on the part of children – over sharing their biological parent with the step-parent (Smith, 1990). Of course, biological parents in intact nuclear families can resent marginalisation in this way too. Indeed, this issue is often raised in self-help books aimed at new parents, advising mothers to continue to give their partner attention and involve him in caring for the baby. This point raises the question of the extent to which tensions that may be a facet of life in families generally are attributed to a particular family structure, i.e. that everything that goes on in a step-family is explained in terms of it being a step-family.

Some have posed the couple relationship as being central to a step-family's functioning (Visher and Visher, 1979), with friction between the couple over issues such as childrearing a cause of unhappiness (Ferri and Smith, 1998). Jaqueline Burgoyne and David Clark (1984) pointed to the way that the stages of 'courtship' (as they refer to it) and 'becoming a family' are collapsed, in that the first stage is as much organised around the needs of children as the second. They also highlighted the way that partners in step-families may find little time for themselves. Yet they noted too 'how strongly pragmatic views overshadow more conventional and popular notions of romantic love' (Burgoyne and Clark, 1984: 87). Perhaps, two decades on from their study, couples may no longer be so philosophical, in the face of claims that romantic love is now the individualised centre of couple relationships. By 1990, for example, Stacey was drawing attention to the conflict between childrearing and the couple relationship in the contemporary 'brave new families' she studied.

In the context of these dynamics, it is said to be a number of years before integration within a step-family occurs – between two and ten years according to, for example, Stern (1978) and Parentline's website (www.parentline.co.uk). Some identify a linear trajectory in how step-family members develop a sense of solidarity (e.g. Papernow, 1993; Robinson and Smith, 1993), while others point to considerable fluctuation over time rather than progressive settlement (e.g. Gorell Barnes et al., 1998; Baxter et al., 1999).

There has been concern about the consequences for children of structural family change. This has resulted in an extensive body of literature addressing and comparing children's development in various family forms (for overviews see Heatherington and Jodl, 1994; Maclean and Eekelaar, 1997; Ferri and Smith, 1998; Rodgers and Pryor, 1998). Much of this takes a problem-oriented approach, and can be based on clinical samples (for a considered critique of this work see Gorell Barnes et al., 1998). It examines family structure in relation to the outcomes for children's behaviour and psychological adjustment, their educational achievement, 'transition' points such as leaving school and home, sexual activity and parenthood, and involvement in criminal activity. There have also been attempts to measure step-parent/step-child relationships. Age and gender are often highlighted as issues in this. Christina Hughes (1991) has reviewed claims that the younger the step-child, the more likely it is that a successful relationship with the step-parent will develop, and that same-sex step-parent/step-child relationships are especially problematic. She concludes that the research evidence is contradictory and ambiguous. She also points to the way that concern with outcomes tells us nothing about the process of these relationships – in other words, everyday step-family practices and how these may interlock with age and gender practices.

While much of the knowledge about children's experiences in step-families comes from asking parents about their children's well-being, and/or conducting clinical and other assessment tests on them, there has been some recent in-depth sociological attention given to asking children themselves how they feel about step-family life (notably Brannen et al., 2000, and see also Gorell Barnes et al., 1998; Neale et al., 1998 for retrospective accounts from adults). The research here reveals some variation in how children view the new partner(s) of their parent(s). Both the attempt to be a clearly demarcated 'ordinary' family household and the construction of elastic and multiple commitments across households are in evidence. Nevertheless, the step-parent/step-child relationship tends to be contingent rather than positional. Step-fathers or step-mothers had to 'earn' their place in the family by finding ways of taking an active and affective part in the children's lives – in other words, step-parenting is achieved through social practice rather than being inherent in social status. Retrospective accounts from adults (Gorell Barnes et al., 1998) also pose this achievement as gendered (a point we return to below), with a higher level of parenting expected of step-mothers (and more condemnation of those who fell short) than of step-fathers, in a context where biological fathers often handed over responsibility for their children's care to step-mothers. Furthermore, as we shall see, quite what step-parenting practice can or should consist of is a sticky issue.

A key question posed for step-parents is how much of a 'parent' to their step-child/ren they can or should be (Giles-Sims, 1984; Ambert, 1986; Marsiglio, 1992). For those adhering to a neo-Darwinist perspective, the answer is simple, because step-parenting practices are genetically driven rather than socially shaped. Martin Daly and Margo Wilson (1998) undertook a secondary cross-national statistical comparison including historical data, and state that a child living with one biological and one step-parent (most usually the step-father) is around seven times more likely to be abused. They argue that universal evolutionary 'natural selection' means that step-parents will be more likely to mistreat step-children and inevitably will nurture them less solicitously:

> *Step-parents do not, on average, feel the same child-specific love and commitment as genetic parents, and therefore do not reap the same emotional rewards from unreciprocated [in terms of genetic posterity] 'parental' investment.*
> (Daly and Wilson, 1998: 38)

In this view, the frequent claims by step-fathers in Burgoyne and Clark's study (1984) that they had imparted some interest, behavioural or personality trait to their step-children and had attempted to be an 'ordinary' family are red herrings: it is not possible for step-families to be the same as 'the family' and for step-parents to be a social parent who cares for and about their step-children in the same way as a biological parent. (See also the review in Marsiglio, 1993, and the debate in Part I of Booth and Dunn, 1994, on assumptions of biological essence.) Daly and Wilson attempt to explain the behaviour of fathers of adoptive children, and those who bring up a child with their partner, without knowing that the child is not their own biological offspring, with the curious assertion that such fathers will unconsciously simulate a genetic relationship (Edwards, 1999).

Other work, however, takes a more considered, socially grounded, approach. A continuing theme of literature addressing the subject over the years has been that there is normative uncertainty around the role of step-parent. Research and 'self-help' literature often point to the way that those involved are relatively ill-prepared in consequence (e.g. Robinson and Smith, 1993; Coleman and Ganong, 1995). In the mid-1960s, the lack of institutionalised norms for the role was emphasised (Fast and Cain, 1966). In the late 1960s/early 1970s, Margaret Mead (1970) observed that there were very few 'alternative moralities' to that of 'the family' emerging to structure step-family relationships. In the late '70s/early '80s, the dearth of normative expectations was similarly remarked on by Burgoyne and Clark (1984: 14): 'As there appear to be few norms structuring the stepparent role in our own society many men and women may find themselves trying to construct a new role de novo'. In the late '90s, Elsa Ferri and Kate Smith (1998: 12) could still comment on 'the normative vacuum in present-day society concerning the actual roles which step-parents are to play'.

Given that step-families have existed for centuries – albeit now predominantly created following divorce or separation rather than a parent's death, and thus often having to deal with the actual presence of a non-resident father – one might wonder what it is about the organisation of family life in Western developed societies that means that such norms have not developed, even over the last third of the twentieth century. Recent sociological theorising would answer this by pointing to the contingent nature of contemporary morality. As we discussed earlier, standard family pathways are said to have been usurped by more individualistic lifestyle construction, and shared family rules and norms replaced by negotiated contextual guidelines. Such an answer, however, raises the further question of why there do not appear to have been any agreed norms prior to this point in time either.

Yet in the face of this supposed individualisation and fluidity, a key point raised by much literature on the topic is that it is not the 'step-' status alone that is an issue. There are major differences in understandings and experiences of step-parenting, between step-fathers and step-mothers, reflecting long-standing gender divisions within (heterosexual) families more widely.

(Step-)fathering and (step-)mothering

A recurring theoretical theme in research on fatherhood is that it is in flux, undergoing a transition from 'ascribed' to 'achieved' (see Furstenburg, 1988; Jensen, 2001). Thus, lack of clarity in quite what step-fathering consists of in practice has been related to the shift towards a less clear formulation of the role of fathers generally (Ferri and Smith, 1998).

Notions of ascribed and achieved fatherhood raise issues of biological and social parenthood, as discussed in 'Legal discourses on family life', above. However, they also go beyond them. Ascribed fatherhood is a relationship that is rooted in the biological tie between father and child, which in itself is seen to constitute the essence of fatherhood. In this understanding, fathering a child literally means providing the genetic input, with little sense of an on-going relationship. Ascribed fatherhood therefore 'fits' with a model of heterosexual family life in which there is a gendered division of labour between parents: fathers are breadwinners, disciplinarians, emotionally distant, while mothers are the nurturing carers. It is argued that, with increased maternal employment and family change, this traditional and institutional form of 'remote' fathering is shifting and breaking down. Frank Furstenburg (1988) in particular, has posed two directions in which it appears to be splitting: 'deadbeat' fatherhood and 'achieved' fatherhood. The disengaged deadbeat father is the result of the growing individualisation discussed earlier, and men's potential economic redundancy as women are drawn more extensively into the labour market. The Child Support Act 1991 is a legislative attempt to deal with this issue with respect to non-resident fathers' financial obligations, while the Children Act 1989 attempts an affective intervention. On the other side of the coin, however, it could be said that family legislation generally positions step-fathers as 'deadbeat', by marginalising them.

Fatherhood as an achieved social relationship is rooted in new expectations that fathers should actively engage with their children as physically and emotionally involved carers (Burghes *et al.*, 1997). The 'father of duty' is being replaced by 'the loving father' (Bertaux and Delcroix, 1992).

The conception of a distinction between 'ascribed' and 'achieved' in understanding the position of fathers has its drawbacks, however. In particular, the overlaying of the social relationship with the biological relationship, even within conceptualisations of achieved fatherhood, does not address the practice of step-fathering. Morgan's (1998) development of the distinction between 'fatherhood' as institutional discourses and representations, and 'fathering' as referring primarily to relational practices, perhaps has more merit (although he also points to their interdependence). It can help to provide more space for understanding step-fathering beyond a purely achieved relationship. For example, the social practice of step-fathering might work towards 'ascribed' fatherhood in all but biology.

Indeed, despite the increasingly 'hands on' nature of modern fathering, the evidence is that the practice of British fathers is still largely seen by themselves and other family members as primarily one of economic provision, with other aspects being additional to this (see review by Lewis, 2000). There is also evidence that, rather than being achieved by themselves, fathers' relationships with their children are mediated through mothers. Numerous studies have revealed fathers' reliance on mothers to interpret children's practical and emotional needs for them (including Backett, 1987; Hutson and Jenkins, 1989; Ribbens, 1994; Brannen et al., 1994; Warin et al., 1999; Gillies et al., 2001). There is little detailed evidence about step-fathers' material, social and emotional practice in relation to their step-children. Ferri and Smith's (1998) National Child Development Survey (NCDS) analysis focused on patterns of parental employment, family activities and practical involvement in childcare and childrearing. They conclude that:

> whether or not parents in step-families actually aspire to re-create a 'typical' nuclear family in the ways in which they organise the main aspects of their family life, this is, in fact, what they appear to do.
> (Ferri and Smith, 1998: 58)

They note the difference in this picture in comparison with that found in Ferri's previous analysis of NCDS data in the mid-1970s, in which step-fathers were much less involved with their step-children in these ways than biological fathers in 'the family'. While the practice of fatherhood may still largely reflect a 'traditional' formulation then, the emphasis on achieved 'fathering' may have created a little more room for the social development of practical step-fathering.

Ferri and Smith's research does not, however, tell us anything about step-fathers' affective involvement, or about any sense of belonging to a family or a bounded household unit. Some commentators feel that this is likely to be circumscribed by the fact that step-fathers are increasingly understanding their position in a situation where their step-children are in some form of contact with their biological father (see Allan and Crow, 2001). While there are no figures on this specifically, the situation for children's contact with their non-resident father generally is indicative. Jonathan Bradshaw and colleagues' (1999) recent work found that 47 per cent of non-resident fathers saw their child at least once a week, and a further 14 per cent once a fortnight, but as they acknowledge, this does not tell us anything about closeness of relationship.

Social class may be a significant feature in this. Some studies suggest that some non-resident fathers' contact with their children can be severely curtailed because of the infrastructure and transportation costs involved (Simpson, *et al.*, 1993; Henman and Mitchell, 2001) – in other words, working-class fathers are most likely to be constrained in this way. However, Mavis Maclean and John Eekelaar's (1997) finding that non-resident fathers in lower socioeconomic groups are more likely to move aside when the mother of their child/ren re-partners would signal that something else may also be an issue in this – that people who are working class may feel that a child needs a father, but that it does not have to be the biological father who fulfils this role if someone else 'steps' into it.

Non-resident fathers' experience is very wrapped up in gender too. Carol Smart (1999) has argued that after divorce or separation, non-resident fathers often continue their reliance on mothers to interpret children's practical and emotional needs to them. They have to learn to achieve a self-sustaining relationship with their children. Edward Kruk's (1993) study of divorced fathers similarly found that they had to redefine their role and identity as father, but that it was easier for those whose practice had been that of ascribed fatherhood before the separation to adjust, because they had already been practising remote fathering (see also Simpson *et al.*, 1995, on divorced fathers renegotiating their practice). The Child Support Act 1991 enforces the financial obligations of ascribed fatherhood, potentially impinging on this element of step-fathers' social practice. The further affective, non-resident parental involvement promoted under the Children Act 1989 can also spill over into other aspects. Indeed, the fact that non-resident parents represent a 'disturbance' to or 'intrusion' into resident parents' and step-parents' ability to create an 'ordinary', bounded, family unit is noted again and again in the literature (see Allan and Crow, 2001). They can be left with no option other than to make families that diverge from 'ordinary' pathways.

Furthermore, as Robinson and Smith (1993: 217) argue:

> *In many respects, step-families are leading the way in redefining gender roles in families because the traditional role expectations for men and women are not workable in the step-family context.*

This argument, which is shared by others, rests on the fact that step-fathers have an ascribed fatherhood breadwinner and authority role undermined by a non-resident father's input and the biological mother's greater legitimacy in child discipline matters. Similarly, step-mothers will have to confront the father's greater legitimacy and experience as child nurturer. Thus, not only is there an absence of societal norms for step-parenting, but it is argued that parents and step-parents have to make democratised and gender-equal (step-)families.

Yet the evidence does not always bear this out (see Ishii-Kuntz and Coltrane, 1992; Ferri and Smith, 1996; Sullivan, 1997), and gendered images of parenting are deeply enduring, not least for step-mothering. Although a step-family in which a step-mother has the main responsibility for the children is much less common, step-motherhood has received a fair amount of attention in the literature. It is generally acknowledged that the issues faced by step-mothers are likely to be far more problematic than those faced by step-fathers, and again this is related to long-standing gender divisions within families generally (see the review in Allan and Crow, 2001). Furthermore, motherhood does not break down so easily into biological/social, ascribed/achieved or motherhood/ mothering distinctions. They are all implicit in each other. For example, unlike fatherhood, the term 'motherhood' carries a package of biological, institutional and active relational connotations (see New and David, 1985), and is not in flux or transition (other than the incorporation of paid work to some extent). Indeed, achieved fathering seems to be judged as the equivalent of mothering rather than being posed in its own terms.

Gendered divisions in parenting roles remain considerable in British families, despite mothers being more involved in paid work outside the home. Analyses of the National Child Development Survey data (Ferri and Smith, 1996, 1998) showed that mothers and resident step-mothers usually took the main responsibility for domestic life and caring. Step-mothers largely operate and are placed within the expectations of mothering practice, and thus, like resident mothers, are said to occupy a central caring role in step-family life in a way that resident fathers and step-fathers do not. While definitions of fathers' practice are ambiguous, mothers' practice is more clearly defined and subject to judgement and accountability. It is this that means that resident mothers bear a gendered responsibility for the 'success' of their step-family, and makes step-mothering especially difficult. Indeed, analysis of calls to a dedicated telephone helpline showed that step- and biological mothers in step-families accounted for nearly three-quarters of all calls received, and they were concerned with others in the family just as much as with themselves (Batchelor *et al.*, 1994).

Hughes (1991) has elaborated the way that step-mothers are subject to the predominant ideology of 'good' motherhood (at least in White British society) as selfless, caring responsibility for children. This point echoes other commentators on the topic (for example, Burgoyne and Clark 1984; Smith 1990; Robinson and Smith, 1993), who can also point out that a step-mother can be in competition with the biological mother in adhering to the ideology. Hughes goes further, however, to argue that this exacting ideology crucially articulates with the 'myth of the wicked step-mother' – which, as with all myths, helps society to define situations that lie outside its normative framework (Visher, 1984). The wicked step-mother myth (think of Cinderella and Snow White) forms the very opposite images to those created by notions of good motherhood. Hughes found that the step-mothers in her study had to take account of and negotiate the disjunction between the two types of image in their everyday actions and dealings with step-children, family, friends and others. Their practices were founded on anticipatory refutation of any possibility of their being perceived as malign, through demonstrable and visible adherence to 'goodness' by putting step-children's needs first. This was in stark contrast to the step-fathers, whom Hughes found to be largely unaffected by any public, popular images of this kind in their understandings and experiences (despite the fact that 'wicked' step-fathers exist in both literature and reality).

This discussion illustrates the importance both of not using the category 'step-family' to explain every aspect of the understandings and experiences of the children, parents and step-parents within them, and of not individualising them entirely as endless vistas of creative lifestyle possibilities. Our own study sought to avoid both these extremes in seeking to explore how parents and step-parents 'do' family practices and make sense of their family lives within the wider social context.

Methodology and sample

The research on which this book is based involved individual in-depth interviews with a range of people involved as resident, step- and non-resident parents in step-family life. The main focus of the book is on parents' and step-parents' perspectives of how they make sense of 'family' and parenting within and across households. We regard their understandings as valuable in their own right in a context where family forms are said to be undergoing rapid social change, and where parents' and step-parents' experiences have received little sustained in-depth research attention. At one point (Chapter 3), however, we also draw on interviews undertaken with the children concerned in two 'step-couple' case studies, in order to explore a particular issue (explained further below).[5]

We took a largely open-ended exploratory approach for a major part of the interviews, seeking to cover aspects of the life histories of individuals, of couple relationships and parenting relationships. Towards the end of these interviews, some more specific questions were asked of everyone, concerning perceptions of more 'public' norms, images and policies around step-families. A series of vignettes was included at this point, attempting to directly pose some of the dilemmas that step-family living may present, and to elucidate both the interviewees' views about the appropriate responses and any direct personal experience of such situations. (We refer to these vignettes at appropriate points in the following chapters, and they are reproduced in the Appendix.) Janet Finch (1987) discusses the use of vignettes in survey research in order to elicit the norms and beliefs about family responsibilities to which people give public assent, rather than their own circumstances and behaviour. In the context of in-depth interviews with people actually in the situation under investigation, we are less certain that a distinction between public moralities and private understandings can be drawn in this way. Our interviewees often spontaneously and seamlessly wove together assessments of what the people in the vignettes 'should' do, with stories about what they or people they knew had done in similar circumstances, sometimes starting from the latter in order to produce the former. Overall, then, our interviews encompassed the organisation and meaning of everyday family life for our interviewees.

This approach to researching parenting and step-parenting and making families enabled us to explore the 'lived realities' of the people we interviewed (Chamberlayne et al., 2000: 1), paying attention to meaning and experience within the stories that they told us about themselves, family members and significant people and events in their lives. Such an approach is essential if we are to understand the meanings and values that people attach to certain activities, interactions and behaviours, and the variety of ways in which they accept, reject, transform and/or ignore public discourses in their everyday lives and (step-) family practices. In this book we have taken a primarily constructionist approach towards our interviewees' accounts, which does not view words and practice as two separate realities that can be at odds with each other in any absolute sense. This means that the issue is not 'the truth' of whether or not our interviewees' actions were in line with what they said. Rather, it is that their accounts are part of 'reality work', by which they 'produce meaningful realities and formulate the social world' (Gubrium *et al.*, 1994: 31). Words and actions are in a reflexive, mutually constitutive, relationship: actions can only be understood through the framework of language, which in turn is constructed within the context of practices and interactions. Thus, because social meanings are, as Janet Finch and Jennifer Mason (1993: 174) put it, 'constructed for *use*' (original emphasis), in that they are conveyed in and shape people's actions, they are important if we are to understand how step-parents and biological parents create, understand and experience their parenting and family lives, within and between households, and within the wider social context.

It is difficult to make sense of step-family life without a knowledge of its antecedents. This applies not only to the way the past may be understood as a material and emotional legacy implicated in the complexity of step-family forms and relational dynamics discussed in the literature (above). Importantly here, it also applies to the way the people involved themselves often engage in the process of making sense by reference to the past. As we will see, step-family members often used similarities or contrasts with their own and/or others' behaviour in the past in order to construct, understand and transmit 'reputations' for themselves and others. Finch and Mason (1993) argue that such reputations built up over time, as a good, wayward or reformed character, are important within families and kin networks in providing a shared structure for the negotiation of kin responsibilities, and as symbols of personal moral identity.

Further, though, we would argue that they also act as symbols of personal moral identity that are built up within research interviews – with the researcher as the audience and implicated in their production (see Holstein and Gubrium, 1995; Walker, 1997). This is evidenced in the evaluative or confessional language interviewees may use to describe their own and others' past or current behaviour, which in turn assumes shared understandings between interviewee and researcher (see further discussion in Ribbens McCarthy *et al.*, 2000). These points about the building and sharing of moral identities within both families and interviews resonate with Morgan's (1996, 1999) concept of 'family practices' as conveying not only the routine 'doing' of family life, but also the perspectives of the person carrying out the practice and those observing it, be they other family members or researchers.

We have discussed elsewhere the details of and rationale for our 'snowballing' process of accessing the people who took part in our study (Edwards *et al.*, 1999b). Our sampling strategy was largely based on approaching people through our, and their, informal social networks (as individuals living in different locations and with different sorts of networks). We did not want to seek contact entirely through formal organisations in order to avoid being associated with the agenda of the agency concerned. Given that we were aiming for heterogeneity, we monitored the sample that our networking approach was producing and attempted to fill lacunae. As part of this, we also attempted some approaches through more formal avenues (for example, a church, a doctor's practice and an Asian women's centre).

An important issue to note is the symbiotic nature of methodology and substantive topic in conducting family research. These links manifested themselves in two main ways (all discussed in further detail in Edwards *et al.*, 1999b). Firstly, we realised that our own definition of the range of situations that constituted a 'step-family', and thus who could or should take part in our research, would have major implications for what we then 'found out' about such family forms. For example, we concentrated on heterosexual couples because we were interested in how far step-family members might work towards 'passing' as an 'ordinary' family (not possible for non-heterosexual families) or considered themselves to be a loose-knit and fluid assemblage. (For research on non-heterosexual families, some of which include step-families, see Weeks *et al.*, 2001, especially Chapter 7.) Additionally, we did not initially include 'live-out' relationships where the resident parent's partner was not living permanently with her or him, but we reconsidered this once we realised this potentially excluded a number of African-Caribbean interviewees. Such definitional boundaries for our step-family study then interacted with our target sample's own definitions, also with implications for what we 'found out'. For example, even with our redefinition, we found it particularly difficult to get Black potential interviewees to agree to be included in our study. Furthermore, refusals to take part in our research generally could focus on the potential interviewees not wishing to think about their family as anything other than 'normal', or not wanting to 'rock the boat' of family relationships.

The second way in which the links between methodology and topic manifested themselves was in the fact that our method of access reflected relational dynamics within and across households. Our intention was to interview people across households, whose members might or might not share any sense of common 'family' identity – what we termed a 'step-cluster'. This choice of research unit was based on the policy concerns around maintaining children's relationships with their non-resident parent after divorce or separation, which we have discussed above, including in relation to how this may constrain step-family members working towards a clear-cut 'ordinary' family unit. In each cluster we sought, but did not always obtain, interviews with the resident parent or co-parent (usually the biological mother), the step-parent (usually the social father) and the non-resident parent or co-parent (usually the biological father). We negotiated access in stages, only asking for contact with others once the interview had been completed with the first contact person. Having agreed to take part themselves, though, interviewees could resist our requests to 'snowball' out to particular members of the step-cluster, or a person 'snowballed' to would refuse to be interviewed when approached.

The importance of gender was evident here, with women largely being positioned as the first point of contact and taking responsibility for mediating access to other step-family members – reflecting their responsibility for family life and continuing relationships with children. Social class was also important. Our access to working-class men in step-clusters, both as partners and non-resident fathers, was particularly curtailed, resulting in 'step-clusters' that consist only of interviews with the resident mother.[6] These often reflected uneasy or distant relationships within the step-cluster, as well as women's responsibility for family life. While uneasy relationships could exist within middle-class families too, these were far less likely to manifest themselves in a refusal to take part in research. In particular, the White middle-class 'liberal' interviewees, who could see themselves as creating 'new' extending family forms and relationships, were enthusiastic and proactive in ensuring our access to all within the step-cluster (even where there were resentments of each other under the surface).

In the event, our sample consisted of 23 'step-clusters', comprising interviews with 46 individuals, with heterogeneous household structures (see Table 1.1).

Given the complexity of household forms, as Table 1.1 indicates, some of our resident biological mothers or fathers were also step-parents, as were some of our non-resident parents too. The children involved could include children from a previous relationship living in the step-family household, children from the current relationship, children born to the non-resident parent within a new relationship, and step-children acquired by the non-resident parent in a new relationship. Children's own relationships could therefore be with full siblings, half siblings, or step-siblings. Their contact with their non-resident parent could vary between none (because the non-resident father was completely absent or

Table 1.1 Interviewees' parenting status

Women

Resident mother of child/ren from previous relationship	7
Resident mother of child/ren from previous relationship plus mother of child/ren from current relationship	11
Resident mother of children from previous relationship plus part time step-mother	1
Half-weekly care mother	1
Half-weekly care step-mother plus resident mother of children from previous relationship	1
Full time step-mother plus resident mother of children from previous relationship	1
Full time step-mother plus mother of children from current relationship	1
Part time step-mother plus mother of child from current relationship	1
Non-resident mother	1
Total women	*25*

Men

Resident father of children from previous relationship plus father of children from current relationship	1
Resident father and step-father	1
Resident step-father	4
Resident step-father plus father of child/ren from current relationship	9
Resident step-father plus non-resident father	2
Half-weekly care father of children from previous relationship plus resident step-father	1
Non-resident father plus father of children from current relationship	1
Non-resident father	2
Total men	*21*
Total overall	**46**

deceased), through some contact (sporadic, such as during school holidays), to high (weekends or shared care) – with roughly equal numbers of children involved in the step-clusters in each contact category. Our sample thus includes a fair coverage of the permutations that step-family researchers attempt to classify in an effort to impose order on diversity. It is also evenly divided in terms of the length of time the step-couple interviewees had been living together in a step-family household, with around a third having lived together for two years or less, a third for between three and five years, and the final third between six and nine years. There is also a balance of married and cohabiting step-couples in the sample, with middle-class step-couples being equally split between the two partnership forms, and two-thirds of the working-class step-couples cohabiting (see below for a discussion of social class).

In terms of the sociostructural characteristics of our sample, we achieved a reasonable gender balance, with 25 women and 21 men. We also had some ethnic diversity: of the 46 individuals involved, the sample was predominantly White, including four Irish and one Italian, but also included four African-Caribbean and two Bangladeshi. The social class mix involved 29 middle-class interviewees, 13 working-class and four currently 'upwardly mobile'. We used a multidimensional 'objectivist' approach to assess our interviewees' social class, incorporating a sense of people as individuals with particular biographies and located in particular households and communities (Osborn and Morris, 1979; Morgan, 1996). This included:

- interviewees' own occupation(s) and educational qualifications;
- the occupations and educational qualifications of their parents and their current partner;
- housing tenure and neighbourhood;
- current social networks.

For most of our sample, these characteristics coincided, enabling us to place them clearly within a simple middle/working-class dichotomy. For four individuals, from two couples, classification was more ambiguous. This related to their overall class trajectory, with movements into more middle-class positions currently occurring (e.g. through higher education studies, or occupational promotion and housing moves). Social class clearly needs to be discussed carefully given the small numbers involved in our study. Within the sample, however, the social class dimension of our findings has been very striking. As the following chapters show, like gender, it recurs across a range of aspects of our discussion, some features of which are only possible within an in-depth study of this sort.

The analysis of the interviews with our sample forms the basis for the discussion of parenting and step-parenting within and across households in the following chapters of this book. We used a combination of deductive and inductive approaches in our analysis of this data, moving iteratively between the two analytic strategies. The more deductive analysis centred on a comparison of responses to some of the more specific questions asked of everyone, as well as a thematic analysis of issues identified as important in existing family, parenting and step-parenting research, i.e. caring, authority/responsibility and economic/material support. The more inductive analysis started from each individual's account, with a search for recurring themes, preoccupations, images and concepts. Only then did we generate categories, building towards a comparison of themes across the different accounts. We have been struck by the way that several aspects of deductive and inductive themes echo each other. These largely concern issues of biological and social parenting, and moral obligations and guidelines for step-family life, and are cross-cut by gender and social class. As we will show, these and the other issues that we discuss key into, and throw light on, broader current debates about the changing nature of parenting and family life.

The structure of this book

In the next chapter, we look at 'family' and the meanings our interviewees constructed about it and attached to it, in the context of discontinuity in relationships and a potential break between experiences of family and household. Our analysis reveals the continuing power of notions of 'family' as a social unit that is constituted and experienced through symbolic and concrete boundaries, involving mutual responsibility, a 'team effort' and commitment. Only in a few cases was a sense of individualisation much in evidence. For the most part, it was notions of 'family' that were important, with the vast majority of our parents and step-parents rejecting 'step-family' as a term or image that applied to their own, or their ex-partner's, situation. Furthermore, some challenged the idea that step-families, and parenting relationships within them, are different from other families. This group largely comprised the working-class parents and step-parents, and this signals one of the key distinctions that runs through other chapters.

Children generally formed a focus in understandings of family, in that our interviewees regarded family as the social unit in which care of children and 'childhood' occurs. This brings to the fore issues of generation and the moral responsibilities of parents and step-parents for children, which may interact with children's own understandings and activities in relation to the adults who care for them. These form the topic of Chapter 3. A key feature of interviewees' accounts in this respect was the overriding moral imperative that parents and step-parents should exercise responsibility for children and try to put their needs first, rooted in a categorical distinction between the construction of moral agency for the 'Adult' and the 'Child'. The constitution of this responsibility, though, was deeply gendered. It is at this point, given the significance of Adult/Child categorisations, that we turn to consider the understandings of the children in our case studies in relation to moral agency. Notions of pure relationships and of coupledom may be in tension with responsibilities to meet children's inalienable needs, however, and the chapter then returns to our adult interviewees to explore their understandings of coupledom in this respect.

In Chapter 4, we focus on considering the meanings our interviewees attached to caring, authority and material provision for children, as areas that lie at the centre of notions of parenting and are subject to concern in public debates about contemporary family life. Once again, class was a major feature of discussions of these issues, with middle-class parents and step-parents regarding biology as a major determinant of emotional attachment and the exertion of authority within and between households. In contrast, working-class parents and step-parents commonly asserted that step-children could and should be loved and provided for 'as if they were your own', as part of the family household. Time was of significance in both viewpoints, with regard to building and maintaining caring relationships with children under changing circumstances, and in understanding, building and maintaining family relationships.

Chapter 5 turns to exploring how 'fairness' was a guiding principle our interviewees drew on in varying degrees and fashions in working out how to 'do family', manage coupledom, and exercise caring, disciplinary and material responsibility for children within and across households. Here too, categorical distinctions between 'Child' and 'Adult' are crucial. While being fair to and between children involves what is just in terms of children's rights, it also encapsulates what is 'good' for them in terms of their (inalienable) needs. Being fair to the adults involved, however, was associated with rights and the justice of the situation, was more negotiable and contingent, and subordinate to the question of what was fair for children. And once again, gender was a major issue in terms of moral responsibility for maintaining fairness.

Our final chapter draws together all the issues discussed in previous chapters, to consider issues of social class, generation and gender in family life, parenting and step-parenting. We consider how the reflexive sociological enterprise can require careful attention to the implications of the language that we use in translating private lives into public knowledge. In particular, we evaluate current theorisation of family life as fundamentally shaped by individualisation and democratisation in the light of our findings.

Notes

1   The only other appears to be Christina Hughes' (1991) participant observation study of families where both partners were step-parents, from an anthropological perspective. Graham Allan and colleagues' (1999) in-depth sociological study of step-families was concerned with extended kinship construction, and Joanna Bornat and colleagues' (1999b) with the implications of step-families for older people.

2   Anthony Giddens (1999) argues that the early 1970s was the moment that the transformations wrought by globalisation began to take a hold, including the impact of processes of individualisation and democratisation on family life. In this view, Jacqueline Burgoyne and David Clark's (1984) 'progressive' step-families were indeed harbingers of change.

3   Some time ago, Elsa Ferri (1984) suggested that this lack of attention to step-families in social policy and legislation is linked to the perception that the greatest problems facing step-families are rooted in roles and relationships of the sort that we discuss later, i.e. that these are a 'private' rather than 'public' issue. This 'private issue' stance was one with which cotemporaneous step-family members agreed (see Burgoyne and Clark, 1982).

4   Christina Hughes' work is a good example of this process. Her published PhD work (1991) led her to write a self-help book (1993), with roots in her own acknowledged experience as a step-mother.

5   Our original intention was to undertake three case-study clusters which involved reinterviewing the step-couple six months after the first interviews with them, and also the children involved and any significant others identified as important by the step-couple. We selected three clusters as encompassing a range of key characteristics and situations in terms of social household structures and length of time together. In the event, in two cases we completed further interviews with the step-couple and with the children involved. In the third case, however, the resident mother was reinterviewed, but before interviews with others could occur she suddenly left her partner and the area, and contact was lost.

6   Other researchers have pointed to the general difficulty of accessing and actually interviewing men, and step-fathers specifically, about intimate and relational issues. See, for example, Julia Brannen (1988), Jean Duncombe and Denis Marsden (1993) and William Marsiglio (1993).

Chapter 2
Being 'a family'

As we discussed in the previous chapter, ideas about 'the family' have received a great deal of scrutiny in recent contemporary political and public debates. There has been extensive discussion about whether or not 'family life' is 'breaking down', with some commentators focusing on diversity and change and others highlighting continuity. The people we interviewed for this study might be seen by some as representing the vanguard of change, the real exemplars of family breakdown and fragmentation, given their experiences of fractured family lives. A number of our interviewees had lived as a nuclear family unit which had then broken up; some step-fathers had never lived as a household with children before; other interviewees had previously been single mothers and had never lived as a couple along with children before. In this regard none of our interviewees had positive adult experiences to underpin expectations of (nuclear) 'family' life, and might be seen as epitomising postmodern family diversity. However, the question arises as to how far they see themselves in this way.

In this chapter, we begin to explore how our interviewees expressed their understandings of their lives, in the context of their interwoven personal histories of shifting parenting and partnership relationships, and changeable household membership and residential arrangements. In particular, did they see the children as now belonging to a new step-family, and did they eschew more established notions of what it means to be 'a family'? In considering these questions, we draw on our own and earlier studies to help identify aspects of what it may mean to 'be a family' in contemporary Western societies, to map out some of the overarching issues involved. We then turn in detail to our interviewees' discussions – both spontaneous and prompted – to analyse how they understood what it means to be a family under changing circumstances. This analysis reveals the continuing power of family discourse and ideals, and presents compelling evidence against recent theoretical assertions (discussed in Chapter 1) about the significance of pure relationships (Giddens, 1991, 1992) and elective affinities (Beck-Gernsheim, 1998).

In this chapter questions of language are crucial, particularly around the meaning of the family in the context of changing household arrangements. While ideas of 'family' undoubtedly have a close relationship with ideas about 'home' and 'household' (Gubrium and Holstein, 1990; Morgan, 1996; Allan and Crow, 2001), each of these terms has potentially quite distinct meanings which can intertwine and diverge, coalesce and dissolve, in subtle and stark ways. While statisticians may continue to concentrate on the apparently less debatable structures of household membership (Sweeting, 2001), our interviewees grappled with the question of how to understand 'family' when its meanings might not map neatly onto household structures.

Ideas about 'The Family' have been hotly contested and discussed within a context of New Right and Third Way politics (as discussed in Chapter 1) and constitute implicit assumptions behind much social policy (e.g. Bernardes, 1985, 1987; Van Every, 1991–92). Some sociologists have sought to move away from using the term altogether, aware that they may be helping to reproduce the ideologies they are seeking to analyse. Anthropologists, too, have argued that the language of 'family' is fundamentally based on a Western model of the nuclear family (Fox, 1967; Robertson, 1991; Hendry, 1999). Indeed, even when a comparative cross-cultural perspective is sought, the framework for analysis may still take the nuclear model as its starting point (Lee, 1999). The use of broader concepts such as 'kinship' may similarly be argued to incorporate Western assumptions about relationships (Adams, 1999). The anthropologist, Rodney Needham (1971), has argued that the concept imposes an illusory uniformity on phenomena that only loosely have anything in common. Some anthropologists have instead sought to use terms such as 'reproduction' to indicate their focus of interest (Robertson, 1991).

Whatever language academics may develop, and whatever conclusions one reaches about the state of 'the family' in contemporary Western societies, *the idea* of family is still very strong. It constitutes a key concept by which people understand their lives, and a very significant and powerful ideal at the levels of both personal lives and public debate. Whether people like or hate the idea of belonging to 'a family', it is difficult – if not impossible – for people to ignore family ideals and discourses in relation to their understandings of their own lives. The discourse of 'family' is a key concept by which people themselves understand their lives, and consequently we would argue that to neglect the significance of 'family' as a concept would be to abdicate our responsibility as social scientists to explicate and analyse aspects of contemporary everyday Western lives.

Jaber Gubrium and James Holstein (1990) have argued that family cannot be regarded as a physical or social entity, although much academic, therapeutic and policy discussion may reify 'the family' in just such a way. They suggest that ideas and discourses about 'family' can be studied, for example through an analysis of how such discourses may link to ideas about 'home' and 'privacy' in a contingent and historically and culturally specific way. Consequently, 'family' can be seen to occur in a whole variety of institutional and social contexts, wherever ideas and discourses of 'family' are re/constructed, asserted and contested. This may occur quite explicitly as an ideological contest or the basis for a moral claim – as can be seen, for example, in the ways in which people living in non-traditional circumstances may want to lay claim to being a 'family' (Weeks *et al.*, 2001). It may also occur in a more mundane everyday way, as an organising concept by which people work out the meanings of their relationships. In these regards, we would argue that 'family' is still very much a legitimate and central topic for social analysis.

While 'family' as a discourse focuses our attention on language, we are not just studying how words are used. 'Family' is a word with very powerful consequences for the ways in which people organise and experience their everyday lives, in the context of what David Morgan (1996) has referred to as 'family practices' (discussed in Chapter 1). In this regard, it is clear that family issues and events figure prominently in people's lives, even for those who live alone – although this does vary in relation to gender and age (Scott, 1997).

As we suggested in Chapter 1, we do not find it productive to draw a clear distinction between discourse and practice. Nevertheless, we have found it helpful at times to emphasise family discourse as a way of examining the power of language, and at other times to emphasise family practice as a way of examining the experience of everyday living activities. In both these regards we find that our interviewees discussed their concerns in relation to what it means *to be* a family and how *to do* family under their changing circumstances of coupledom and parenthood.[1]

In conducting our interviews, we consciously avoided introducing a language of 'family' in our own questions or prompts, as we wanted to see how and when this language was used spontaneously, in quite a taken-for-granted, unproblematic way. We were thus able to analyse how this language was used by our interviewees on their own terms. Additionally, towards the end of the interviews we asked some explicit questions about what family meant to our participants, and whether or not they saw the children's current household as a step-family. Both the spontaneous and prompted discussions provide insights into how our interviewees understood what it means *to be* a family, and this is the focus of the present chapter. From our readings of the transcripts, we also identified inductively themes that occurred across different interviews, which can be seen to constitute aspects of family practices. These issues can be understood as our interviewees' constructions of what it means *to do* family under changing circumstances, in the everyday mundane concerns of bringing up children, whether living with them or apart. These aspects will be discussed in Chapters 4 and 5, but first we will consider more general evidence about what it means *to be a family* in contemporary Western culture.

The social de/construction of 'family'

> Deconstruction is a way of working backwards from the taken-for-granted realities of everyday life to the contexts and practices that constitute them, documenting the production process.
> (Gubrium et al., 1994: 47)

In their concern to avoid the imposition of implicit Western assumptions through the use of the language of 'family', anthropologists may dissect 'family' into a number of constituent elements of social life. In particular, an anthropological perspective may focus not on 'family', but on issues of reproduction (the bearing of, and caring for, children), residence, sexuality and material provision, as separate features of social life that may be patterned in quite variable ways in different societies. Within Western societies we have a particular version, in the nuclear family, of how these aspects may be ordered and overlaid. But even here, Rayna Rapp (1982) has argued that we can distinguish two uses of the word 'family', one narrower and one broader. The narrow version refers to the nuclear, residential unit, composed of two generations. The broader version refers to kinship ties more generally, and is not tied to the household in the same way. In everyday language, Rapp argues, people may slip easily between the two aspects of usage. Indeed, the possibility of using the word in such ambiguous and contingent ways may be an important aspect of dealing with tensions and ambivalences about close relationships around kinship and reproduction.

With regard to family in the narrower sense, previous studies suggest that the social construction of family involves a number of aspects. While we endorse Jaber Gubrium and James Holstein's (1990) argument that family cannot be seen to be a physical object, and should not be reified by academic writers, we would argue that everyday 'family' discourse is concerned with constituting family *as if* it were indeed just such a coherent and solid entity. First and foremost, then, 'family' signifies a social unit, which is constituted and experienced as such through processes of internal cohesion and external boundaries (Ribbens, 1994).

In using the term 'boundary' we are drawing on anthropological definitions which refer to a symbolic social entity demarcated by various concrete criteria. Some of these may be quite obvious, such as a front door that may customarily be left open or shut, and some may be less obvious, such as appropriate forms of dress or language. Boundaries in this sense can also have important implications for more subtle aspects of social interactions, such as issues of identity, or forms of knowledge that are considered valid. There are also likely to be significant issues of power in relation to boundaries, such that the anthropologist Sandra Wallman (1978) suggests that boundaries are likely to signal areas of confusion, ambiguity and danger in social life.

Amongst sociologists, the notion of 'family boundary' has been critiqued in relation to its usage within family systems theory (Gubrium and Holstein, 1990). Criticisms have focused on the way 'the family' is reified as a distinct, concrete entity with an inside and outside, that can only 'really' be known by 'insiders', and may even be regarded as having a 'super-personality' of its own. While we find much of value in these discussions, these notions are not just derived from academic and professional writings, but can also relate to individuals' everyday understandings and concrete experiences (David *et al.*, 1993; Edwards, 1993; Ribbens, 1994). Our present concerns are therefore close to what Morgan (1985) refers to as people's personal and affectual boundaries. In our own usage of the notion, we are seeking to explore how individuals, as members of collectivities, may sometimes construct and experience clear boundaries, and at other times fudge or reject them. As Graham Allan and Graham Crow (2001: 155) comment:

> *Different boundaries are drawn around different sets of kin depending on the meaning 'family' has in the context in which it is being used. Like the boundaries of inclusion and exclusion constructed around different communities, these boundaries around families are not watertight or unchanging, although some formulations are more 'solidly' constructed than others.*

People may vary as to how far they draw minimal or strong boundaries around their notion of their family unit, and how far they expect this to coincide with the physical boundaries of the residential unit. If they take a minimalist approach, they may see family almost as a loose assemblage of people. Within this approach, Western post-Enlightenment ideas of 'the individual' may be particularly strong, and would be more in line with theories of individualisation (as discussed in Chapter 1). If individuals take a strong approach to boundaries, they are likely to place a much greater stress on the family unit, and to expect this to be strongly reinforced by the significance of residential boundaries. This places considerable emphasis on the current time period, since this (step-)family unit is very much something that is being built in the present. In this formulation, children who have a biological parent living in another household represent a particular 'threat' to the strength and maintenance of the family boundaries. It may also be more difficult to deal with a long-term time orientation, since the past signifies the relevance of the parent who is not resident, and the future signifies the relevance of the 'family' project over generations, implicating wider relatives (particularly grandparents) whose relationships may be especially complex and ambiguous for step-family households (Bornat et al., 1999a).

Apart from issues of external boundaries, the family as a unit also raises issues of internal cohesion. Here we are faced with the significance of gender and generation as two fundamental axes of heterosexual family life,[2] such that the 'family' unit is based on a fundamental social division between adults and children, cross-cut by gender expectations. Internal cohesion may be a particular source of concern for people living in changing households. (Issues of gender have been discussed in Chapter 1 with regard to mothers and fathers; issues of generation and the division between Adult and Child will be discussed further in Chapter 3.) In such circumstances, generational relationships may be seen as more complex if they are not understood as symmetrical in terms of the different historical or biological significance attached to particular adult–child relationships, or indeed child–child relationships. As discussed in the previous chapter, gender expectations may also change as social, biological and residential links shift around relationships with children, raising ways of providing and caring for children which may not just map onto gender patterns established in an earlier nuclear family household (see Chapter 4).

Another relationship which may be seen as cutting across the internal cohesion of the unit is that of the couple. Understandings of coupledom may or may not be seen to be in conflict with the project of constructing a family unit. The couple may be seen as the foundation of family life, or alternatively, as constituting a separate element that is more to do with individual fulfilment and the pursuit of romantic happiness (as we explore further in Chapter 3).

There are thus a number of key relationships, which are shaped by people's ideas about how (far) to demarcate external boundaries, and how (far) to be concerned with the internal cohesion of the family unit. These have important consequences for people's notions of what it means to be a family and to undertake family practices.

Constructing 'family' is not just about identifying the relevant members. The quality of the relationships involved is also a key defining issue. A family is expected to be caring and nurturant of its members (Collier et al., 1982; Dalley, 1996) and there is a pervasive view of family life as involving something akin to a team effort (Gubrium and Holstein, 1990). Within the overall hierarchical division of adults and children, and in the context of expectations of appropriate gender identities, the distribution of resources and exertions is meant to be based around love rather than self-interest. There may thus be a core tension between an orientation towards communal needs and equitable but individualised principles (Clark and Chrisman, 1994). This raises issues about reciprocity, obligation and mutual support in the context of specific family-based identities and histories (Finch and Mason, 1993).

These various understandings are played out in everyday life in the context of mundane everyday issues, such as money or time, which run through all the analyses of our interviews. Some of the details of these various day-to-day practices will be explored in subsequent chapters. In the process, we will show how these aspects of family may be teased apart to reveal the exertion and thought involved in 'being a family'.

Yet people's discussion of 'family' suggests that it is meant to be natural and effortless, based on biology and/or natural affection by adults for children in their care. The different aspects of 'being a family' are meant to be mutually reinforcing, with things coming together rather than being in tension. The end result may be a fine 'balancing act' (Ribbens, 1994), but this is meant to be achieved by an invisible production (Graham, 1982), its naturalness locating it outside the province of law and contract (the State) or self-interest (the marketplace) (Collier et al., 1982). By contrast, feminist writers have explored how far 'families' are socially constructed, such that even intact nuclear families can be shown to be the result of a great deal of effort and production, particularly by women (Ribbens, 1994).

This sense of the inevitability and naturalness of families may be reinforced by a sense that this is how things have always been. One of the key characteristics of a family is that its members have a strong orientation to time past and future, rooted in particular family traditions and histories (Morgan, 1975, 1996). In this regard, family life may be seen as underpinned by a traditional form of authority, with patterns over time that do not need to be considered or asserted. It is this everyday taken-for-grantedness of 'family' that leads to a sense of its inevitability, but also its value (Langford et al., 2001).[3]

For step-families this mutually reinforcing package of family discourse and practices may be more difficult to sustain as one coherent set of ideas, and there are no clear guidelines about how or what to hold together. Residence and household boundaries become blurred; biological parenthood and social parenthood become potentially separated; care as female nurturance and male providing become contested; past and future time trajectories are broken; lines of mutual support and obligation become highly controversial; and traditional authority fails to provide guidelines about how to behave. Many of these issues we pursue in later chapters, but next we turn to consider how our interviewees could still identify strongly with 'family' as ideal despite (or perhaps because of) the experience of changing relationships and living arrangements.

What does it mean to be 'a family'?

In considering how our interviewees spontaneously used the word 'family', as well as how they responded to our direct question concerning what family meant to them, the overwhelming image evoked was that 'family' involves a unit and is about 'togetherness'. Furthermore, in the responses to the prompted question, it is apparent that 'family' involves commitment. This association with ties that bind suggests that part of the point of being a family is that it is the antithesis of pure relationships, and involves something more dependable than this.

In their study of middle-class families, Bill Jordan *et al.* (1994) found that this commitment is not just a matter of obligations to, and ties with, particular individuals, but involves a sense of the family as a unit, and of 'putting the family first'. Additionally, the unit is expected to differentiate between the parts played by its individual members, although how this gets worked out can involve considerable tension and effort.

At the same time, among the interviewees in our study there were variations in how people prioritised different aspects and understandings of being a family. Sue (White, middle class, half-weekly resident mother) was the only interviewee who explicitly distanced herself from the idea of 'being a family' in her re-partnered household with her children. Part of this seemed to reflect her mixed feelings about the notion of 'family' at all:

> It's almost I have this horror that when we're [self, new partner and children] *driving along in the car, that people will think that we're a very straight normal family! I want to put a little banner on the car saying, 'We're not', you know! 'It's not as you might think! They're not his! We're more interesting than that!'*

In part, it also reflected her own personal history and sense of having 'failed' once before at being a family:

> There's a part of me that would like it, obviously, to play happy families. But I think of us more as a household of people trying to have relationships! Um, and that there are family aspects to it, traditional family images about it ... because I think for me I still carry slightly that I've failed my first attempt at family. I'm not even calling it a family this time round. I'm having a second stab at a household of people living together.

Sue was a minority of one in our sample, with others espousing the idea of 'being a family' much more wholeheartedly. A few applied the term to other groups of people more broadly e.g. 'the family of the church', but in such cases it was again being used in a very positive way, to indicate something about other groups that mirrored their understanding of what it means to 'be a family'.

The family unit

In many interviews the word 'family' was used early on to refer to the interviewee's life as a child, unproblematically identifying a unit of specific people. For example:

> I was born in Northampton '61. Family moved to Cambridge, round about '64 I believe, and lived there basically all through my growing up.
> (Geoff – White, working class, upwardly mobile, father[4] and step-father[5])

This sense of an identifiable group of people, that can be easily understood by others, occurs spontaneously in many other contexts in the interviews.

When you introduce them to people who've not met them before, how would you describe everybody to them?

We just describe ourselves as 'the family' now, yeah, especially since we've been married.
(Catherine – White, middle class, mother[6])

The bloke who was in charge of it [the homeless hostel he was living in with his partner and her child] *... he said, 'You're the only family that's come in here sort of got any manners'*
(Neil – White, working class, father and step-father)

There was seven of us altogether buying this house. Um, and then after a year all that changed again! ... And then there was another family moved in with us, moved out...
(Lorna – White, middle class, mother)

As Allan and Crow observe, 'the sense of self which an individual has is frequently hard to separate from their sense of the family unit to which they belong' (2001: 11), but this is something that may differ considerably, both in terms of people's understandings of 'self' and their understandings of 'family'. There may thus be variability in how far ideas about family are prioritised over notions of individuality, and how far the unit is seen to be strongly bounded or to have a more open sense of fluidity. Some interviewees did allow for a sense of individuality within this unit, to varying degrees. Geoff, for example, suggested that family is:

A collection of people who are related and live together and do some things together and do some things separately.
(Geoff – White, working class, upwardly mobile, father and step-father)

A few of our interviewees articulated a loosely bounded notion of the family unit (akin to Judith Stacey's 1992 discussion of a postmodern form of extended family), suggesting that this could be beneficial to the children involved:

I think the more a child has an opportunity to start relationships with adults, with other people, the greater their ability to survive life in a healthy happy way. There's always somebody else with a better idea of doing something that you've got, and shared parenting helps in those sorts of things.
(Bob – White, middle class, step-father and half-weekly resident father)

Some used the language of 'extended family' to refer to the wider range of relationships they had developed. Much like Stacey's 'brave new families', Lorna described the range of 'rellies' (relatives) who would be coming to her wedding with her new partner, Pete:

(Chris) [ex-partner] *told me yesterday he was* [coming to the wedding]. *His mum's coming and his brother and wife and baby. Yeah, and it probably will be a bit strange introducing some of Pete's Welsh rellies to them. But I thought, well, they're part of our extended family, so it would be weird not to have them there.*
(Lorna – White, middle class, mother)

These more diffuse views of 'family' were, however, expressed by a small minority in our sample. The view of the extended family as a loose-knit set of relationships across re-partnered households was only found among some of the more liberal, middle-class interviewees. Indeed, this itself was reflected in our fieldwork right from the early days of the study, with such liberal interviewees keen for us to talk to people across households, while others drew much clearer lines about who they considered relevant for us to interview (Edwards *et al.*, 1999b).

For most people, then, 'family' referred to something more clearly defined, and this was the case also for the two non-resident fathers in our study who had not themselves re-partnered. Both of these men discussed 'family' in terms of a unit to which their children belonged, but that they themselves were outside of. Daniel, for example, was puzzled by his son's use of 'family' to refer to the trio of (non-resident) father and two children, even suggesting that his son's idea of 'family' was incorrect:

> They [the two children] *call it a family. Nick especially. But he doesn't distinguish between us as a family and Jessica and Bob* [Nick's mother and step-father] *as a family, they're all family. He said it several times actually ... I remember it specifically 'cos I thought, that's a strange thing to say, Nick. 'Cos there was no female, there wasn't like me and a woman that I could see as a family unit ... So he doesn't really have a distinction of what a family is I don't think. I don't think of it as a family. I think of it as me and my kids. I distinguish between that.*
> (Daniel – White, middle class, non-resident father)

For Daniel, then, blood ties with his children were not sufficient in themselves to constitute 'a family'. Similarly Dino regarded himself as outside of 'family', even though in his case he did have a new partner (living in Italy).

> *I like to see a family. But I don't see myself – I'm too free you know ... Well, the family should be one man, and woman and children. It doesn't matter if they're married. Me and Eva* [daughter] *we are just me and her. Well it's not really a family. Because a family should be like that. It misses something ... without father and daughter or father and son or daughter. That's a family.*
> (Dino – White, Italian, middle class, non-resident father)

For many of our interviewees 'family' implies something that is greater than the sum of its individual parts and relationships:

> *A unit of individual components ... it's that word, 'unit'. You all work together for the benefit of the unit, the family.*
> (Lisa – African-Caribbean, middle class, mother)

Jessica's notion of 'family', discussed spontaneously early in her interview, raised strong positive images of togetherness in the home, overriding potential divisions due to differences of biological parentage:

You know, most of the time all six of us are squashed on that sofa together, all like squashed up, and we have a good giggle. And we have our maths game we play on a Friday night, and it's sort of Connect 4. And they really like the six of us doing family things together.
(Jessica – White, middle class, mother and half-weekly resident stepmother)

This sense of the family unit could be expected to function as something people would put before their individual needs:

Doing things to help the common good rather than individual needs.
(Ben – White, working class, upwardly mobile, step-father)

You've got to work together as a unit. No good pulling one way, you've gotta pull in all ways, else the unit falls apart. As far as I'm concerned the family is a unit, and they've gotta stay as a unit, else it'll just fall apart.
(Trevor – White, working class, step-father and non-resident father)

In the prompted discussion, some interviewees were quite explicit in drawing boundaries around their idea of family. Gill's discussion neatly encapsulates many of the elements that other interviewees distinguished: she uses an organic analogy to imply mutual support and to emphasise inside and outside.

I suppose in my interpretation, we're all together, it's like the one unit where we all work together. Like one brain cell. It's like we're all together and each comes first. You know, our main priority is us before the outside.
(Gill – White, working class, mother)

The notion that this unit provides the basis for support against a potentially hostile world is apparent in a number of discussions.

It kind of conjures up images of sort of a self-sufficient unit, that doesn't lose contact with everybody else but can survive on their own.
(Ben – White, working class, upwardly mobile, step-father)

A mutual support union

In their emphasis on reciprocal ties and obligations, some of these quotes also highlight another aspect of understandings of family, implying mutual responsibility and support. John (White, middle class, half-weekly resident stepfather) used the word 'symbiotic' to describe the interdependency of individuals within a family unit. A large number of interviewees defined the word 'family' in terms of mutual duties and expectations.

When you live in a family all of a sudden you can't do what you want. You've got roles and responsibilities and obligations.
(Rob – White, middle class, step-father and father)

Kate also emphasised this aspect of family relationships, but without such a sense of loss of individual freedom, and more of a sense of mutual advantage:

> *I suppose a group of people who've got reciprocal ties and who have different dependencies on each other.*
> (Kate – White, middle class, mother)

Many interviewees stressed the significance of family members caring for each other and being supportive – being 'willing to do anything for each other' (Louise – White, working class, mother). The phrase, 'being there' for each other was often used, and as we have discussed elsewhere in more detail (Ribbens McCarthy and Edwards, 2002), 'being there' is a subtle and complex notion, that includes ideas of potential availability and psychological attentiveness, providing an ontological security in the world (Gunilla Hallden, 1991; Ribbens, 1994). Both Sally and Trevor described the word 'family' in terms of a reciprocal duty to be available to help and reassure other family members:

> *It really is just doing things for each other and encouraging each other, and being there for each other. That's really nice, and that's why I feel a family.*
> (Sally – White, middle class, mother)

> *You're there for each other, there's no good being selfish, 'I want this, I want that, I'm gonna have this, I'm gonna have that'. You've got to be there for both.*
> (Trevor – White, working class, step-father and non-resident father)

Mary also referred to family in positive terms as a source of shared and mutual support:

> *Being there for each other, helping each other, even if it's just washing up or something, doing something for each other.*
> (Mary – White, middle class, mother)

The key significance of children

In looking at the ways in which people used the word 'family' spontaneously in the interviews, it appears that 'family' is identified as the social unit in which the care of children occurs, and thus as a site of 'childhood', in both emotional and residential terms. The 'childhood' at stake may be either that of the current generation of children, or of the adults when they themselves were children. This then has consequences for kinship networks and also for the individual's social identity, which may be positively or negatively evaluated. But these various features of 'family' are generally taken as quite unremarkable. The following quote from Kim encapsulates many of these aspects, while Simon's quote illustrates the kinship implications, particularly in the context of locality:

> *Right, well to begin with I was born into a family with two parents. Um, my father was an alcoholic. So he left my mother when I was six, and we stayed in the house.*
> (Kim – White, working class, upwardly mobile, mother)

> *Basically Dad's family were Manchester based and moved to Derby,*
> *Mum's family, brothers, sisters and Mum, were born in Leicester, and*
> *they all moved to Derby, so pretty much a lot of my uncles and aunts,*
> *you know, live in Derby, and if they don't live there they live in Sheffield.*
> (Simon – White, middle class, step-father and expectant father)

Paula makes one of the very few references to 'family' in the context of a couple relationship without children, but this is immediately followed by her intention to have children. Here she is discussing the decision that she and her partner Chris made to move away for a period, apparently creating a new sense of a bounded unit:

> *Going to Australia was trying to see whether it was the situation or*
> *whether it was us! ... So for four years we had a different relationship*
> *altogether. It really cemented our relationship as a family. And I wanted*
> *kids of my own.*
> (Paula – White, middle class, mother and non-resident step-mother)

For a few interviewees, the mutual responsibility of being a family derives its purpose quite explicitly from the project of caring for children:

> *It's basically a living arrangement that involves bringing up children.*
> (Rob – White, middle class, step-father and father)

> *Accepting that as a fairly lucent and open relationship, but as a basis for*
> *a sort of springboard for kids to grow up in an equally open and aware*
> *way, which gives them a basis for living, realistically.*
> (Jonathan – White, middle class, resident father[7])

A team effort

We have suggested that both gender (discussed in Chapter 1) and generation (discussed further in Chapter 3) are core structuring dimensions of heterosexual family lives. We would argue that, as deeply embedded features of family relationships, they seriously compromise Antony Giddens' suggestion that family policy can move towards a view of families as 'democratic', based on a model composed of individuals who can be seen in some ways as equal citizens.

> *The family is becoming democratized in ways which track processes of*
> *public democracy.*
> (Giddens, 1998: 93)

'Families', we suggest, are specifically composed of individuals who are seen as differentiated rather than equivalent. In many of our interviews these features of 'being a family' were taken for granted and unremarkable. However, some people explicitly suggested that the mutual support union of 'family' entails complementary roles and duties rather than similarity.[8] This is akin to the view of Clark and Chrisman (1994: 75–6), who suggest:

> Our own a priori view is that a communal rule, that is, feeling responsible
> for and responsive to the other's needs without expecting repayments in
> return, is the ideal that most people hold for their intimate relationships...
> [R]esults revealing that a global sense of equity is associated with
> satisfaction in a relationship or with the stability of relationships are not
> necessarily at odds with people holding the view that resources in
> intimate relationships ideally should be distributed according to the
> respective needs of members of that relationship.

In Chapter 6, we discuss more fully these differing ways of theorising family relationships.

The interviewees in our study did indeed emphasise the notion of a team effort:

> I think we function really well. All of us playing differing and
> complementary roles. We function really well and I pride ourselves on it.
> (Tina – White, middle class, mother)

> A family is a unit. It's just doing things together, you know. It's just like a
> little business really; you all do your little bits, don't yer? You know, you
> all do your little jobs and it all should work out at the end of the day,
> hopefully.
> (Neil – White, working class, father and step-father)

Togetherness and shared activities

Neil's quote also highlights a particularly pervasive image of family discerned in these interviews (as well as in other studies, such as Langford *et al.*, 2001, Gillies *et al.*, 2001). The language of 'togetherness' – living together, working together, growing together, eating together or doing things together – was a recurrent theme in defining family.

> A group of people living together in a house, sharing their life, doing
> things together.
> (Martin – White, middle class, step-father and resident father)

Other interviewees were more specific in outlining particular activities that they associated with being a family. For example, Mary emphasised the significance of meal times for cementing family relations:

> What does the word 'family' mean to you?

> Well, living together, eating together. I'm a great advocate of family meals.
> It doesn't happen often these days. I think Sunday lunchtimes, I'm a bit
> of a stickler about that. I do like a family Sunday lunchtime where
> everybody sits down together ... My family ideals come from my parents.
> It was always the sort of family that had a family roast on a Sunday.
> (Mary – White, middle class, mother)

For some people, their feeling of 'being a family' was particularly strong when they were together outside the home, and perhaps when being seen by others as a family:

I always think of a proper family of people that all talk together and go out together ... I think when we go out, me and Alan and Jack, I think we're a family then, but I don't feel, well, we never really go out all together really [with older sons from first marriage]. *But even when I'm out with my boys I think, well, they're my family.*
(June – White, working class, mother)

Other studies have suggested that parents may express awareness of their family relationships when they are publicly visible outside the home. This might be associated with a sense of vulnerability in such contexts, which might either reinforce a sense of being a family, or negatively challenge people's family identities (see, for example, Mauthner, 1994; Ribbens, 1994; Miller, 2000).

Commitment and ties that bind

The mutual support system of the family was also explicitly described by our interviewees as having an enduring quality that could survive individual faults, bringing about a sense of security and solidity. This view was prevalent in interviews despite participants' experiences of changing family and household structures. Elizabeth, for example, prioritised 'commitment' in her understanding of 'family', while Tina emphasised support:

A group of people with a certain commitment to each other.
(Elizabeth – White, middle class, resident step-mother and mother)

I think what's important about family is that, as I was saying, they were really, really supportive. I could abuse them. You can do that with families. You can muck them about and piss them off, and they still come back for more. You can be forgiven all these horrendous things you put them through and you can expect it all back from them too.
(Tina – White, middle class, mother)

Family bonds are thus represented as resilient and able to withstand upsets and arguments. Several interviewees felt that being a family involves tolerance and acceptance that may entail putting up with, and getting away with, behaviour that might damage relationships within a less committed group. Lorna, somewhat humorously, characterised family relationships as ones that you had to put up with:

You know, couple and a bunch of children, and we have to live with each other whether we like it or not!
(Lorna – White, middle class, mother)

The significance of enduring family membership could, however, be evaluated in variable ways, implying a sense of support and security, or a sense of duty, responsibility and loss of freedom. A few men, particularly, seemed to experience family in terms of responsibility and lack of choice – images that arose spontaneously in the unstructured parts of the interviews:

Having children means you have to give up being selfish, I think, to a certain extent, and um, by taking on a relationship which has got children in, you have to be less self-centred. I mean I can't sort of do all the things that I would like to do, erm, because I can't just say to Sue, 'Oh, do you fancy going to Paris this weekend?' or something.
(John – White, middle class, half-weekly resident step-father)

And my feeling of entrapment, if you like, in the [work] field and the [geographical] location and so on, which weren't actually what I'd been aiming for. I'd much rather have been elsewhere in the country.
(Jonathan – White, middle class, resident father[9])

Security

For many interviewees, the enduring mutual support union of the family conjured up more positive images of security and safety. In this respect, family could be seen as a kind of sanctuary from the outside world. Rather than focusing on the reciprocal obligations and restrictions of family life, the mutual benefits of security and stability were emphasised.

Having a unit where everybody feels secure and safe and loved.
(Margaret – White, middle class, mother)

Well, it just means sort of like a bit of a haven, where you can be as relaxed and uncaring about pressure as you like ... and it's sort of like security as well. When you feel low, you can be built up and you're sort of cosseted.
(Jo – White, middle class, father and step-father)

Security, stability. Um, loyalty. Not necessarily getting on all the time but knowing that you've got family who are there for you. Yeah, security and, er, somewhere to go when all else fails.
(Paula – White, middle class, mother and non-resident step-mother)

The bases of family life

Generally, then, there was strong agreement amongst the interviewees about family as togetherness, although they varied as to whether they evaluated this as a source of comfort or pressure. They also varied in their characterisation of this unit, with shifting emphases on the significance of blood or marriage or ties built up over time.

Fixed, or achieved over time?

A number of people gave a traditional definition of the word 'family', centring on relationships of biology and marriage. Some people responded by outlining the structure of a conventional nuclear family, suggesting that family meant a mother, father and children. For instance, Paul's interpretation of the word 'family' starts from the common emphasis on togetherness, and being a unit, but proceeds to emphasise a traditional view:

Family I'd say for me is a group of people living together as a unit. Having a head of father, mother, children, basically.
(Paul – African-Caribbean, working class, father and step-father)

Other conventional definitions of family focused more on the criteria of blood or marriage as indicators of family status. For Mark, blood ties constitute family, and thus his current household (composed of his pregnant partner and her son) does not yet fit this definition:

I don't know, I see blood relatives more as family.

Would that be different if you were married?

I don't know, maybe it would. And it may be different when the baby's born. Then we're more of a unit. We're bound by something more than love.
(Mark – White, middle class, step-father and expectant father)

It is notable that for Mark, family is explicitly about enduring ties that bind and cannot be broken, constituting 'something more than love', which is why blood relationships are significant. (We will return in Chapter 4 to differing understandings of the significance of biological ties.) Similar considerations may be important for Sue and Karen. Sue also focused on the significance of biological relations, while Karen included both blood and marriage in her definition of family, using a language of being 'tied together':

Family is blood ties more I think, you know. So your actual birth family. That can be separate from the household structure.
(Sue – White, middle class, half-weekly resident mother)

If you're tied together by blood or marriage, it's your family. Your history and everything.
(Karen – African-Caribbean, working class, mother)

Karen hints, here, at the significance of time and a shared history underpinning family ties. While many interviewees saw processes over time as highly significant, with family being something that develops, a few suggested that family is something that may be achieved through building relationships rather than being ascribed through birth or fixed by marriage:

That you all live together and you grow and you learn from each other ... I think it's a thing of growth.
(John – White, middle class, half-weekly resident step-father)

Overall, then, togetherness may be seen as something that is either fixed and rooted in ties that bind such as blood or marriage, or something that is achieved over time through the development of emotional bonds and commitments – although the former view predominated in our interviews.

Positive feelings

For some interviewees, the nature of family relationships – whether rooted in blood, marriage or shared histories – matters less than the nature of the emotional ties:

> *It doesn't matter what shape or form it is as long as all the love's still there.*
> (Louise – White, working class, mother)

> *You just ensure that they're safe and well looked after, and that there's a strong loving bond that blends it all together.*
> (Pete – White, middle class, father and step-father)

While the notion of ties that bind could be seen to emphasise restriction rather than enduring support and commitment, such negative images were in a small minority among our sample. Other studies (Morrow, 1998; Gillies *et al.*, 2001; Langford *et al.*, 2001) asking similar questions about the meaning of family with different samples of interviewees (more likely to be living in intact nuclear families) found even greater idealised notions of family relationships as warm, secure and loving. This almost seems to amount to a view that a family not living up to such an ideal does not constitute a family at all:

> *For most interviewees it seemed impossible to define 'family' in neutral terms. The word 'family' was suffused with strong ideological overtones and was experienced in a powerful and emotive way. Relationships that did not live up to the ideal might not count as 'family' at all.*
> (Gillies et al., 2001: 30)

Such idealised images of 'family' may help to explain why the interviewees in the present study distanced themselves from the word 'step-family', and it is this issue which we consider next.

The 'step-thing': not being 'a step-family'

It was very striking that, across the board, our interviewees were not comfortable with the term 'step-family'. Only one couple, Kate and Rob, confidently described their current household as a step-family, and Rob as a step-father. Notably, Kate worked in the field of family support, and so may have been more prepared to define and draw clear categories around different family forms. Other interviewees gave a number of reasons why they felt the term 'step-family' was not appropriate to describe their household.

Where 'step-' language was used spontaneously in our interviews, it was generally in the context of particular relationships, rather than 'family'. In this regard, 'step-' language might be used in quite a technical and instrumental way, in order to 'place' and define such relationships for others. Geoff, for example, referred to one of his uncles as his 'mother's step-brother', while Catherine asserted a recognition for her new husband's status in the context of her children's school, by describing him as their step-father to the headmaster. Pete used the 'step-' language in the very first sentence of his interview:

> *Well, I'm now in a situation where I've got two children of my own and three step-children.*
> (Peter – White, middle class, father and step-father)

However, later in the interview he said that he hated using the words 'step-dad' and 'step-children' and would only use them when talking to 'someone like yourself'.

This 'step-' language is used in the context of relationships most easily by Sue and John, who seem to give it explanatory power with regard to their family experiences, which may reflect Sue's professional experience as a social worker. Elizabeth is another interviewee who spontaneously referred to her 'step-sons' and implied that they constituted a 'step-family', but only in the context of reassuring her husband how well they were doing by contrast with most step-families, whom she suggested are generally seen as 'going off the rails'.

This marked reluctance to use the 'step-' language, because of its pejorative overtones, is in line with the interviews discussed by Joanna Bornat and colleagues (1999b). These authors suggest that people may need a term without liking it, and that the lack of a well-understood and stigma-free language creates difficulties for people in describing their relationships. In general, their interviewees did not seem to want their experiences labelled or made subject to generalisations; 'step-' failed to reflect their feelings of individual and unique relationship experiences.

In line with these earlier findings, few of our interviewees spontaneously used the word 'step' to characterise their own or their children's households or relationships. Nevertheless, towards the end of the interviews, we asked everyone whether or not they saw themselves as a step-family. This question clearly 'made sense' to people, and they could discuss why they rejected the term in relation to their own lives. It is the responses to this question that we consider next.

Positive claims to being 'a family'

Many interviewees rejected the term step-family in order to lay claim to the positive connotations of being 'a family'. For instance, Karen and Paul (a step-couple) were both keen in their individual interviews, to emphasise how closely they conform to the traditional, 'normal', family, and that this is how others see them:

> *We think of ourselves as a normal family. 'Cos even when we introduce each other, he says that Isis is his daughter.*
> (Karen – African-Caribbean, working class, mother)

> *We don't live like that* [as a step-family]. *If anyone sees us they wouldn't be any the wiser.*
> (Paul – African-Caribbean, working class, father and step-father)

Sally feels that the word 'step-father' inaccurately implies that the relationship is insignificant:

> *The name 'step-father' makes him sound not really that important, but I feel he's more to them.*
> (Sally – White, middle class, mother)

Others were aware that the word 'step-family' was indeed applicable to their household, but felt more comfortable themselves with the word 'family'. Several people also described how their relationships felt 'too natural' to be anything other than 'a family':

> *I suppose I automatically think of ourselves as a family, um, more than a step-family, although I know we're a sort of step-family 'cos of the situation ... It just seems so sort of natural that we're together and that, um, the boys are sort of coming home from school and relating together and playing cricket or whatever, that it just seems like a family to me.*
> (James – White, middle class, step-father)

> *No, I think ... we are like a family, although he's not obviously their dad, he plays that role, and I don't think of him as being their father or anything like that, it's just natural.*
> (Sally – White, middle class, mother)

The irrelevance of biology

This emphasis on the 'naturalness' of social parenthood relationships by these middle-class interviewees, shades over into a more positive assertion by a number of working-class interviewees that biological ties are not important to being 'a family'. (Classifications of social class were discussed in Chapter 1, and differences around these will be discussed in more detail in Chapter 4.) The term 'step-' was thus resisted because it defines relationships on the basis of biology rather than commitment and closeness. For example, Louise (White, working class, mother) is clear that Neil is a father, not a step-father:

> *You don't think of Neil as a step-father?*

> *Not in the slightest, no. I think a father, the way I see a father is it's not so much just because like when men say, 'Oh that's my daughter, she's got my blood she has', sort of thing, like that kind of way ... I don't see it so much because it's their sperm and five minutes.*

Dawn (White, working class, mother) also rejected the term 'step-father' because it emphasises an irrelevant biological distinction:

> *So do you think of Trevor as a step-father?*

> *No, I don't look on him as a step-father, no. He's as good as their own dad really.*

The pejorative overtones of being a 'step-family'

The quotes above highlight a strong distinction made between being 'a family' and being 'a step-family'. While some interviewees might use the 'step-' language to describe specific relationships accurately (as discussed above), the use of the term 'step-family' was overwhelmingly rejected. Most of the interviewees drew on negative constructions of step-families, or compared them less favourably to being 'a family'. Being a 'step-family' might be felt to imply the existence of problems:

> No [not a step-family], *I mean I think maybe if you start encountering problems. I think as it is now things have been relatively good so I haven't really.*
> (Gina – White, working class, mother)

Several people referred to the classic portrayal of step-parents as wicked to illustrate the derogatory connotations of the word 'step-'. For example, Margaret mentions the fairy tale of Cinderella and wicked step-fathers, while Jo refers to the legacy of talk about wicked step-mothers:

> *I don't like the word 'step', I think that's what it is. I struggle with that word. I don't like the word 'step-family', I think it's horrible. I suppose Cinderella spoilt it really. I mean, in one sense I'm aware that we are, but I don't like to think of us like that because it puts James as the wicked step-father and I don't like that.*
> (Margaret – White, middle class, mother)

> *It's a pejorative term, 'step-' anything, because of the wicked step-mother and all of that. I mean it's a term that I sort of know I have a reaction.*
> (Jo – White, middle class, father and step-father)

Other interviewees focused on more contemporary understandings of step-parents as cruel and uncaring to explain why they do not identify with the term:

> *I think the actual word, 'step-father', I think you hear so many bad things about step-fathers, I think as soon as someone mentions that, what goes into people's head is not good things, you know. Because you read or hear, you know, so many bad things about that.*
> (Neil – White, working class, father and step-father)

> *I think it's that 'step-' thing. You just imagine this sort of step-mother or step-father with a stick beating the children.*
> (Jackie – White, middle class, mother)

Simon (White, middle class, step-father and expectant father) felt that the word 'step-family' implies distance. He described the term as an unnecessary categorisation that impedes the development of family relationships by creating 'barriers' within a family:

> *It's all, it's titles and labels, not into that, you know, couldn't even tell you what it meant to be honest ... I don't think it's important to be labelled, there's too much of this labelling going on, you know, you're that, you know, and what I'm hoping is because I'm calling them brothers and sisters that they will all get on. Rather than putting perhaps a barrier, you know, a possible barrier.*

Unqualified to be a (step-)family

Other interviewees rejected the term 'step-family' on the grounds that it was not applicable to their circumstances, with most of these discussing marital status. For example, Ben (White, working class, upwardly mobile, step-father) explained how not being married contradicts his definition of a step-family. In response to the question, 'Do you think of yourselves as a "step-family"?' he stated:

> No, I don't. Well, um, only because 'step-' conjures upon some kinds of changes in marriage. A step-mother as being married to your dad, but not your real mum. I see 'step-' as having something to do with marriage, so no.

These definitions sometimes focused as much on the reasons why they do *not* qualify as a solid *family* unit, as on why they do not qualify as a *step*-household. Both Mary and Frank (a White, middle-class step-couple) focused on the status of the absent parent, suggesting that the definition of step-family does not fit if the children's father still takes an active role – perhaps implying that the family boundaries will be clearer:

> I think my idea of a 'step-family' is when one of the parents has died, and a mum or a dad then becomes a step-mother or a step-father. But when they've got both parents alive I can't actually see them as being step-relations.
> (Mary)
>
> No. I live with the person who is the mother of Annie and Carl and I live with them too, but they're not my children and they're not my step-children.
> (Frank)

Are step-families different?

The majority of interviewees thus firmly rejected the term 'step-family' to describe their situations, comparing themselves with a more positive imagery of 'family' against which they felt they did or did not qualify. Nevertheless, although they emphatically rejected the term, a question concerning possible differences between step-families and other families, was clearly felt to be meaningful. Responses were quite sharply divided, and social class was again a key element.

Step-family relationships are not as emotionally meaningful

We suggested above that many of our working-class interviewees asserted strongly that step-relationships were as emotionally meaningful as biological ones (we discuss this further in Chapter 4, and see also Edwards *et al.*, 1999a). By contrast, middle-class interviewees focused on biology as a major factor that distinguished step-families from other families. Most of these interviewees emphasised the significance and strength of genetic relationships between parents and children, in comparison with the lesser intensity of 'step-'relations. Biological links were thus felt to relate to the depth of emotional ties. For example, Martin explained how the biological tie is characterised by a deep emotional bond:

> There is something special between a child and a true parent that you can't replace.
> (Martin – White, middle class, resident father[10] and step-father)

Both Elizabeth (White, middle class, resident step-mother and mother) and Tina (White, middle class, mother) emphasised the unconditional nature of biological ties in contrast to less solid step-relations. Biological ties are thus seen as more capable of withstanding anger, paralleling the earlier discussion of family relationships:

> You can't take things for granted [with step-children] than with your own children [sic]. I mean I think a lot of it's to do with what happens after you've been angry, 'cos if you're angry with your own child you can sort of give them a cuddle at some stage, and everything seems to come right again sometimes. You sort of resume the relationship, whereas if you're angry with step-children it lingers, it doesn't really go away.
> (Elizabeth)

> Yeah, that thing about being able to abuse and shout and still come back for more. You can't take that for granted. You can't do that in the same way.
> (Tina)

John (White, middle class, half-weekly resident step-father) implied that the emotional connection is not the same in step-relations, with a difference in 'investment' (perhaps also implying a different time orientation):

> I'm sure there must be some differences ... because you're dealing with two parents that it's their children. You know, they have their own interests in what their children do. I mean, Sue will get more excited if Katie's read a book or Nikki's done a high jump, or whatever. Whereas I don't really feel that. I've got nothing to be proud of, haven't got the same investment.

While Simon (White, middle class, step-father and expectant father) does believe that there may be differences (despite his emphatic rejection of the term 'step-family' quoted above), he speculates about the benefits of not being a genetic father:

> In fact, it may be better for the kids ... I can sort of like be their friend and do things with them, you know, and then on the other hand I can be sensible, and I'm always very reasonable, well, I always try to be reasonable, and I think that that also helps as well, and maybe a lot of this is because I am not, in inverted commas, 'their real dad', I am, in inverted commas, 'a step-dad'.

Complexity and conflict

Nevertheless, Simon implied elsewhere in his interview that he experiences considerable pleasure when his step-daughter calls him 'daddy', and that he would love her to take his name. However, such a shift in terminology is made complex in the light of the continuing relevance of her 'real dad'. Many interviewees distinguished step-families from other families for just such reasons, by pointing to their propensity to be more complex and complicated. Sarah focused on the elaborate structure of a step-family and emphasised the multi-faceted nature of relationships within it. In her discussion she slips between different uses of the word 'family' in much the way that Rapp (1982) discusses, but here the extended relationships involved are more variable. She also describes different boundaries that are relevant, but in a way that prioritises and centralises the new household unit:

> *There are so many different dimensions going on. So many other people involved in a step-family. With a normal family you've just got one set of parents and that's it. But in a step-family you've got parents, previous partners, grandparents, so many other factors that make up that other family. It's like two rings, isn't it? The inner ring is the family and the outer ring is all the other people that make up that family.*
> (Sarah – White, working class, mother and part-time step-mother)

Bob also highlighted the complexity of step-family life, although (like Simon above) he was keen to stress the potential benefits of the differences in step-family living:

> There has to be [differences] *because the relationships become more involved, more complicated. But that doesn't mean to say they're any worse, they can in fact be a lot better. It can actually be a learning, growing experience.*
> (Bob – White, middle class, step-father and half-weekly resident father)

Others, however, saw the complexity of step-family relationships as providing the opportunity for more conflict. Step-families were seen as more 'risky' and particularly susceptible to problems. For instance, Jo (White, middle class, step-father and father) and Margaret (White, middle class, mother) both described the difficulties associated with step-family relationships. Interestingly, neither referred to their own personal circumstances, but drew on more public conceptions of what it means to be a step-family:

> *I mean, the complications like the scenarios suggest* [referring to the vignettes included in the interview guide] *are endless. There are differences I think because you have more than two adults being parents. And adults are then competing and acting quite badly sometimes ... I can see that there's an awful lot more risk of things going wrong and risks of conflicts between personalities of adults.*
> (Jo)

> *I'm sure there are a lot more hiccups initially, I'm sure. I've read situations in books. I think it's hard, I think it's hard on the step-parent.*
> (Margaret)

Conflict was a particularly prominent theme associated with step-families. Like Catherine (White, middle class, mother), many people emphasised the increased potential for friction faced by step-families, feeling this might make the unit difficult to sustain:

> I mean, I know step-families that the parents don't like the children and the children don't like the parents and it drives one out, and that sort of thing.

As Margaret implies in her quote above, however, and as Paul (African-Caribbean, working class, step-father and father) states explicitly, some interviewees feel that such issues are a matter of initial adjustments from one household structure to another:

> Initially, I would say. In terms of the offset. You may see that differently if you knew the single mother or the single father. There might be a little bit of a struggle to start off with and probably after the first two or three years things will settle down and then they'll be like normal families.

Resisting difference

These constructions of step-families as different due to biology or complexity, and somewhat problematic as a result, were very largely a middle-class preoccupation. Jessica (White, mother and half-weekly resident step-mother) was the only middle-class interviewee to question the significance of step-family difference, which she did by stressing the heterogeneity of all families, regardless of household structure:

> I think there's differences between every family, you know, whatever ... I think each family's going to be different whether you're a step-family or not.

By contrast, the majority of the working-class interviewees challenged the idea that step-families are necessarily different from other families. Distinctions were either attributed to volition – a matter of attitude or behaviour – or minimised, or refuted altogether. For example, Karen (African-Caribbean, working class, mother) and Neil (White, working class, step-father and father) both emphasised the importance of consciously deciding to be a family rather than a step-family:

> Apart from the third party there doesn't have to be any difference at all. And if your mind-set is to bring your family up as a family then that's how you'll do it. But if it's your mind-set to bring your family up as a step-family, which means that the other partner doesn't really have full responsibility, then that's how it will be felt.
> (Karen)
>
> I think it's how you do it from the beginning. How you perform when you start, you know.
> (Neil)

Other interviewees felt that there may be differences, but questioned their significance:

> *Well, I mean it's only a name. There isn't really a great deal of difference. The attention that's given might be slightly different. It's not really different enough to really note unless there's sort of reasons for it, such as some of the cases before* [referring to the vignettes]. *It does depend on how they act.*
> (Ben – White, working class, upwardly mobile, step-father)

For Gina (White, working class, mother) and Trevor (White, working class, step-father and non-resident father), the suggestion that step-families are different was in itself problematic and likely to undermine internal cohesion. Gina felt that defining a step-family as different automatically devalued its status, and marginalised it by comparison with 'normal families':

> *No, I don't think they should be ruled out ... So no, I think you should class step-families as a normal family. Like as if there was mother and father and children. I think they're just as close-knitted.*

Trevor felt that distinguishing between step-relations and family would create internal barriers within the household, and vigorously argued that this would in itself be harmful:

> *There can be differences, there ain't no differences really. There's no good you thinking of 'em as a difference, step-families and families, but as a family. You should look at them as a family, not a step-family. Because once you start drawing a border line, as far as I'm concerned that's when you start getting problems. 'They're my children, you're only their step-mother' or whatever. That's when you start getting problems. There shouldn't be a line, they should be a family, and that's it.*

Making sense of 'family' under changing circumstances

In both their spontaneous and prompted discussions, our interviewees used a pervasive language of 'family' as a key concept by which to understand their close relationships. In this chapter we have teased open our interviewees' understandings of what it means to 'be a family', and found their themes resonate closely with those of other studies based on different samples, despite the changing circumstances of our interviewees' lives.

A number of different elements can be seen to be involved in the ways people understand 'family': it is a coherent unit which functions as a mutual support union centred primarily on children and childhood; it involves a team effort, togetherness and commitment. For our interviewees, family may be seen as fixed by blood or marriage ties, or as something that develops over time. Most ideas of 'family' emphasised the significance of the unit as greater than the sum of its parts, while some expressed a more fluid notion placing greater emphasis on individuality.

A widespread feature of these 'family' understandings is the emphasis placed on ties that bind – that these are indeed a crucial aspect of the meaningfulness of family. A few interviewees saw such ties as restricting the choices of family members to make their own individual decisions and 'do their own thing'. However, the great majority discussed such ties as desirable, as a key source of security in both practical and emotional terms. Despite their own personal experiences of change, our interviewees identified 'being a family' precisely in terms of something dependable and long lasting, and resisted the idea that being a step-family meant anything different from this. Furthermore, their ideas of family prioritised support and obligation, constructing family as 'a community of need'. This is something which Beck-Gernsheim (1998) argues to have been a feature of pre-industrial families, contrasting this with the post-familial families of elective affinities of contemporary Western societies. Our quotes demonstrate the pervasive continuing relevance of just such a view of family amongst the interviewees of our current study (with only one rather ambivalent exception), despite the fact that we might expect them to be key protagonists for the view of family as based on elective affinity. (How coupledom and romance are understood within the context of family is explored in Chapter 3.)

Interviewees thus overwhelmingly rejected the notion of 'being a step-family', with many espousing the idea of 'being an ordinary family'. However, this personal rejection of the term did not prevent them from discussing whether or not there are differences between step-families and other families (in response to our direct question on this issue). Some interviewees felt that there was indeed the potential for differences, either due to the variable significance of biological relationships, or due to the potential for greater complexity in step-family relationships. However, a social-class difference occurred around this issue, with working-class interviewees asserting that biology is largely irrelevant to parenting relationships as these are experienced in everyday family life. They also felt that it could be positively harmful to see their family relationships as different, which was part of the grounds for rejecting 'that step-thing'. Such differences in the context of social class will be explored in more detail in Chapter 4.

Although our numbers are small, in this chapter we have started to discern some of the tensions that exist for our middle-class interviewees, as they are torn between different elements in their understandings of what it means to 'be a family', elements which they find difficult to hold together in their changing household and parenting circumstances. The preferred attitude of our working-class interviewees was to see such difficulties as largely a matter of attitude. This view facilitated a much easier demarcation of the boundaries of the new unit, with ideas of 'family' coinciding with household residence. Some of our middle-class interviewees, by contrast, had a much more diffuse sense of family boundaries (particularly apparent among our more liberal, professional interviewees). Others were torn between a desire to assert clear boundaries with regard to the new household unit, and a belief that blood ties do make a difference and have to be recognised as giving rise to legitimate claims in relation to children, whether or not they coincide with household residence. But whatever approach was taken, 'being a family' was a central preoccupation.

Throughout these various ideas of what it means to be a family, we have suggested the centrality of the presence of children, with family seen as the key site for the experience of childhood. In the next chapter we will explore in more detail the significance of generation for these accounts of family lives under changing circumstances, and consider how ideas about the Child and the Adult in contemporary Western societies underpinned a moral imperative within them.

Notes

1   This dual focus has parallels with David Morgan's (1996) distinction between 'family' as noun and as adjective.

2   For discussions of gay and lesbian couples who are living with, and bringing up, children, see Jeffrey Weeks *et al.* (2001) and Gill Dunne (1997). These studies show that, while gender expectations may certainly shift in such households, ideas of generation may parallel those of heterosexual households.

3   Our discussion here resonates with Bettina Apthekar's (1989) concept of 'dailiness', but her discussion is concerned with rather different epistemological issues.

4   When we refer to a father, we are always referring to a man who is living with a child or children from his current relationship, rather than a child or children from a previous relationship – unless we specify otherwise. The children involved are thus living in a household with both their biological parents.

5   When we refer to a step-father, we are always – unless otherwise specified – referring to a man who is living with children that are not his own biological children but are the children of his current partner.

6   All mothers were living with all their children – unless otherwise indicated.

7   In Jonathan's case, the children with whom he resided were children from his first marriage as well as his second, current marriage, so we describe him as a resident father.

8   The notion of differentiated complementary roles and duties, at first sight may have some resonance with a functionalist view of family (notably Parsons and Bales, 1955; Goode, 1963), and echoes notions of rational economic trading within families (notably Becker, 1981, 1996). These theories of family life, however, do not take into account whether this is how people may consciously comprehend 'family'. The theories state that complementary differentiation is going on, whether or not people see themselves as acting in this way, and/or that complementary role specialisation is the best and most 'efficient' form of organisation and socialisation for both families and society as a whole. Furthermore, while our interviewees might stress differentiation and complementarity, this does not necessarily refer to the gendered division of labour at the heart of functionalist and economic rationality models.

9   See Note 7.

10 Like Jonathan, Martin was a resident father living with children from his first marriage, but unlike Jonathan, he was also a step-father, living with his second wife's children from her first marriage.

Chapter 3

Putting children first? Adults, children and coupledom

This chapter centralises issues of generation that were touched on in the previous chapter, where we saw that ideas about children and childhood are important in understandings of 'being a family'. In this chapter we examine debates about the social construction of childhood in contemporary Western societies, and how this sets up a fundamental dichotomy between the Child and the Adult. We will consider the significance of moral agency and accountability in relation to these social categories, which posit children's needs as taking overriding moral precedence. We explore how our adult family members positioned themselves morally in their discussions with us. We will also set this alongside an exploration of how the children we interviewed for case studies (see Chapter 1) positioned themselves in relation to agency and moral responsibility.

In intact nuclear families, issues around children's needs are understood in such a way that they are expected to reinforce ties and solidarities between the (biological) parents of the children involved. Both parents are expected to have a 'natural' commitment to the needs of the child/ren who are the outcome of the romantic coupling. Coupledom and parenthood are meant to be part of a mutually reinforcing package – although even for intact families, experience may well not live up to this expectation. In contrast, for repartnered families, there is a strong public discourse (as discussed in Chapter 1) that raises the possibility – even the expectation – of tensions and rivalry between a step-parent and children. In the second part of this chapter, therefore, we turn to consider the significance of the couple relationship for our adult interviewees in the context of caring for dependent children.

Adult and Child as moral categories

Central to understanding our interviews is the distinction between Child and Adult. These categories are constructed by reference to one another, so that we know what it is to be a Child because it is to be Other than Adult (i.e. as Adults we understand Children in terms of their difference from us) and vice versa. It is important to be clear that we are using these terms as social categories here (signalled by our use of capitalisation). We are not implying any biological essentialism – indeed, we would want to distance ourselves from such a view. Nor are we implying any moral evaluations around these categories. Consequently, when we describe (below) some step-parents as taking the position of 'Child', we are referring to a social category, not moralising about their narrative by inferring that they are being 'childish' or failing to shoulder their 'Adult' responsibilities. We do not intend any developmental model either, such as may be found, for example, within therapeutic discourses that may position the counselled as needing to 'work on' her or his Inner Child in order to develop and become fully Adult.[1] Indeed, the images of Adult and Child we identify arise out of our interviewees' own narratives, rather than being preimposed categories.

Attention has been paid in recent years to the social construction of childhood. There is considerable agreement within this literature (see reviews in Lynott and Logue, 1993; Jenks, 1996a; Hendrick, 1997a) that, in contemporary Western societies, the Child is seen as different from the Adult, and that childhood has been institutionalised and portrayed in particular ways in recent centuries. A key theme is that of the separateness of childhood (e.g. Ennew, 1986; Hockey and James, 1993; Pilcher, 1995; Jenks, 1996b; Hendrick, 1997b; James et al., 1998), whether it is the construction of 'home' as the appropriate place for children, their exclusion from paid work and segregation into educational establishments, their compartmentalisation within the judicial system, or the construction of particular sites such as playgrounds for any (accompanied) forays they might make into public spaces. Underlying this institutionalisation of separateness, these writers suggest, are themes of the dependency and vulnerability, and also the incompetence and immaturity, of children (Archard, 1993; Moss et al., 2000).

This construction of the Child as Other can be traced both to the rise of developmental psychology, which constructs models for normality for children, and to the Enlightenment conception of the Adult as 'autonomous, emancipated and rational subject' (Moss et al., 2000: 240). Some argue that this separate institutionalisation is dependent on a high level of economic security at both national and individual levels (e.g. Boyden, 1990). Such experiences of childhood both across and within particular societies may be socially patterned around class and race (e.g. Burman, 1994; Glenn et al., 1994; Lareau, 2000). Overall, though, in Western societies childhood is constructed and idealised as a separate phase of life, a time of freedom and spontaneity, in which the only *responsibilities* required of the Child are to experience and enjoy childhood, and to pass the appropriate developmental and educational milestones successfully as the years progress (although even these responsibilities lie primarily with the parents/ mother).

Peter Moss and colleagues (2000: 240) point to the centrality of family, and parental/maternal relationships, for this understanding of the Child:

> This dominant discourse has constituted childhood as located within the private domain. It has constructed the child as dependent and individualized, with a recognized and necessary place in the family but not in society.

While we query such a positioning of 'family' as somehow located outside of 'society', this does highlight how notions of childhood are bound up with family in ways that emphasise their separation from Adult 'society'. Barbara Walkover (1992) discusses 'the family as an overwrought object of desire' in referring to couples' decisions about whether or not to have children. Her discussion points to the ways in which children are both idealised as the ultimate source of meaning in life, and dreaded as creating impossible responsibilities in terms of satisfying their emotional and material needs. Walkover argues that childhood is constructed so that parents feel individually charged to resolve such tensions, and suggests that they are burdened with an overwhelming moral obligation to ensure that the child is 'number one' (1992: 181).

Legislation and policy reinforce this understanding of the Child as being distinct from the Adult, as well as integrally connected with family. An emphasis on children's rights, whether understood in protective or assertive terms (Hendrick, 2001), and children's special treatment within the law (Kilkelly, 2001a, 2001b), both assume that the Child requires distinct consideration in terms of age, level of maturity and intellectual and emotional capacities. At the same time, the Human Rights Act 1998 provides legal recognition within the UK for the right to respect for private and family life. Within this, the relationship between parent and child is given priority and protection. Parental rights can only be overridden if they are seen to be in conflict with the child's individual interests. The needs of children are thus given the status of public accountability (Home Office, 1998).

Much of the literature on the social construction of childhood concentrates on the practical everyday and institutionalised ways in which the separateness of the Child is manifested, and the consequences for children. There is also discussion about the historical origins of this particular Western construction of childhood, including Christian ideas of children as different from adults in their moral state as well as in their capacity for rationality. Initially this stemmed from ideas about original sin, but later shifted to more contemporary notions focusing on the Child as innocent.

The significance of the historical notion of childhood as based in the Child's moral status may merit further attention, even if this moral construction has become more secularised during the twentieth century. Spencer Cahill (1990, 1998) draws on the work of Irving Goffman to understand the positioning of children as being outside moral agency. Goffman himself saw social life as intrinsically moral, in the sense that social actors feel obliged to follow the ground rules of any particular interaction setting in order to preserve and maintain their sense of their social selves (Rawls, 1987). The actor thus seeks to 'sustain a viable image of himself [*sic*] in the eyes of others' (Goffman, 1971: 185). Goffman continues (1971: 186):

> *These norms to which the individual is concerned to demonstrate a* relationship of his own choosing *are norms about personal qualities, norms at the centre of our official religious beliefs, which designate the virtues and qualifications the individual ought not to deny through his behaviour.* [emphasis added]

While Goffman centres his notion of moral agency around the nature of social interaction, this revolves around key valued qualities in any particular social context. Furthermore, the agency that is apparent through individuals' placing themselves in relation to these qualifications 'by their own choosing' does not apply to the situation of children. Instead, their relationship to these qualities is held to be the responsibility, not of children themselves, but of their relevant adult caretakers – as Cahill discusses with regard to children in interaction with adults in public places. In such settings, children are not expected to appear at all without adult supervision, because they are not positioned as competent social actors who can be expected to behave within the moral obligations required for the maintenance of social interaction. Rather, it is the adult caretakers' own social value that is at stake. It is they who are held morally accountable for the actions of children in their care, although the key requirement is for adults to demonstrate their acknowledgement of their moral obligations by showing that they have *tried* to control their charges – since children may not always obey their instructions. Children thus do not qualify 'for the special, socially autonomous (first person) status of adult persons' (Shotter, 1993: 124). Adults are under a moral obligation to account for things in an acceptable manner if they are to avoid being treated as socially incompetent and sanctioned accordingly. Children, by contrast, are 'non-persons' (Cahill, 1998).

Jenny Kitzinger (1990) suggests that the notion of innocence positions the Child as passive and without agency – although she also goes on to discuss how children's lack of agency is part of the much wider power dynamics of children's social structural position. It is important to note, however, that when writers point (by contrast) to 'the actuality of children … as active social agents' (Scott *et al.*, 1998: 692; see also Smart *et al.*, 2001), such capacity for action by children is not necessarily the same thing as moral agency and accountability (as we discuss further below). Furthermore, the 'actuality' of children's social agency is not the issue for us here. Rather, it is the images of children being invoked that are crucial for the present discussion.

The (potential) 'evilness' of children poses dilemmas for contemporary constructions of the 'innocent' Child, with particular implications for the age of criminal responsibility (which is tending to increase across Europe – Kilkelly, 2001a). David Archard suggests that, while there is a moral dimension to ideas about childhood innocence, this does not entail notions of moral *accountability*, because the Child is without knowledge:

> [The child's] *purity is that of ignorance. The innocent do not sin because they do not know how to. The child cannot be tempted because it has no understanding of wrong-doing. Thus, the innocence of the child is, in an important sense, an empty one.*
> (Archard, 1993: 37)

References to the evil nature of children – as seen, for example, in discussions of the James Bulger case[2] (Jenks, 1996a) – do not *necessarily* therefore mean that children themselves are held to be accountable. Calls to 'police' or protect children can be seen as a sign of their renewed and enforced separation; in doing so, adults avoid putting children into positions in which they can make choices, which is an intrinsic component of exercising moral agency[3] as we discuss below. It may be that such reactions depend on the degree of evilness ascribed to children. While children as 'little devils' (Ribbens, 1994) may still be seen as (morally unaccountable) children (akin to the 'impish' child of 'potential evil' that Jenks describes as the Dionysian child), James Bulger's killers may be depicted as 'evil beyond comprehension' (Scott *et al.*, 1998: 695), as standing outside Child-like 'nature', and thus not children at all.

While the significance of the moral construction of the Child may have been underemphasised, the significance of the concomitant construction of the

Adult as responsible moral agent has passed unremarked. This may relate to a neglect of theorising adulthood. Where adulthood has been problematised, it has been largely in terms of a set of markers, including legal rights and practical accomplishments, which young people need to achieve in order to leave 'adolescence' behind, or which the Adult may lose as she or he encounters old age (Hockey and James, 1993; Pilcher, 1995). Yet it is the significance of this construction of the Child as being without moral agency, and the Adult as morally accountable, that is fundamental to an understanding of the moral content of the narratives we heard from our interviewees. Further, these categories may also be significant for understanding the nature of the contemporary family and intimate relationships in general because, as we go on to discuss, they lead to a moral imperative that essentially is non-negotiable and overrides any alternative morality of care of the (individual) self.

The moral imperative of meeting the needs of the Child

Given the extent of the public scrutiny and debate concerning contemporary family lives, the centrality of moral issues in our interviewees' accounts is not surprising. While some of the scrutiny proclaims its intention not to moralise about people's private lives, it is the 'needs of the child' that are accorded overwhelming moral and legal priority. As Janet Finch (1989) points out, family lives in general are an area where people's moral identities are at stake. Bill Jordan and colleagues suggest that, when we ask people to talk about their family relationships, we place them in a position where they face 'dual threats to moral adequacy and interactional competence' (1994: 76). Yet the significance of dependent children to the work needed to sustain morally adequate identities is often overlooked, both by those who theorise family lives and intimacy, and those who theorise the nature of contemporary morality – issues to which we shall return in Chapter 6. Here, though, we lay out the ramifications of moral identities around the categories of Child and Adult for our interviewees. Such moral content in people's accounts, briefly, is evident in: our interviewees' use of evaluative language; their use of contrast as a narrative device; their use of self-disclosure or the confessional. We also consider the part played by cultural assumptions about what constitutes moral behaviour as a good parent (for further discussion see Ribbens McCarthy *et al.*, 2000).

We have argued, then, that to be Adult is to be positioned firmly as a moral agent, and as such, adults must exercise responsibility and be accountable for themselves and for the care of others who are not Adult. In our interviews, these categories lead to an overall moral imperative, namely that *adults must take responsibility for children in their care and therefore must seek to put the needs of children first.* This is such a strong moral imperative that it seems to have been impossible for anyone to disagree with it in the accounts we have heard. This is not merely a guideline for action, it is an unquestioned and unquestionable imperative, not open to negotiation, comprising a number of key elements for the sustaining of a moral identity.

To be positioned as a moral Adult requires that the narrator must present her- or himself as *having tried* to live up to the overall moral imperative concerning the prioritising of children's needs. There may be reasons why the individual was not able to do this fully, but the crucial point is that the interviewee presents her- or himself as having tried: 'You try to do your best, be there for the kids, help 'em, guide 'em' (Dawn – White, working class, mother). None of our interviewees took the position of saying that they 'don't care'. While this might be implicit in a few interviews in places, nobody could avoid positioning themselves in relation to this morality in some way. Nobody could ignore it, and everyone subscribed to it in some format in at least some part of their interview.

The way in which adults can be seen to be trying to fulfil this powerful moral obligation is revealed when they are in a position to *make choices,* although it is crucial to understand here that the choices are not neutral. To make moral choices is not like choosing within the marketplace between different brands of washing powder, and in the context of our present discussion, there is almost no choice actually available if one is to maintain one's moral identity. Nevertheless, to be Adult is to be in a position to make moral choices, so that to present oneself as being without choices is to present oneself as powerless, and not fully Adult. The effort involved in making, or trying to make, moral choices around the care of children, is itself indicative of caring about children. To be morally deficient is to imply that you had a choice and did not even try to pursue the moral option.

No-one in our interviews presented themselves as morally unworthy in this way, although presenting others as morally unworthy could be an important device in telling a moral tale about oneself (Ribbens McCarthy et al., 2000). Of the 46 adults we interviewed, no-one contradicted this morality, and no-one was able to avoid engaging with it at some level (although we will consider below some interviews in which this sense of the moral imperative is less apparent). Only the two women in our sample who were not involved full-time in the lives of their children (one a full-time non-resident mother, the other a half-time 'non-resident' mother) were in a position to be able to pursue an alternative, more individualistic, morality around self-care, which some men also emphasised (and which was far more muted for the half-time mother). In this regard, we have concluded that it seems to be more possible for men, rather than women, not to engage with this moral imperative.

It is also instructive to note, however, how differently a working class couple originating from rural Bangladesh discussed moral themes, in the sense that their accounts were not characterised by individual decision-making. Attia had married Rashid after her first husband died, and she was left as a young mother with children and no male provider. It was the people around them who decided that Rashid was the appropriate person to marry Attia. Doing the right thing was not so much related to a sense of an individual making moral choices, because neither of them were given much option. The right thing was jointly decided by members of their community. Rashid's story is implicitly moral in that he married his cousin in order for her to maintain a respectable position in the community. This action was not presented as an individual moral decision however – his tale does not position him as the author of his own moral biography. In this regard, his interview does not show signs of individualism in terms of being morally accountable for a self made through his own choices (discussed by Jordan et al., 1994).

The overarching theme of moral responsibility for children does not mean to say that our other interviewees told the same, or even similar, moral tales at the level of putting this into practice. People varied in how they thought actual choices should be exercised within the *non-negotiable obligation* to seek to put children's needs first. For example, some of our interviewees particularly stressed the theme that 'children need (biological) parents', whilst others took the view that 'children need (social) families' (discussed further in Chapter 4). In addition, understandings about the actual practice of this moral obligation tended to be deeply gendered. Jordan and colleagues (1994) similarly found gender divisions in family-based ethical guidelines, as one might expect, given the wider evidence of the gendered nature of contemporary parenting and family lives. Thus, we do not see such divisions in relation to moral obligations as gendered in any essential way. Rather, as will become clear, they are related to the differing social construction of motherhood and fatherhood (and their 'step-' equivalents).

The gendering of moral tales

Men's moral tales, as biological or step-fathers, are often concerned with being a provider – 'I have without doubt been a good, if you like, provider for [my step-children]' (Frank – White, middle class, step-father) – and also with having authority, although this authority might be compromised in the complexity of step-cluster relationships. Other men stressed the importance of being in control as a rational and effective moral decision-maker:

> *It's a conscious decision a lot of the time to make sure that one* [set of children] *doesn't get more than the other.*
> (Bob – White, middle class, half-weekly resident father and step-father)

They might also frame moral issues in terms of acting 'maturely' (i.e. the language of responsible Adulthood).

Other men might tell a tale that places them less categorically in the position of responsible Adult, but they might still make some strong moral claims in their accounts. The interview with Daniel (White, middle class, non-resident father), for example, contains strong elements of being a Child. Daniel often suggests how naive he is, and that he does not know what to do in situations, saying: 'I don't feel that I have finished being young'. This unknowing position, however, has affected his ability to exert authority in relation to his children and their step-father. Nevertheless, he does see himself as having some serious adult responsibilities towards his children, most especially around finances: 'I'll pay for my kids, I know I've got responsibilities and I'm quite happy with it'.

While Daniel integrated his naive Child and responsible parent identities quite easily within his account, other men found their position fraught with tension, because of the conflict between taking responsibility for children and having the freedom to pursue individual goals. John (White, middle class, half-weekly resident step-father) yearns for freedom and spontaneity, but when the children are around he says he cannot help but feel 'dreadfully responsible' for them. This is self-imposed. Nevertheless, he poses his desire to disappear off on his motorbike as 'dreadfully selfish', and sees the obligation to be responsible imposed by being a step-father as rescuing him from this. For other men, too, moral responsibility was exercised through giving up the pursuit of individual pleasures.

Other moral themes expressed by men in relation to children included the responsibility of working out how to do the right thing in developing relationships with children, listening to children and being aware of their feelings, and ideas of providing guidance, or being a good role model in general:

> *I suppose I feel responsibilities towards* [my step-son]. *I have to provide him with a roof over his head and those basic kinds of things that I feel I ought to provide. And I think I ought to be a role model to him. I think it's important that I can go to work everyday and I'm not getting drunk and all that kind of stuff. You know, setting an example.*
> (Mark – White, middle class, step-father)

Yet another aspect was a gender-specific stance of active passivity, of *laissez-faire* and not being too heavy handed:

> *If I were strict and put my foot down it would cause trouble. It's not worth it. Let them get on with it.*
> (Martin – White, middle class, resident father and step-father)

The moral tales of women, as step- or biological mothers, were organised emphatically around the theme of accepting responsibility (which could, but did not always, include authority). Accepting responsibility was Tina's (White, middle class, mother) definition of a good parent, while children were defined as non-responsible:

> *I think it's knowing where responsibilities are. And accepting them so that the children don't end up having to be responsible.*

Elizabeth (White, middle class, resident step-mother and mother) equates 'growing up' (being Adult) and being in relationships with taking on moral responsibility, since children cannot be held accountable. In discussing her husband, she says:

> *He's very good with the children. And I don't think he would ever blame them for anything. I mean that, in that you can't blame a child.*

She emphasises (but, like John above, takes for granted) her obligation to deal with responsibility once she had acquired it:

> *I was just going to have to do the best I could, which I suppose is the way I approached it.*

The meanings of responsibility, however, generally differed between the women's and the men's accounts. The creation of a stable family unit was a strong moral theme for several women, requiring considerable emotional work, mediation of relationships, and organisational skills. It was a vital element in exercising responsibility for children, and often linked to major themes of commitment and obligation. Sometimes, though, these could be in tension, as in Kim's (White, working class, upwardly mobile, mother) worries about whether to draw in her partner to create a family or sideline him from her daughter's life as a protective measure in case the relationship does not last:

> *I still do worry that he'll go and* [my daughter]*'ll have some sense of loss.*

Several women also stressed that a potential new partner was only acceptable if he was also right for the child/ren. Gina (White, working class, mother) maintained that unless her new partner had been right for her young son Dan, then their relationship as a couple could have had no future:

> *You know, if you didn't love Dan, you and me wouldn't happen ... You know, we come as a package.*

In women's accounts, then, telling a moral tale could involve a clear statement about how their own happiness had to take second place to the needs of the children.

Moral bypass routes or amoral tales?

As part of our interpretation of moral tales, we conducted a search for negative cases (Hammersley and Atkinson, 1995), considering those that seemed to be least concerned with our identified moral imperative.[4] Of the 46 adults we interviewed, the person who seems to have given the least priority to the overarching obligation to put the needs of children first was Jo (White, middle class, step-father and father). Jo very rarely positions himself in his interview as a moral Adult. Nevertheless, he does not seem to tell an immoral tale, in that he avoids positioning himself as morally unworthy. Instead, he uses a number of routes to present himself as being outside the moral arena (routes we have already seen operating at times in other interviewees' accounts above).

The first, and perhaps most powerful way in which Jo does not construct himself as moral Adult is by positioning himself as being a Child, presenting himself (like Daniel above) as being unknowing, inexperienced or simply not accountable. He also (like Martin above) adopts quite a moral active passivity, being 'easy-going' and taking a *laissez-faire* stance. The other major way Jo presents an amoral tale is to use to an individualistic discourse stressing a duty of care for himself – 'I think you just have to look after yourself' – combining this with the implication that moral issues are often not relevant because there may be no choices involved if you are to survive in a situation. Mark (White, middle class, step-father) also used an individualistic discourse in his interview, but accompanied by the confessional device of owning up to being 'selfish', thus heading off potential accusations of moral deficiency.

There are also moments in Jo's interview where he hints that children's needs are given too great a priority, but without stating this explicitly. This can also be seen with another step-father:

Probably Sue is concerned what her children feel and what her children think and doesn't want to upset them. I probably don't have that attitude. I mean they're children and to a certain extent they don't have a lot of choices ... they've got to learn that they can't have everything that they want.
(John – White, middle class, half-weekly resident step-father)

For John, this attitude justifies him sometimes putting his preferences over and above the children's.

Nevertheless, all our male interviewees acknowledged the moral requirement to put the needs of children first. Even with Jo there are brief occasions when he engages with the morality of children's needs, and the idea that these should take priority. There is also an implicit (gendered) morality apparent around the theme of being the good provider: like John and Mark, Jo talked about having to cope with economic realities because of the pressures of his job.

Overall, then, we have identified several ways in which some men might not position themselves as moral Adults, but without presenting themselves as morally unworthy. These moral bypass routes are:

- to place themselves in the position of Child;
- to stress an individualistic discourse concerned with a responsibility towards one's self;
- to suggest an absence of real choices;
- to use a confessional style to demonstrate their current moral integrity.

Amongst the women interviewees, the account that initially struck us as placing the least emphasis on holding a moral position as a responsible adult parent was that of the only full-time non-resident (White, middle-class) mother in our sample, Mandy. Clearly she does not have to face the inescapable sense of responsibility expressed by resident mothers. While Mandy was aware that others may see her as rather passive in relation to her children's lives, she suggested that this constitutes a realistic response to a lack of power and choices: 'Well, it's just out of my hands, you know'. There are also a number of other ways in which Mandy bypassed the position of morally responsible Adult and parent. She described herself as having been damaged by her unhappy childhood, which had prevented her from growing up and reaching Adult maturity. She also identified this as the root cause of her prolonged ill-health. Nevertheless, the morally creditable side of Mandy's story concerns the effort she has made to overcome this childhood damage and improve her health. Furthermore, she also did at times clearly position herself as a morally Adult parent, in terms of putting the needs of her children first. For example, her younger son had been worried about leaving her on her own when he decided to follow his older brother and live with his father:

I just had to say, well, you know, 'Don't worry about it'. I didn't want him to feel guilty and that's what he wanted to do.

When asked what the word 'family' meant to her, Mandy made strong moral statements about what it entails:

It means hard work, it means tolerance, and I think it means communication.

In some other women's accounts the moral content seems to be quite subdued (or at least, differently framed). They have in common distressing stories of unhappy childhoods, and/or very difficult experiences in adult life, combined with considerable material struggles. Dawn, Sheena and Sarah (all mothers) told tales that included some sad or harrowing events, spoken in a flat, emotionless manner, with a sense of their having no control and few real choices. This raises wider issues about how people may feel able to tell such tales, given the potential emotional content and implications for both narrator and listener. It also suggests the likelihood, however, that the interviewee may expect the moral content of the story to be blindingly obvious, such that no special devices are needed to position the narrator morally. Just to stay with the children and meet their needs could thus be understood as a moral achievement:

The house was paid for and they were fed.
(Sarah – White, working class)

Dawn (White, working class) uses a contrast with her own childhood in an orphanage to position herself morally:

You know, I brought them up, whereas I wasn't brought up.

Indeed, Jordan and colleagues (1994) suggest that brevity is an indication that interviewees do not feel the threat of 'double jeopardy', whereas lengthy discussions tend to be produced where speakers are struggling to establish their moral identities.

In some respects, then, these women, like the men discussed earlier, also tended to position themselves as Child, through their emphasis on their ignorance, innocence and powerlessness. However, unlike other accounts where the emphasis on lack of choices may serve as bypasses to neutralise the moral imperative and tell an amoral tale, these issues appear to have the reverse effect in these women's tales. This is because some are stories of struggles to deal with Adult responsibilities as mothers, despite their damaged childhoods and lack of power and abilities. Ultimately, these are clearly moral tales. What is also notably different from the men's accounts, however, is the absence of any individualistic discourse as an alternative to the moral imperative of children's needs, other than (to varying extents) that of the two women interviewees who were not full-time resident mothers.

We have examined here some aspects of those accounts that are most muted in their presentation as moral tales, and considered how these still position the narrator morally, or what bypass routes are deployed to avoid a position of being morally unworthy. Yet the very presence of these bypass routes suggests the power of the absolute moral imperative for responsible adults to put the needs of children first. We thus have a moral imperative (adults should take responsibility for children) as an unchallenged consensus in our accounts, dependent on the categories of Adult and Child. We do also have an alternative morality apparent at times, however, particularly in some men's accounts, which is close to the idea of duty to oneself, or the pursuit of self-development, which is dependent on a notion of the self as autonomous and separate. Perhaps a more relational sense of self – which may be patterned by gender, class and race (Ribbens McCarthy and Edwards, 2002) – may not set up the alternatives in quite such an oppositional stance (Nutt, 2002). Indeed, this alternative morality of care of the self was difficult to find in the women's accounts. As Lynn Richards observed in her study of suburban families in Australia, 'nobody suggested that a good mother has her own life' (1990: 149). This gendering of the morality around children's needs is hardly surprising in the light of continuing evidence of the overwhelming part played by women/mothers in caring for children, mediating family relationships, and helping children deal with changing household circumstances (for a review see, for example, Crow, 2002b).

Children's (moral?) agency

Our parent and step-parent interviewees overwhelmingly drew on, and expressed, a discourse of children's needs as taking priority over those of adults, with adults having the responsibility to ensure these needs are met. This is not to say, however, that they constructed children as necessarily passive and without agency. At times they painted a vivid picture of children asserting their own perspectives and feelings in ways that had a major impact on relationships and decisions within and between households (as can be seen in our later discussion of coupledom). This is not the same thing, however, as suggesting that children were positioned as being responsible, or morally accountable, for such effects.

As we noted in Chapter 1, there has been recent attention paid to children as active agents in family life. This emphasises how they can exercise care and responsibility, rather than regarding them as passive dependants of their parents. In particular, Carol Smart and colleagues (2001) have argued that children are competent moral agents in post-divorce family life, engaging in active sensibility and sentient activities, rather than fitting the dominant conceptualisations of their being passive recipients of their parents' behaviour. This has implications for our arguments above about the importance of Adult/Child categories and moral accountability. At this point therefore, we turn to our interviews with some of the children in our step-clusters.

Our discussion here in relation to children's agency in step-family life, however, is somewhat different from that of Smart and colleagues, in that we are concerned not just with moral agency but also with moral accountability. The interviews with children in our research were not, in our terms, 'moral' in quite the same way as the accounts we heard from their parents and step-parents. The six children we interviewed – Katie, Nikki, Fred, Zoe, Ellie and Max – were drawn from two case-study step-families in our main sample.[5] Although both families were White and middle class, they represent quite different situations, each displaying aspects of the complexity of relationships and household arrangements that the literature characterises as comprising step-families.

For three years, Katie (aged 11) and Nikki (aged 8) had been moving half-weekly between their father's and their mother's households. On their father's side they had a step-mother, Jessica, and two step-siblings, Nick and Grace, close to them in age. On their mother's side they had a step-father who had been having a relationship with their mother for the past two years, but they had only been living all together for the past six months.

Fred (aged 13), Zoe (aged 11), Ellie (aged 11) and Max (aged 8) had been living together for three years, since Lyn and Martin moved in with each other. Fred and Zoe's mother, Lyn, was divorced and they lived with her and Martin. They had regular contact with their father two-and-a-half weekends every month. At their father's house they were involved in another step-family, as his partner had two sons from a previous relationship. Ellie and Max were Martin's children, and their mother had died six years previously. Although we have said that these children's situations represent complex step-family relationships and household arrangements, different from 'ordinary' families, the children did not see their lives in this way. Katie explicitly characterised her family as 'normal':

I think it's just like a normal family really, because we all do respect each other, respect each other's privacy and everything, and we will listen to each other, help each other out, look after each other and everything. So I don't think there's any real difference, it's just I have an extra brother, an extra sister, an extra mum and an extra dad really.

Indeed, when the children were asked at the end of their interview if there was anything that they would particularly like to stress or add, Katie said:

That a step-family's just like a normal family really. Things are basically the same.

Fred, Zoe, Ellie and Max seemed aware that there might be differences associated with living in a step-family, but all found it difficult to articulate how such differences were, or might be, experienced. Ellie and Max gave positive accounts of their family lives and referred to Lyn throughout as 'mum', as if they were a conventional family. Max, however, struggled to explain why he would be more likely to go to his father for a cuddle:

Well mostly dad because he's kind of like my proper parent. 'Cos my mum [i.e. Lyn], she's kind of like broke up with a different man and it's kind of hard.

While in response to a more direct question Max had suggested that there were no real differences between step-families and other families, he expressed an awareness that relationships may not be the same as in other families. His use of the term 'hard' seems to reflect his difficulty in identifying and explaining such differences. Fred, Zoe and Ellie all made a distinction between their own experience of step-family life and the problems that other children might face.

Ellie, like Katie (above), described her family as 'normal', but drawing on negative 'step-' associations she said:

> Some people don't really like their step-parents. But I do.

Similarly, Zoe said:

> They might not ask them to help them with their homework or ask for cuddles and things. They might not speak to them much.
>
> Is that how you feel about Martin?
>
> No I speak to him a lot.
>
> Right, so that would be other people, other step-families?
>
> Yeah.

By associating complexity and problems with step-families other than their own, the children conveyed their sense of being a relatively ordinary family. In fact Fred, Zoe, Ellie and Max seemed to want to portray themselves as ordinary carefree children in their interviews, perhaps aware that step-children can be seen as hard done by. For example, in response to the final 'anything else' question, Fred responded:

> Only that I get treated fair by everyone and there's nothing really bad about it.

Overall then, in terms of the essential values of family life as they saw it – respect, care and fairness – all six of the children felt that their step-family lives were the same as 'ordinary' families, rather than different from them.

The children's discussions as to who they thought of as family, however, show an interesting contrast. This mirrors the sorts of debates we noted in Chapter 1, as to whether contemporary family life is focused within clearly demarcated boundaries or seen as more elastic and diverse. Fred, Zoe, Ellie and Max worked with a more tightly defined unit. When asked who they saw as 'family', they identified the members of their immediate household, including their parent and step-parent, sibling and step-siblings. Only Fred transgressed the household boundary to include his father, while Zoe identified her step-sibling's father as 'someone else who is also important', but not as family. All four children were explicit in their definition of family as people who live with you and support you, and they had to be prompted to include relatives other than immediate family.

In contrast, Katie and Nikki held a far more 'open' notion of family. In addition to their biological and step-parents, they listed their father's mother ('gran'), his numerous brothers and sisters and their partners (as aunts and uncles) and their children (their cousins); their step-mother's parents (as grandparents), her brother and his wife and their children (also as cousins); and their mother's parents ('nana and grandad') and her sister (their aunt). They saw most of this extended family regularly, and the 'step-'sides seemed to intermingle. Katie gave this example:

> Nick my brother, who is also my step-brother, stays over at our cousin Mark's house [their father's brother's child] 'cos they're a similar age.

Their step-sister, Grace, whom Nikki was particularly close to, sometimes came to stay at their mother's house when they were there. Katie and Nikki were immensely proud of having such a large family. The only drawback they could see was in the future, when they would have to take responsibility for 'kin-keeping'.

> Katie: *I like it* [having a big family]. *It's going to be a bit annoying when we're older when we have to buy Christmas cards or presents for everyone.*
>
> Nikki: *Yes, mum has that trouble.*

This association of adulthood with having and taking responsibility for undertaking caring activities is a feature of all the children's accounts of their step-family life. The Adult/Child categorical distinction that we have identified as crucial for our parents and step-parents, keying together moral agency, responsibility through making choices, and meeting needs through care, is evident. The children were undoubtedly active in the way they lived and were parented within and (for those who were) between two households, as we note further below, and could display a moral awareness. However, this is not the same as taking moral responsibility and being accountable for family life in the terms that we have elaborated. Indeed, when any of the children did speak of taking moral responsibility for meeting the needs of a family member, they implicitly posed themselves as the symbolic Adult and the subject of their care as symbolic Child. This positioning is also evident in work on young people's moral values, which shows that young people can place themselves as more mature, responsible and Adult by reference to the immaturity of younger siblings or less responsible behaviour of friends (Holland *et al.*, 2000; Gillies *et al.*, 2002).

The fine distinction between agency and accountability, and its basis in the Adult/Child categories, is illustrated below. The children's agency, and indeed the power they could exert in the interstices of step-family life within and between households, was evident. Talking about who sets the 'rules' in each of their households, Max assessed which of his parents were most likely to let him do something:

> And if I asked my dad if I could have a friend round to stay the night he'd probably say no. Or if I want to sleep in the same room as someone dad might probably say yes, I mean no. If I asked mum she might say yes.

Likewise, Katie and Nikki skilfully evaluated the likely reactions of their different parents, and could act accordingly if they were feeling unwell or if they wanted something:

> So if you're ill who would be the first person you would think to tell about it?

Nikki:	Mum.

Katie:	Mum's more sympathetic than dad is. Dad will like [shrugs her shoulders].

Nikki:	Dad's like 'Go to school and see how it is when you're there'.

Katie:	Yeah, he won't go 'ohhh'. Mum will say 'Oh do you want [to stay off school]?'

...

And what about if you wanted to ... say, you wanted to go up to town with a friend. Who do you think would be the person most likely to let you do that?

Nikki:	Actually it would be Jessica [their step-mother]. Once we all went together on our own, me and Katie, Nick and Grace.

Katie:	... Jessica was like 'Oh, I'll give you a lift then and I'll pick you up from town' and everything ... I think if like I had to go somewhere or something I'd go to either [mum or dad]. Well, dad because he probably wouldn't give me the money. Mum would give me the money but she probably wouldn't let me go, but dad would let me go but wouldn't give me the money!

As we now discuss, however, these sorts of instances of the children's ability to exercise agency in how they are parented are not necessarily accompanied by moral responsibility and accountability. The children did display the moral reasoning that Smart and colleagues (2001) point to as a feature of the accounts of children living in post-divorce circumstances, manifested in the espousal of the ethics of fairness, care and respect. These ethics can be seen in the earlier quotes from Katie and Fred about the essential values of their family life. Ellie and Zoe also drew on a notion of fairness in talking about which of their parents they would go to for help or to ask for something. Ellie stressed that she would treat both parents the same: 'I think it would be equal'. Katie and Nikki drew on an ethic of fairness in their concern that their parents had equal shares of them, in a similar fashion to that described by Smart and colleagues, with Katie saying of their life across two households:

I don't think it's like the brilliantest really good way but at least everyone gets to see us. And like mum doesn't feel that she's missing out and dad doesn't feel like he's missing out, and we don't feel like we're missing out really.

Zoe, however, felt strongly that co-parenting arrangements involving equality of time between households would not be 'fair' on children:

I don't think it's very good for the children to be travelling from one house to another. They should be settled in one place.

This sort of moral awareness and reasoning, however, is not the same as taking responsibility for step-family life being fair. While the children may desire and positively evaluate fairness, this does not mean that they wish to exercise the decision-making responsibility for meeting needs fairly, and the accompanying accountability that characterises Adult moral agency:

Katie:	*Sometimes* [mum and dad] *make you decide where you want to sleep, on Christmas Eve or something.*
Nikki:	*Yeah, and you're like oh, oh, if I sleep over there I'll make mum feel kind of lonely, and if I sleep at* [mum's] *house, dad – one year I was like, oh, I don't know which house to sleep over.*
Katie:	*That's the worst thing. If they just decided and said.*

The issue of fairness in step-family life is an important one generally, and we will have more to say about it, from the parents' and step-parents' perspectives, in Chapter 5.

In the few instances where the children did talk about themselves as voluntarily taking the initiative in being responsible for and attentive to the care needs of other family members, they took on the symbolic position of Adult in their account. Being Adult could concomitantly involve placing their parent as a Child as well. Katie, for example, could reverse roles and play responsible Adult to her father on occasion:

Once he told me off because I forgot my keys or something like that. And say if he forgets his key I will do the same to him and I tell him off, and things like that.

Taking up the position of Adult was evident in many of the responses that the children gave to the hypothetical dilemmas about step-family life we posed in vignettes (see Chapter 1 and Appendix), and in their discussion of more abstract, generalised questions.[6] For example, in considering whether it was ever a good idea for step-parents to adopt their step-children, Zoe spoke from the position of parent when answering:

Um, if their real parent wasn't treating them very nicely, you'd want to adopt them so if anything happened it would be official.

The children's taking up of the position of Adult on their own terms was in stark contrast to Katie's reaction to a question about whether she thought that her mother might talk to her or her sister about any worries and problems:

No, I think it would be like putting pressure on us a bit if she told us. I wouldn't want her to.

While the children we interviewed might take up the position of Adult as they chose, it appeared to be too much if it involved a moral responsibility for caring and meeting their parents' needs. Zoe's disapproval of the concept of co-parenting demonstrates a similar sense that children should not be burdened in any attempt to ensure fairness between adults. In sum, the children wanted their parents to act as the Adult with ultimate moral responsibility for putting the Child(ren)'s needs first, as indeed Smart and colleagues (2001) also found. A question about what a 'good' mother and father should be like elicited the following responses:

Katie: *Firm but nice. I think she'd know where to put the line. I think there should be some rules, some boundaries there. But then there should be care and everything. There should be like interest in school work, willingness to help and things.* [And a good father the] *same sort of thing I think, yeah.*

Fred: *If they think anything's wrong they should like speak to* [their children] *and put them on the right path.*

Children's moral awareness and agency, therefore, do not appear to operate in the same way as they do for the adults who are caring for them, in that they do not involve the key interlinking of the three elements: moral agency, responsibility through making choices, meeting needs through care. However, in making our arguments about these differences, we need to be cautious. Our sample of children is very small and not particularly diverse or representative. Nevertheless, it is clear that while the children we interviewed could display moral awareness, reasoning and activity, they did not have their moral identities at stake in the accountable way that the parents and step-parents felt themselves subject to. Furthermore, our discussion of their views shows the importance of the Adult/Child categorical distinction that we have identified as crucial in constructing moral responsibility in family life.

We now return to the adults in our sample, to look at the ways they discussed issues of agency and accountability around the Adult/Child distinction in the context of their couple relationship. We might perhaps expect to find a greater emphasis here on the needs and wants of Adults.

'The coupley bits': couple intimacy and family life

A major question raised in relation to the requirement for responsible adults to put the needs of children first is whether or not this leaves any room for adults to prioritise their own needs in terms of their couple relationship. If the arguments about pure relationships (Giddens, 1992) and elective affinities (Beck-Gernsheim, 1998) discussed in Chapter 1 have relevance, we would expect to find such notions in the context of the personal histories of re-partnering and new coupledom. Every step-cluster in our study included at least one person who had been through the experience of ending a significant relationship in their lives, and choosing to embark on a new one. One might therefore expect to find discourses of 'romance' or 'self-fulfilment' to be apparent. Although responsibilities to children are sidelined in the discussions of Anthony Giddens and Elisabeth Beck-Gernsheim, our interviewees had to take account of the fact that there were dependent children involved as major figures in the contexts of their (potential) projects of the self and coupledom. As we have argued, in some of the men's accounts particularly there were definite overtones of an ethic of care of the (individual) self. But the possibility that this project of the self may lead to relationships formed through 'elective affinity' leads to the question of *which* particular individuals are being elected for affinity. Our adult interviewees might focus on their desire to be with another adult, but in deciding to live together they could hardly ignore the fact that there were other pre-existing attachments and responsibilities involved: importantly, child/ren.

Almost all of our interviewees did express a sense of having taken on a new couple relationship that might require its own investment of time and energy, and that had something to offer them as individuals. One male interviewee was exceptional in that, for him, couple intimacy as a separate element within, or alongside, family life just did not appear to be a priority. Instead, his interview revolved around the children, wider family and ex-partner relationships. He only addressed the question of a separate couple intimacy when asked directly about it, when he stated that he did not hanker after it.

There may be similar issues for adults in intact nuclear families about how far coupledom is seen as part of the family project or as in tension with it. For our interviewees though, 'being a couple' and 'being a family' have the potential for being harder to hold together, occurring within different personal histories of changeable couple relationships. As with other potential sources of tension, however, our interviewees varied a great deal in terms of how far such issues were apparent. Alongside this, the agency of children is also very apparent as a major factor in how far it is possible to reconcile the new couple project with the pre-existing family project.

Coupledom as the basis for 'family'

For several interviewees, the meaning of coupledom was such that there seemed to be no perception of tension between couple intimacy and family life with children. Even when we posed a vignette that we had written specifically to stimulate discussion about such tensions, some of our interviewees interpreted the situation we had described as being about other issues altogether.

The construction of coupledom as the foundation for family life was particularly apparent and explicit for some of our interviewees who were active members of religious organisations. Lyn and Martin both come from Jewish families, while Margaret and James, and Karen and Paul, are active Christians who met through their churches. James (White, middle class, step-father) happily refers to a quotation that allows him to pose love for Margaret as being the best thing he can do for her children:

> A quotation which I love is the question, 'What's the way a father can be the best father to his children?' and the answer is, 'To love their mother', which I think is lovely. They've got a mum who they're very close to and they know that we're very close and our relationship is very very important and they know that we love each other, and I think that probably helps them, gives them reassurance and stability after, you know, a very difficult year or two, before when their dad was dying and the year after that.

For her part, James's wife Margaret (White, middle class, mother) felt that there had been some tensions after she fell 'madly in love' with him, particularly in relation to her eldest son, who she felt had taken on the role of 'head of household'. She described how she considered and prayed about her decision to marry James, and 'it seemed absolutely the right thing to do'. At the same time, she says she would not have allowed herself to fall in love with someone who would not be good for her children:

> *The minute we announced our engagement, the oldest one found that quite hard ... I thought, well what can I do? I actually can't live without James, and I thought I will go mad if I can't marry him so I won't be any good to them anyway ... they really need a father figure, particularly as teenagers ... [I don't think] I would've fallen for someone who hadn't got on with [the children], I don't think I would've let myself. I've got a feeling. It's always been very important to me, how a man got on with children.*

Others too, not necessarily with religious underpinnings, may see the new couple relationship as good for children, providing them with greater security and a new sense of family. When Dawn's (White, working class, mother) previous relationships had begun to break up, she felt they were not a family any more, whereas 'family' is about 'joining in and being close, you know, it's a family and all getting on'. Now, with her new partner, Trevor, she feels 'it's been a good thing for the kids, 'cos he likes the kids and the kids like him'.

Similarly Sally (White, middle class, mother) is very conscious of how much she feels her children gain from her relationship with Michael, who has only recently moved in to live with them:

> *Michael and I support each other ... it really is just doing things for each other and encouraging each other, and being there for each other. That's really nice, and that's why I feel a family, the kids have changed since he's been here, they are a lot happier.*

Taking on the children along with the parent/partner

Another dimension of interviewees' accounts that expressed no indication of tension between coupledom and family was the general agreement, between the adults and children involved, that the step-parent was as committed to the children as to the partner. As the commitment to the new partner developed, this was understood as implying an equally developing commitment to her or his child/ren.

Kim (White, working class, upwardly mobile, mother), for example, had had a fraught on–off relationship with Ben. For her, having an established and acknowledged couple relationship means that he is committed to a family relationship. Thus the coupledom she desires encompasses her daughter, rather than being a separate intimacy. For Kim, the only source of tension lies in the way state benefits operate, which mean that she would be financially worse off if she were seen by the relevant agencies as having a cohabiting partner.

Some people acknowledge the possibility of tension between the couple relationship and the children's needs, but they feel it is up to them to manage this and prevent such tensions developing. The new partner has to ensure she or he loves the children, and the existing parent has to monitor the new relationship so that it includes the children's needs:

> I think, you know, that you can't just have a relationship with the woman. The children are there and therefore in the same way as you're developing a relationship with the woman or the mother, or the man if it's the other way round, you've got to develop a relationship with the children. They can't be appendages.
> (Pete – White, middle class, step-father and father)

> I want what's best for the kids as well at the end of the day. I think it made me like that, knowing that if I accept somebody into my life that heavily, it's got to work, in all ways, otherwise I wouldn't do it.
> (Sally – White, middle class, mother)

Including the children before everything else

If there is a conflict, however, most interviewees felt that responsibility for children has to override personal desires for couple intimacy, as children must not be made to feel excluded or insecure. One of our vignettes proposed the scenario that a child from a previous relationship might go to live with his grandparents as a way of dealing with tensions and ensuring the viability of the new family unit (see Appendix). This was viewed almost unanimously by our interviewees as something that was quite unacceptable.

Some of our interviewees imposed an absolute obligation on the new adult to love the children and be committed to them – there was no choice about this. Paul (African-Caribbean, working class, step-father and father), for example, was very explicit about how seriously he took his new commitments both to his new partner, Karen, and to her daughter, Isis:

> I had every intention from the start to treat Isis as if she were my own ... And from day one, I said to Karen, even before she said anything about Isis, 'I love you, and I will also love Isis as my own.' So Karen didn't have to ask me, 'Well what about Isis?' From the time I knew she had Isis I considered that I loved Karen and I would love Isis.

For others, the issue is seen more in terms of acceptance rather than love as such. Catherine (White, middle class, mother) feels that her children and her third husband are equally important to her, and wants them all to 'accept' each other so that no-one is excluded. But poor relationships between her husband and her children were presented as a major reason for the breakdown of her second marriage.

> Although the kids come first, I wouldn't want them to get rid of, in this case Simon, or Simon to get rid of them. I would like them all to accept each other really ... [My second husband] made the eldest's life hell, and we were just arguing all the time.

At other times, it is presented as a matter of luck or circumstance that there is no tension between coupledom and family. The adults can have their couple time together without any detriment to the children, since the children are regularly elsewhere at times when the couple are together. In this way, couple time can occur without the children experiencing any sense of being excluded. For Sally (White, middle class, mother), specific couple time is facilitated by her children's regular weekend visits to their father:

> We're lucky as far as we're concerned to actually get every other weekend. A lot of couples don't ... I mean, I love 'em to bits, but I do like to have that space as well ... It's good for Michael and I to have our time.

All in good time

For some people, couple intimacy was something that could only be recognised as a priority at particular phases within the overall trajectory of the family project, either as the new partnership was formed, or as children grew older. Tensions might thus be discussed as a matter of transition, sorted out over time. The strength of initial feelings in the new couple relationship was one aspect of this, while dealing with children's reactions to it were another.

Lyn (White, middle class, resident step-mother and mother) described the early days of her relationship with Martin in the following terms, suggesting an intense period when any tension was to do with their own feelings of insecurity, rather than the children's:

> I think when Martin and I were first together, you know, when the relationship's new you're very very inseparable. I think we devoted an inordinate amount of time to each other. Not to the detriment of the children, but you know, with a new relationship you're very possessive with each other. But perhaps we'd get slightly miffed with each other for spending too much time with the children.

Others suggested that step-family life meant that it was difficult to find the time initially to invest in the couple relationship:

> If you're marrying with ready-made children, then there's no time to get to know each other really. You have to make that time, really. Sometimes it gets pushed to the back.
> (Mary – White, middle class, mother)

Jackie (White, middle class, mother) described a great deal of tension initially, as her eldest daughter, Emily, appears to have regarded her new partner as intruding on her close relationship with her mother:

> That was very difficult. Extremely difficult ... Emily was unwilling to have anything to do with him basically.

However, eventually:

> Emily sort of realised that underneath, this person she saw as taking her Mummy away from her, underneath was okay. I think that was a turning point.

In the other direction, some interviewees suggested that the time for being together as a couple would come later. Frank (White, middle class, step-father), for example, said he could wait for their couple time to come later:

> *Sometime or other Mary and I will be able to get that motor caravan and drive to China you know.*

This sense of the couple relationship being put 'on the back burner' during the children's years of dependency may be found with intact nuclear families too (Ribbens, 1994).

Distancing the couple relationship

For some people, sidelining the couple relationship could be carried to the point where the couple relationship was kept separate from the notion of 'family'. Underlining these situations was an understanding that if anyone was going to feel excluded and marginalised, it would have to be the new partner. The child/ren had to be the priority.

In some cases, this separation between parenting and partnering occurred because the resident mother and/or her new partner continued to regard herself and her children almost as a single-parent family:

> *I just happen to be married to their mother and* [her children] *live with us*
> *... If I'd hated her children I would still have married Mary.*
> (Frank – White, middle class, step-father)

Sarah (White, working class, mother) had experienced several relationships before she met Dave, her current partner. She was quite explicit that she wanted him to be her partner, but not a father to her eight children, and it was many months before he even met her children:

> *I just wanted someone there for me. For whatever I might have wanted.*
> *I didn't want a dad for the kids. They'd had enough dads.*

In response to our standard question about who she sees as her family, she did not include Dave:

> *My family I see as my children. My children, that's really who I see as family.*

In the other direction, Kate (White, middle class, mother) discussed her doubts about how far to allow her new, inexperienced, partner to take on a direct parenting role with her child:

> *It's a bit hard, it's almost experimenting on your child. The idea of letting somebody else make mistakes on your child.*

The part played by the children themselves could be significant too, in determining whether and how the couple relationship was incorporated into family life. As discussed earlier, many of our interviewees described hostility and difficulties arising as a result of the attitudes of children to a new partner or a new step-sibling. Sometimes this would be from one particular child, and it might centre on a sense of intrusion into the relationship with the child's mother or, less often, the child's father.

Some interviewees explicitly discussed how 'lucky' they were that such rejections and hostilities by children had not been apparent, and that relationships had developed well. For some of those who had experienced hostility between the new partner and the children, these tensions had eventually been resolved or abated, and were now seen largely as something in the past. For others, however, these tensions remained, and could be seen as a continuing threat either to the couple relationship as a separate element, or to the viability of continuing 'family' life at all.

Continuing tensions: coupledom as incompatible with family life

The majority of our interviewees were able to reconcile coupledom and family life in some way, or at least keep any tensions between the two within manageable limits. For some, however, tensions were felt to be such that they could not really be reconciled.

The two non-resident fathers who had not re-partnered constructed coupledom as separate from family, or as difficult to reconcile with parenting relationships. Daniel (White, middle class, non-resident father) explained:

> *I wouldn't plunge into another relationship if you can possibly help it because I think it confuses kids ... I don't think it's a good idea to jump, for anybody, either partner, to jump into a relationship if there are kids involved.*

Paula (White, middle class) – the only non-resident step-mother we interviewed[7] – described her difficult experience of trying to sustain a couple relationship with her husband, who was also maintaining his fathering relationship with his children from his first marriage:

> *If I was to do it again, I wouldn't! If we get divorced, I'm not ever again getting involved in a relationship with somebody else's kids! Unless they've grown up and left home.*

We also described above the case of Sarah (White, working class, mother), who had constructed her new relationship with Dave as being separate from her family life with her children. She had also previously been a resident step-parent herself, when Dave's daughter Leanne had come to live with them. The tensions that resulted, however, had eventually proved impossible to resolve, and Leanne had moved out again. They continue to resurface on the weekends when she comes to stay. Resentments from Sarah's own children in terms of what they saw as an intrusion by Leanne were part of this. In addition, Sarah herself did not necessarily feel obliged to like Leanne, and her advice to people in similar circumstances would be:

> *Don't assume that if you get on with someone you're going to get on with their children ... And if you don't get on, accept it. See it for what it is. There's nothing that says you've got to like someone. You can still have a good relationship even if you don't get on.*

Even for Sue and John (White, middle class), who have half their time alone as a couple, uncomfortable compromises have to be made, because John finds it hard to cope with the reduced space for coupledom that occurs when Sue's children are around.

> *Keeping a relationship together is difficult, but you've got to do it with children, you know ... I kind of resented [her children] a little bit. It was just this extra layer of things to get through to have a relationship ... I've told Sue that I don't think I'd ever have stayed in a situation where I had the children every seven days a week because I just wouldn't be able to deal with it all ... You've got to vie for attention with these other creatures here. But we don't have that problem really, when Sue and I are together for three days a week by ourselves.*

Sue, in a somewhat different direction, was aware that she had given up the time she had for individual self-fulfilment without her children, when she and John set up home together.

Other interviewees indicated that, if there is continuing tension between the couple relationship and the parenting relationships, this has to be dealt with by prioritising the care of the children at the expense of coupledom. In the case of Kate and Rob (White, middle class), tensions with Kate's son, Liam, had been a source of great difficulty from the start of their relationship, and had never been resolved. Rob described how he had felt like an outsider in the household for some time, and suggested that step-parents 'have to be a bit self-sacrificing in terms of their relationships with their partners'. When he and Kate had a daughter, Jasmine, a different set of alliances developed: he spends time with Jasmine, and Kate continues to spend time with Liam. Consequently, Rob feels that the couple relationship has almost disappeared under the priority of parenting relationships. When he and Kate had time alone as a couple on holiday, he suggests they found it difficult to relate to each other:

> *and all of a sudden I thought, it's just me and Kate. Who is this person? What am I supposed to do with her? I can't talk about Liam, I can't talk about Jasmine ... What am I supposed to talk about? In fact it felt strangely odd.*

Conclusion

Overall, then, we find great variability in these interviews about the place of coupledom, and the ways in which it is constructed and experienced alongside the 'needs of the children'. Coupledom might be seen to require its own investment of time and energy, but this is not necessarily regarded as being detrimental to children. Many of our interviewees understand the needs of children, and the meanings of family and coupledom, in such a way that these ideas can still constitute a mutually reinforcing package. If, however, investment in the couple relationship is seen to be detrimental to children, the dominant view is that it has to be kept in its place, and/or subordinated to the overriding priority of meeting the needs of dependent children. As we shall consider further in Chapter 5, the needs and wishes of adults can only fully enter the picture if they are understood as necessary towards meeting the needs of children. As with earlier studies of family lives, 'what's best for the children' (Cornwell, 1985) continues to be a crucial theme. Indeed, it may be that uncertainty about the morality of relationships for re-partnered parents highlights and contributes to this unquestionable moral imperative around the needs of children. While such 'needs' are not necessarily written in stone (Woodhead, 1990), the power of their rhetoric is such that it is difficult even to begin to raise questions about how we have constructed them, or to imagine that they could be questioned.

In this chapter, we have suggested that this moral imperative arises from the ways in which we have constructed the social categories of Child and Adult in contemporary Western societies. We have examined the consequences for the ways in which our interviewees positioned themselves morally in their accounts. Within these processes, gender appears as a very strong feature, with greater possibilities available to men than to women in terms of bypassing responsibility and accountability for children's needs without sacrificing one's moral identity. The residence of the children might at times cross-cut this, however, with non-resident mothers apparently finding greater discursive space for such moral bypass routes. While some may hear these interviewees as telling an immoral tale when they employ bypass routes or stress an alternative morality around self, it is important to reiterate that such immorality was not present in terms of the narrative itself.

While our interviewees may have felt particularly vulnerable to threats to their moral identities given their changing household circumstances in a context of fierce public debates, it is also important to consider how far we are simply finding more general themes of family lives writ large here. While the levels of tensions and difficulties are quite striking at times in our interviews, these are not necessarily different in kind from the experiences of those living in intact families. John Gillis (2000), for example, discusses evidence that men may feel marginal to the home, strangers within the family (see also Ribbens, 1990, 1994), with a sense of rivalry with their own children for the attention of the wife/mother. Mothers living in intact families may similarly discuss dilemmas about how far to draw their children's father into active involvement in childrearing (Ribbens, 1994). The sort of ideals around understandings of 'family' that we discussed in Chapter 2 make it difficult for family members generally to voice such tensions, whatever their circumstances. Perhaps it is more realistic to see family tensions as normal rather than pathological or unhealthy (Bernardes, 1997). Nevertheless, tensions were not always apparent in our interviews amid very variable understandings and experiences of parenting children in changing circumstances.

We have also referred at various points to the significance of economic circumstances and social class with respect to the ways in which childhood and children's needs are constructed. Social class is also significant in relation to the ways in which our interviewees discussed the more practical details of everyday life in relation to the care of children, as we now go on to consider in Chapter 4.

Notes

1   It should, however, be noted that some of our interviewees themselves used the terms within such a discourse. See, for example, Mandy, discussed below.

2   This was a case that attracted a great deal of public attention and debate in the UK, and still does, in which James Bulger, aged under three, was murdered by two boys aged ten.

3   Indeed, in Ribbens' earlier research (1994), some mothers suggested that children have to be helped to learn the skill or capacity to make choices.

4   For more detailed discussion of this search for negative cases and the complexities of some of these accounts, see Ribbens McCarthy *et al.* (2000).

5   Katie and Nikki were interviewed together because Nikki wanted to take part in the research but did not want to be interviewed on her own. Katie would have been happy to be interviewed on her own, but was equally happy to undertake a joint interview. Fred, Zoe, Ellie and Max were interviewed separately.

6   Smart *et al.* (2001) base their chapter discussing the way children draw on the ethics of fairness, care and respect largely on responses to hypothetical vignettes.

7   Our focus on current parenting relationships led us to design our sample around a step-cluster of resident parent, resident step-parent, and non-resident parent. This led to our drawing a boundary, however, that excluded any non-resident step-parent involved. In the case of Paula, we were explicitly pressurised by Chris to include her in the study. For further discussion of such sampling decisions, see Edwards *et al.* (1999b).

Chapter 4

'Doing family': caring, authority and material provision

In previous chapters we have considered some broad issues concerning what it means to 'be a family', and understandings of the social categories of Child and Adult. Now we turn to consider more closely how our interviewees discussed the concrete minutiae of 'doing family' (see Chapter 2) in the context of living with, and relating to, children over time. We do this using the themes of 'caring', 'authority' and 'responsibility', concepts that lie at the centre of contemporary notions of parenting.

Issues of child care, discipline and financial upkeep of children were often discussed spontaneously during the interviews, as well as being directly prompted through specific structured questions and vignettes. These themes were thus built into the research from the outset, as areas of concern in public debate, but our interviewees attached their own meanings to them, largely ordered by prominent sub-themes of biology, time and commitment. Gender and social class were also important in relation to interviewees' understandings and experiences of parenting children, structuring the different resources individuals drew on, both symbolically and practically in their everyday family lives. In this chapter, then, we forefront issues of social class that have been touched on in previous chapters.

Caring

We begin by discussing the theme of caring, particularly in relation to variable, socially patterned, understandings of the significance of biological ties. We then go on to consider the importance of time and attention as being symbolic of caring.

Caring for children

The concept of 'care', in relation to children and family, still almost invariably refers to care undertaken by women, and is understood implicitly in this frame of reference. Discourses of femininity and motherhood are closely interlinked with definitions of selflessness, sensitivity and warmth, traits which are seen as constituting a predisposition to care (Skeggs, 1997). In recent years there has been a cultural shift towards using the gender-neutral term 'parent' when discussing childrearing activities but, as many have pointed out, this reflects few significant changes in the status and responsibilities accorded to mothers and fathers (Burman, 1994; Ferri and Smith, 1996; Lupton and Barclay, 1997).

As we discussed in Chapter 1, the meanings and expectations attached to fatherhood have shifted over time, promoting a new image associated with active caring. Fathers are now constructed in legal and social policy terms as fulfilling a crucial role in meeting a child's emotional needs, representing a move away from traditional conceptions of distant, authority figures. Nevertheless, as we have highlighted, this new focus on the role of fathers in families is contextualised by the fact that it is mothers who predominantly assume responsibility for the day-to-day care of their children. Fathering is still something the majority of men are required to fit around full-time employment, leading them to rely heavily on mothers to facilitate and mediate relationships with their children.

The gendered nature of parenting often becomes more conspicuous during and after family breakdown. It has been argued that changes in understandings of fatherhood have been triggered by the increasing numbers of fathers who now live apart from their children after divorce or separation (Smart and Neale, 1999). Fathers who do not live with their children are often obliged to renegotiate their fathering role in order to secure a sustainable relationship (Simpson *et al.*, 1995). For some fathers, this is seen to require a more active display of emotional commitment, a demonstration of caring that may be regarded as imperative when a step-parent is also involved. These gendered dimensions were implicit in our analysis of parents' and step-parents' views of caring for children, which largely focused on building or maintaining caring relationships with children.

As many have noted, representations of parenting, or more specifically mothering, are founded to a large extent on the amalgamation of 'caring for', as an action, and 'caring about', as an emotion (Tronto, 1989; Smart, 1991). Traditional constructions of 'the family' have relied on the invisibility of this distinction. Despite frequent references to the term 'care', current legal frameworks fail to define the precise meaning of the word. For example, the 1989 Children Act requires active interpretation to establish whether references to 'reasonable care' imply the physical meeting of need, emotional attachment or both (White *et al.*, 1990). As Carol Smart (1991: 489) suggests:

> the supposed 'naturalness' of the activity of caring is precisely what has taken it outside of moral philosophy and indeed out of the perusal of the sociologist.

Although the practical elements of caring for children were discussed during the interviews, it was emotional attachment to children that emerged as a particularly prominent theme in interviewees' spontaneous accounts. During the interviews we actively sought to elicit accounts of everyday childcare, probing about domestic routines and expectations, but while we received descriptions of who was responsible for what, interviewees appeared to place more significance on who cared about whom, and how this was demonstrated. Caring about children, in terms of feeling, demonstrating and receiving love and commitment, was constructed as a vital characteristic of parenting, with emphasis placed on the role of the step-parent in generating caring relationships with step-children. This emphasis on emotional attachment between parents and children reflects the more general interest in love and intimacy highlighted by writers such as Ulrich Beck and Elisabeth Beck-Gernsheim (1995), who point to the increased significance of emotional bonds established with children in the context of less secure couple relationships (see Chapter 1). The focus on caring about, as distinct from caring for, is further intensified by what Steph Lawler (2000) has termed a 'psychologisation' of childrearing. She notes how the current public preoccupation with children's emotional needs eclipses physical caring, to the extent that it is often portrayed as peripheral in contemporary representations of parenting.

In the context of family breakdown and re-partnering, taken-for-granted assumptions about caring for and about children are made more visible in people's attempts to renegotiate parenting roles and construct new families. Pivotal to these negotiations is the concept of biology in defining and legitimising family and step-family relationships, with interviewees assuming varying perspectives on the meaningfulness of genetics to parent–child relationships. For some, biology represented a central feature of parenthood, identifiable as a special bond or attachment to a child that is naturally occurring rather than actively created. For others, genetic ties were relevant only as reference points for confirming the status of a relationship developed over time, most commonly through the assertion that children can and should be loved as if they are 'your own'. While such contrasting positions may, at times, have been associated with gender and parental status, more remarkable was the patterning of these views along social class lines.

As we discussed in Chapter 1, our categorisation of class draws on a number of dimensions in an attempt to generate a situated assessment, leading in almost all cases to a clear placement of individuals as either working or middle class. The significance of social class within this sample was striking, in that some views were confined to interviewees from one or the other social class. In this chapter, we will provide evidence about this social patterning within our sample, moving on in Chapter 6 to consider the wider relevance of this, as well as any possible explanations. Social class patterns were discernible across a wide range of topics and themes in the current study, but were particularly prominent in interviewees' discussions of biology, with middle-class interviewees focusing on the significance of blood ties, and working-class interviewees questioning their relevance.

Caring: blood is thicker than water

The importance of biology in defining a parent's emotional involvement with a child appeared to be an exclusively middle-class concern amongst our sample. From this perspective, the genetic tie between a parent and child generates a more intense and enduring emotional connection, in comparison to step-relationships. Absolute commitment and loyalty are associated with biological parent–child relations, with biological parents portrayed as naturally more protective of their own children. For example, Lyn (White, middle class, mother and resident step-mother) made a clear distinction between parenting her biological children and 'taking on board' step-children:

> There is no doubt that there is a big difference between your natural children and other children that you take on board. It's just something that, you know, your own children there's such an incredibly close tie. You know, you feel with them for everything. And it's not the same for

other children. I think you grow to love other children. I'm sure you do. I would say I'm very fond of Ellie and Max. But I do think had they been two very difficult children, maybe it would never have worked.

For Lyn, step-parenting reveals the difference between caring for and caring about children. As primary caretaker, she accepts responsibility for meeting Ellie's and Max's physical and emotional needs, but while she stresses her fondness for them, she can not equate this with how she feels about her own children:

I know that I'm different to Ellie and Max than if they were my real children ... I'm sure there is that deeper protection of blood relationship. It's something that's inherent.

The theme of biological ties runs throughout Lyn's account of their family situation. She explained how there is an inevitable alliance between her and her two children which is matched by an equally inevitable alliance between her partner, Martin, and his two children. According to Lyn, these natural affiliations translate into particular ways of behaving and relating, which everyone has come to accept. She describes how Martin's children, Ellie and Max, ask Martin for the practical things that she herself tends to provide:

They still go to Martin. And he tries desperately, he doesn't want it to be like that. And sometimes he will come in from work and Max will go up to him and say 'What's for dinner?' And he says, 'Why don't you ask Mum? She's cooked it'. But I suppose it's a learning process. You go through a phase where it bothered me. I thought, 'Well I'm doing all the donkey work and they go to somebody else'. But I accept that now because I accept how it is for me and I accept how it is for them.

This acceptance seems to centre around a reached understanding that biological ties are natural and unavoidable. Having initially worried and puzzled over her relationship with Ellie and Max, this eventual realisation and acceptance of the significance of biology was experienced by Lyn as a liberation, freeing her from the feeling she 'wasn't doing things right'. The notion that it is important to be able to acknowledge the link between biology and emotional attachment was shared by the majority of middle-class interviewees, sometimes alongside a sense that this view might be seen as controversial or politically incorrect. For example Mark (White, middle class, step-father and expectant father) felt his comments about the imminent birth of his baby might sound 'ridiculous':

We're bound by something more than love. It sounds ridiculous to me. But it does make a difference to me. Blood ties. I think I've learnt that over the years regardless of what I do my parents still see me as their son. And nothing will break that. And regardless of what happens between me and my sister they're still my brother and sister. At the end of the day, blood is thicker than water.

Kate (White, middle class, mother) similarly suggested that prioritising genetic ties over social relationships might be questioned or refuted, but described how her stance on this issue had been revised in the light of experience, feeling that her partner (Rob) could not feel the same emotional attachment towards her son (Liam) as he felt towards his own daughter:

> *Yeah, I mean I used to deny this politically, but I think having the biological tie does make a difference. Although it's not necessarily a straightforward difference. Although I suppose it's not a completely unqualified emotion that you feel as a parent for a child. Although it can be very strong. I mean I don't think Rob would, for example, would put Liam's interest first before anything. Which I would put Liam's interest before most things. Anything, yes.*

Understanding step-relationships as lacking the emotional depth and commitment of biological parenting was a liberating insight for some interviewees, but this recognition could also be experienced as a pressure to compensate or hide true feelings. For Jo (White, middle class, father and step-father), the relationship with his step-daughter felt artificial in comparison to the more 'natural' emotion he felt for his biological daughter:

> *I find myself trying and I don't like it in myself either. I feel like I'm being false.*

However, most interviewees who stressed the association between biology and deep emotional attachment saw different relationships within step-families as less problematic, and more an inevitability to be accepted and worked around. Some described the checks and balances they made within the family in order to meet the children's needs and keep things fair (see Chapter 5), while others focused on the role that non-resident biological parents play in maintaining a close caring bond with their children, supplying the emotional depth not achievable through step-parenting. As Frank (White, middle class, step-father) explained, his role as a step-father is limited to practical caring for his step-children, leaving their father to sustain the natural emotional bond experienced between father and child:

> *I do provide for them on a practical day-to-day basis, but I don't provide for them in a parental loving arrangement. That is something that I couldn't and wouldn't attempt to take away from their father.*

Middle-class non-resident parents themselves also tended to emphasise the existence of an enduring tie forged through genetics, suggesting that biology accords them a secure status as a parent:

> *Whatever people say, I think there's a strong genetic tie ... I think eventually people do want to know who their dad is, and regardless of whether they even get on with them, there's a tie there that isn't broken.*
> (Daniel – White, middle class, non-resident father)

> *Well the boys, they'll never be emotionally attached to Elizabeth* [their step-mother] *in the same way.*
> (Mandy – White, middle class, non-resident mother)

Social ties and biological analogies

Underlining the significance of class, this view was noticeably not shared by Trevor (White, working class, non-resident father and step-father), who had very little contact with his biological children. He made it clear that social rather than genetic ties were of primary significance to him, expressing little commitment to his children from previous relationships, while emphasising his emotional attachment to his step-children (see Chapter 2).

For some interviewees, then, created rather than ascribed relationships with children were perfectly capable of overriding the primacy of blood. In sharp contrast to what appeared to be a middle-class focus on biology as a determinant of emotional relationships, working-class interviewees were considerably more inclined to dispute the relevance of genetic ties to step-families, often pointing to the relatively insignificant contribution a biological parent might make in comparison to a sustained, caring relationship with a step-parent. For example, Gill (White, working class, mother) described the significance her nine-year-old daughter placed on the nurturing she received from her step-father:

> I said to Tony, 'How do you feel when Josie calls you Daddy, or the first time she called Daddy?' And he was keeping Josie going, he was saying, 'Oh, all emotional and, oh, it makes me want to cry'. And she was laughing and she said, 'Well you are my Daddy'. And I said, 'Well he didn't make you'. I said, 'He didn't plant the seed'. And Josie turned round and said, 'He didn't plant the seed but he watered the plant'. And I thought that's a good way of explaining. He's the one that's there for you and he's the one that's looking after you. So he really is the Daddy.

Josie had had no contact with her biological father since she was born, and according to Gill, had shown very little interest in him over the years. Gill described how the relationship between Tony and Josie had developed in the two years they had lived as a family, passing through an initial awkwardness to become a close father–daughter bond. Before she met Tony, Gill had spent time as a foster parent,[1] and from her perspective, emotional attachments between children and parents are built through active nurturing. Her prioritisation of social relations over biological ties was also reflected in her observations of changes in her own relationship with Josie:

> Like I notice now, we went round a friend's house the other night and she was getting tired. It was Tony's knee she got on to. You know sometimes I feel it's like Daddy's girl. Most of the time the two of them get on really well. They head off down to the shops and sometimes I feel a bit out of it ... And I just wonder ... I don't know whether she would be as close to me as she used to be. It's maybe not that she's not as close, it's just that it's the both of us.

While Gill clearly feels biology has little relevance to emotional attachment, she is aware of the significance others may place on it. Tony's status as a step-parent is particularly visible given that he is African-Caribbean, while Josie's biological father is Chinese. Gill herself is Irish, and Josie spent her first seven years in Ireland before coming to England. While Gill noted that it was impossible for them to pass as a traditional family, she was pleased that other parents at Josie's school recognised Tony's role as a father:

> He said, 'She's really bright, top of the class'. He was sort of blowing a bit about her. And they said 'Is that your daughter?'. And I said, 'Now if that happened in Ireland, there's no way that anybody would have said, "Is that your daughter?" They would have looked at you and they'd have known it wasn't' ... I suppose they must have thought, 'Well he's her step-father'. But rather than saying step-child or step-father, it was, 'Is that your daughter?'

The importance of having the step-parent's caring role recognised was an issue for many other working-class interviewees, who firmly refuted the idea that step-relations were in any way inferior to biological ties. There was a strong sense amongst these interviewees that step-parenting was unfairly distinguished from 'normal' parenting and was therefore misrepresented. The language of biology was drawn on here, not to underpin references to a liberating acceptance of difference, but to underline the capacity for step-parents to establish close emotional relationships (and see Chapter 2):

> I suppose they are a step-family [referring to one of the vignettes], you know, you can't get away from it, but I look on 'em as my own ... he's just as good as their own dad really.
> (Dawn – White, working class, mother)

Working-class step-fathers were particularly keen to emphasise their commitment to their step-children, suggesting that becoming a step-parent should involve accepting the child *as if* they were your genetic offspring. For Trevor and David, for example, caring for your step-child as you would 'your own' represents an important guiding moral principle. (Again, David is discussing one of the vignettes.)

> Just because the son is not the new father's blood relation, he shouldn't feel rejected, he should treat him as his own and make him welcome in the family ... You don't just marry the other partner, you accept their children ... our family is myself and Joyce [wife] and five children, three of them hers and two of mine, and there should be no difference between them.
> (David – White, working class, non-resident father and step-father)

> I will be their step-father [after his forthcoming marriage], but I think and feel of 'em as mine, not as nothing else ... and I feel of 'em as me own, take 'em in as me own, and that's just it, nothing other ... if you don't take them as your children you might as well not start.
> (Trevor – White, working class, non-resident father and step-father)

The principle that step-relations should mirror conventional parenting is an indication of the power that notions of biology and kinship have in shaping understandings of step-families and parenting more broadly. As is evidenced through the more middle-class emphasis on biological ties, parenting is often constructed as a 'natural' experience associated with instinctive actions and intrinsic, unconditional emotions. Even while other interviewees challenged the significance of the blood ties to parenting, most drew on biological analogies to frame their relationships. By comparing step-relations to biologically defined parent–child relationships, these interviewees are acknowledging the meaningfulness of genetic ties, while at the same time undermining the 'special' unique status of biological parents. In particular, evoking the language of biology conveys enduring commitment and obligation, distinguishing the relationship from the conditional nature of other social relationships.

The recourse to biological analogies also reflects a wider cultural preoccupation with defining family relationships, with 'natural' blood ties representing the template against which step-parenting is evaluated. As outlined in Chapter 1, biological relationships are actively privileged through policy and legislation that seeks to maintain and re-enforce the rights and obligations of biological parents after divorce or separation (Edwards *et al.*, 1999a). Technological advances in fertility treatment and the subsequent increase in those seeking donor insemination have also sparked furious public debates about a child's 'right' to know their biological parents (Bunting, 2001). However, while biology was a central theme ordering interviewees' accounts of parenting and step-parenting, the length or amount of time spent with a child was also identified as a crucial factor determining emotional attachment.

Time to care

The step-families involved in our study included people who had lived together for varying amounts of time, ranging from a few weeks to a substantial number of years, yet even those with a relatively short family history pointed to time as an important factor in the building of relationships. Similarly the ages of step-children were rarely mentioned, beyond occasional references to a lack of shared history in the case of older step-children. Thus, the significance of time for our interviewees appeared to relate to subjective perceptions of quality and quantity rather than to 'objective' time-scales or chronologies. The view that spending time with children is integral to developing close emotional attachments spanned across our sample, but again interviewees' understandings followed a clear pattern related to social class.

For working-class interviewees, time and commitment were the key elements defining parent–child relationships, regardless of biological status. From this perspective, step-relations, given time, have the potential to become indistinguishable from 'natural' parent–child relationships. Middle-class interviewees were more likely to accord a different significance to time, regarding it as crucial in developing good step-relationships, but incapable of synthesising biological ties.

Reflecting their concern with genetic status, middle-class interviewees tended to distinguish the specific, unique nature of parent–child relationships from close but conditional relationships that might be built over time. So while the indisputable, ascribed status associated with biology was assured, time was regarded as the substance underpinning close relations. For example, Jo, the step-father who discussed the missing genetic dimension of step-parenting in terms of falseness, also emphasised the substance of the relationship he had built with his step-daughter over the years. While he did not see himself replicating the bond he 'naturally' has with his own daughter, he implicitly suggested that the different quality of the relationship, established over time, may rival his step-daughter Eva's connection with her biological father:

> I think Eva and Dino have got a good relationship now. He hasn't got that relationship that I've got with Eva in the same sense. He doesn't have that.
> (Jo – White, middle-class, father and step-father)

Many interviewees, particularly step-fathers like Jo, regarded time as a resource that could be invested to produce a future return in the form of a close relationship with a child. Making this form of investment was generally seen as a long-term strategy demonstrating commitment, both to the child concerned and to the family as a whole. A number of (mainly middle-class) step-fathers explicitly drew on financial metaphors to describe or evaluate their relationships with step-children, describing time and emotional involvement as 'investments', while weighing up parenting in terms of 'costs' 'trade-offs' 'pay-offs', 'benefits' and 'end products'.

Many step-fathers explained how they had consciously sought to 'build' a relationship with their step-children, feeling that the success of their future family life was dependent on their capacity to develop this emotional attachment. This spending of time represented more than the passive presence often associated with traditional fathering (Smart and Neale, 1999). It was generally suggested that the children themselves had to want to spend this time with their step-fathers, but that it also required an effort on the part of the step-father to engage with the child/ren. One step-father, Rob (White, middle class, father and step-father), described how he actively and consciously sought out activities and interests that he could share with his step-son, such as going to football matches or playing the guitar. Paul explained how he established an initial bond with his step-daughter through dedicating time to the relationship and building a friendship:

> When we first got married I'd come home and read to her, play about, sing, whatever. And that was mainly my role. The role I played in her life. Sitting there listening to her ... We'd already built a very close relationship.
> (Paul – African-Caribbean, working class, father and step-father)

Devoting time was generally interpreted as a demonstration of caring, but rather than viewing the spending of time as a deliberate strategy to build relationships, mothers were more inclined to see time as forging an enduring two-way emotional attachment. Many described themselves as having become very close to their children as a result of the extensive time they had spent with them, often as lone parents before meeting new partners. Time spent by step-fathers with children was seen as a significant indication of emotional investment and commitment, particularly by working-class mothers:

> *I've come into contact with men that have had very long relationships with women who have then split up, and they've known that child for years ... I think biologically or not you can form very strong attachments to a child.*
> (Kim – White, working class, mother)

> *The way I see a father, as someone that's always been there and always given them love and caring, you know, the guidance that they need.*
> (Louise – White, working class, mother)

The link between time and emotional attachment was also discussed with regard to fathers and their children, with a number of mothers noting how much more time their ex-partners spent with their children since they had separated, compared to a previous lack of involvement. They felt having a step-father on the scene had been beneficial for their children, precipitating closer father–child relationships, with fathers demanding more time with their children in an attempt to preserve their role. Carol Smart and Bren Neale (1999) identify the construction of a prodigal father, who sees the light and develops a better approach to parenting, as part of a wider discourse that valorises post-divorce fatherhood at the expense of the enduring primary care provided by mothers. However, the interviewees in this sample constructed an image of the transformed father, less to promote the contribution he made to post-divorce parenting, and more to present him as realising the error of his ways too late. Jackie (White, working class, mother), like several other women, described her ex-partner's renewed commitment to their children in terms of his having 'missed out' on the quality time they now share with their step-father:

> *I will say that since they go to their father's every weekend, he's taken over the fatherly role much better than he ever did when we were together ... For me actually it was quite sad really because the things we did with them it would have been nice to have done with their father. Just simple things like skimming stones in the river and things like that. But that was just sort of like a fleeting sadness really. Because they've still got that now even though it's not with their father. And they've got another relationship with their father. Which is quite good ... Yes. I mean he's missed out on that. The children haven't because there's another person that's taking that role. So they're getting that now.*

As Jackie's quote indicates, time was not only seen as a resource parents give to children to demonstrate their emotional commitment, but was also inextricably linked with the love and closeness individuals derive from family relationships. This interpretation of time as a resource was structured around the principle that you have to give in order to receive, generating complex dynamics and tensions within step-families. Time, as a form of closeness, could be identified as the source of competition and resentment, bound up with notions of fairness and children's needs. While many of the interviewees noted the strengthening effect that time has on family bonds, several also focused on particular needs or desires for individual attention and nurturing, revealing a tension between time spent as a family and time spent building or reinforcing specific relationships. The significance of time to the creation and management of relationships appears to derive from a sense that caring for and about may initially be uncoupled in step-relationships, leading to a need to 'knit' the two together over a period of time.

This construction of time as a precious but limited commodity is also a prominent theme in the step-family literature, reflecting the notion that step-families are more complex and less bounded than conventional nuclear families (Visher and Visher, 1979; Robinson and Smith, 1993). In images of traditional nuclear families, time may be portrayed as flowing in a more 'natural', even way – although here too it may be discussed as a resource that must be 'fairly' allocated (Ribbens, 1994). In contrast, step-family time is depicted as a problematic practice that must be consciously worked out. Self-help books for parents and step-parents offer copious advice on managing time and forward-planning within step-families (Atkinson, 1986; Burnett, 1991; Hayman, 1994; National Stepfamily Association, 1995). Although our interviewees were divided along class lines as to whether time or biology represents the real core of the parent–child relationship, time was broadly regarded as a symbolic resource that can create, foster and maintain emotional caring between individuals within the family.

Authority

While caring for children is more often located within the remit of motherhood, notions of authority and discipline have a more traditional association with fathers (Tosh, 1996). Although understandings and expectations of fatherhood have shifted over the years to become increasingly associated with psychological caring and nurturing, fathers are still likely to be perceived, and to perceive themselves, as taking a major role in guiding, protecting and disciplining children (Warin *et al.*, 1999; Langford *et al.*, 2001). While this role is also generally regarded as an essential duty of all parenting, issues of authority within step-families may be compromised by situated notions of legitimacy and responsibility.

Interviewees' discussions of responsibility and authority focused predominantly on the rights and obligations of step-parents to maintain control within the household. Again, class differences were visible in accounts of who could legitimately discipline children, and how that discipline should be exercised. The meaning of responsibility and authority in parenting was closely linked to the issue of caring and emotional attachment and, as we have discussed, such everyday understandings were shaped by the significance that individuals accorded to biology and time. In line with their emphasis on biological ties, middle-class interviewees were more likely to associate authority with genetic status. They also appeared more likely to correlate discipline rights with time, in terms of years committed to parenting. In contrast, working-class interviewees were more inclined to emphasise the responsibility of adults to control and protect children, portraying step-parents as automatically acquiring authority as committed, caring adults.

Discipline: status and appropriateness

For many interviewees, issues of discipline and authority within the step-cluster were complex, requiring broad moral principles to be applied in the context of status and appropriateness. Discussions focusing on a step-parent's right to discipline children were directly elicited by Vignette 1 (see Appendix), a story about a mother coming home to find her young daughter distressed and alleging that her step-father had hit her. In response to this vignette a number of interviewees, both middle and working class, expressed their concern that this step-father had overstepped the mark in terms of authority. As the following quotes demonstrate, the biological relationship between parent and child may be accorded central significance in interviewees' evaluations of the appropriateness of the step-father's actions, but this focus on biology was interwoven with issues of legality, gender, time and the validity of corporal punishment generally:

> *I would've said legally he's not actually allowed to do that is he?*
> (Margaret – White, middle class, mother)

> *It's hard to say because even with natural parents they often say fathers are much stricter than mothers. So you've got to put that into context as well. The whole problem here is the fact that he's not the natural father. If he'd have been the natural father it probably wouldn't have been a problem.*
> (Lyn – White, middle class, mother and resident step-mother)

> *I mean being strict doesn't mean you hit. I mean I'm strict with Liam as I say and I don't hit him. In fact I think it's the worst possible thing. And in terms of a child's response to a step-father ... to make the child frightened of him, I'm not quite sure that that's a good response. If a parent, a natural born parent that you've known all your life, hits you, then it's a shock and you may feel negatively about it. But you've at least got a background of fairly loving behaviour to fall back on. A step-parent doing such a thing with a relatively small background, I think you're on very dodgy ground really.*
> (Rob – White, middle class, father and step-father)

For many middle-class interviewees, a clear line demarcated the virtually unquestionable authority of the biological parent from the less defined role of the step-parent. Margaret's sense that a step-father has no legal right to smack a child parallels Lyn's statement that step-parents lack 'natural', ascribed authority. But as interviewees strove to assess the legitimacy of the step-parent's actions in the vignette, they drew on more than simple biological status. While Lyn constructed the 'problem' around biology, her suggestion that fathers often enforce stricter discipline served, to some extent, to warrant the step-father's actions. From Rob's perspective, the act of physical punishment is in itself inadvisable, but a 'natural born parent' acts within a different historical and emotional context.

Authority and time and familiarity

Like Rob, many other interviewees identified the length of time a step-parent had been involved with the child/ren as an important factor in determining how involved they could or should become in discipline matters. As discussed earlier, time is powerfully implicated in emotional attachment, and caring and closeness in turn are seen as an essential context for administering discipline. The principle, that children should only be punished by a loving parent was based on a belief that a family relationship, characterised by love and affection, both engenders respect from the step-child and ensures that discipline is administered for the correct reasons. For example, in relation to Vignette 1, Lorna and Margaret both felt that discipline measures such as smacking were inappropriate and even dangerous unless the step-parent had a fully committed and loving relationship with the child:

> Because I think, being a step-parent you might worry that it's possible that they didn't love the kids enough, wouldn't you, until you'd had a long established relationship.
> (Lorna – White, middle class, mother)

> I suppose in the area of discipline particularly, if people were allowed to sort of lay into a child, and they're not really very committed to that child, I think you could see more cases of child abuse. I suppose if you've had a bit of time to actually live with the child and get to know it and hopefully win its respect.
> (Margaret – White, middle class, mother)

As well as experiencing an emotional attachment and commitment, step-parents were also expected to establish good relationships with children to ensure they were not resented. Some interviewees expressed outright suspicion of a step-parent who assumed a substantial authority role before the foundations for an emotional relationship were properly established:

> People walking into ready-made families I don't trust, I never have trusted. You have to work at them ... I mean there would be a lot more groundwork to the whole thing rather than just moving automatically straight in.
> (Bob – White, middle class, half-weekly resident father and step-father)

Other interviewees discussed the groundwork step-parents necessarily have to complete in terms of learning new parental skills. For example, in response to Vignette 1, Sue (White, middle class, half-weekly resident mother) explained how lack of experience may have led the step-father to smack the child inappropriately:

> He's still fairly new to it isn't he? He may not have the other resources or other ideas about it.

Adult authority

While middle-class interviewees discussed issues of discipline and authority with reference to themes of biology and time, working-class parents and step-parents were considerably more likely to focus on the status of children, constructing them as dependent and in need of adult guidance. In making this clear distinction between the responsible status of adulthood and the less developed, naturally subordinate position of the child, interviewees regarded adults within the step-family as necessarily holding responsibility for and authority over children. This position was most visible in the responses given to Vignette 1, with working-class interviewees particularly centring on the specifics of the incident rather than principles of biological status and familiarity. The contentious issue for these parents and step-parents was whether the child had deserved the punishment, how hard she was hit, and whether she was telling the truth. Many felt that the mother (Angela) should support the step-father (Patrick) if the punishment was warranted:

> If it was for a reasonable wrongdoing that the child's done wrong, then Angela should say to the child, you know – 'serves you right'.
> (David – White, working class, step-father)

> Talk to Patrick. You know, 'What happened? Why was the mark on her leg? Was she naughty? Did she deserve it?'
> (Gina – White, working class, mother)

> If it was done because she deserved it, then she shouldn't do nothing, she should say, 'Well you deserved it', end of story.
> (Trevor – White, working class, non-resident father and step-father)

> Ask Patrick why he'd hit her, whether she'd been naughty.
> (Dawn – White, working class, mother)

> He may well have smacked her for something that she did wrong so it could be perfectly innocent.
> (Frank – White, middle class, step-father)

Obviously, responses to this hypothetical situation were ordered around different perspectives on corporal punishment, but the notion that step-parents should have an automatic right to smack a naughty child appeared to derive from a particular construction of children as amoral and clearly set apart from adults (see Chapter 3). This understanding of children as 'little devils' (Ribbens, 1994) also generated a suspicion among some interviewees as to whether a child's allegations could be trusted. Kim suggested that children do not always tell the truth, while Paul discussed children's capacity for deviousness:

> I wouldn't say immediately take the child's word for it. Because I remember my aunt had a similar situation with her husband. She came home from work, the child was lying on the floor saying 'Daddy hit me'. Daddy would never ever have done anything like that. She'd actually banged her leg.
> (Kim – White, working class, mother)

> If it's left, then they can then play one off against the other. Children today are getting very wise. They could make things very hard for Angela and Patrick.
> (Paul – African-Caribbean, working class, resident father and step-father)

For interviewees drawing on this construction of children as being in need of adult control and guidance, concern might be focused on the extent or severity of the punishment meted out, in terms of whether smacking hard enough to leave a mark was acceptable. In this case, the lack of a biological relationship could be seen as a relevant factor in making the action even more unacceptable.

This orientation to the basic right and duty of adults to exercise authority leads to a stress on building a 'united front' – something that can be a significant issue in intact nuclear families too (Ribbens, 1994). In this view, disagreement between parent and step-parent on issues of discipline could have a serious negative impact on children. The significance of a united front was commonly expressed in response to Vignette 4, a story in which a teenage step-daughter becomes resentful about her step-father's involvement in disciplining her. For these interviewees, lack of unity was dangerous in giving children an opportunity to play the parent against the step-parent, thus weakening the stability of the family unit. Reaching joint agreement was presented as an essential method of containing children's natural urge to take advantage and manipulate situations to their own ends:

> I think it's got to be an all-round thing. Discipline in all areas. Because I think step-children will walk all over them. And if there's no respect from an early start I think they will get a lot of things thrown back at them. I mean you've got to gain respect, like children have got to respect adults. I mean you're an adult, they're a child.
> (Gina – White, working class, mother)

> I think they'd have to come to an agreement about the discipline otherwise the children are going to play one off against the other all the time.
> (Mary – White, middle class, mother)

Joint agreement may also invoke a step-father's right to discipline the children and to expect support from his partner. Several people referred to the significance of new responsibilities taken on by the step-father, suggesting that a right to discipline should accompany the responsibility of childcare. Two interviewees (a couple) explained how, in their own circumstances, authority was divided equally between them:

> Discipline was sort of like, whoever will deal with it. It didn't really matter whether he dealt with it or I dealt with it.
> (Karen – African-Caribbean, working class, mother)

> When I and Karen got married she said to her I had as much right to discipline her and give her instructions as Mummy basically.
> (Paul – African-Caribbean, working class, father and step-father)

A less strategic notion of joint agreement was also emphasised by middle-class interviewees through the more negotiation-focused concept of couple consensus. In this context, emphasis was placed less on presenting a united front to children and more on mutual decision-making as a method of managing relationships and preventing friction. The interviewees who talked about joint agreement in this way focused on the negative effects of conflict on the step-couple rather than on the child. From this perspective, disagreement can generate resentments amongst adults, while couple consensus strengthens a relationship. Most focused on the role of consciously reached consensus to avoid potential problems, advocating the principles of negotiation and joint agreement that are prominent in counselling literature and step-family self-help books (Atkinson, 1986; National Stepfamily Association, 1995):

> They need to come to some understanding about whether it's acceptable for Patrick to hit. And then if they can't come to an agreement, then I think they would have some problems.
> (Sue – White, middle class, half-weekly resident mother)

Mother calls the shots

In contrast to this focus on consensus and joint agreement between parenting adults, other interviewees emphasised the mother's role in determining discipline, and the step-father's role in respecting her greater rights in this area. From this perspective it was felt that the mother should guide the step-father and regulate how he intervenes in disciplining the children. For example, one mother explained how she actively monitored her partner's exercise of authority:

> I've always got an extra ear listening out for if the situation turns, or if Mark says something I don't agree with then I'm sorry but I tend to say, 'I don't agree with that'.
> (Lisa – African-Caribbean, middle class, mother)

It was also suggested by various interviewees that step-fathers should avoid any attempts to impose serious forms of discipline (like smacking), leaving the decision of how to deal with step-children's misbehaviour solely for the mother to sort out:

> He'll tell them. But if they need discipline then it's me that gives it.
> (Jackie – White, middle class, mother)

This emphasis on the mother maintaining overall control of discipline appeared to mirror the previously noted middle-class concern with biological status. According to these interviewees, serious problems can arise if a step-parent becomes too involved in disciplining the children, potentially damaging fragile family relationships by testing biological allegiances, increasing tensions between the couple and provoking resentments from children. Parents and step-parents discussed these possible dangers by relating them to their own personal experiences, often explaining how particular flash-points had revealed the precarious consequences of the step-father becoming too involved in discipline matters. Middle-class step-fathers were particularly likely to distance themselves from a disciplining role having learnt from previous encounters:

> When I heard Zoe speaking to Lyn like that I said to her, 'Don't speak to your mother like that. You don't speak to you mother like that.' And Lyn went mad at me. 'What are you doing, telling my child not to speak to me like that? It's my business. Just because your children are angels.'

This was very early on in our relationship. So once that happened I haven't done it ever again. It happened once and I learnt that's not what I can do. So I don't do it.
(Martin – White, middle class, resident father and step-father)

So we avoid the arguments. I mean I'm aware that this is probably going to be a passing phase. But we could destroy our relationship here and it would never recover. So I'm always trying to stand back. I mean I tell myself I'm doing it because it's the best way to approach it. Because I'm not his father and he knows that. But I think it might be because I don't like confrontation ... I think it would get out of hand, so I just try and avoid it. Like I said, we just had the one big argument where he said, 'You're not my father'. And I realised I'd made a big mistake.
(Mark – White, middle class, step-father and expectant father)

Despite the reservations many step-fathers felt about becoming actively involved in disciplining step-children, it was generally felt that step-parents should be able to exercise at least some authority. Some interviewees who felt that overall control of discipline matters should rest with the mother, also described how step-parents could make an important contribution as background support. Interviewees described how step-parents could effectively reinforce the authority of the parent and also provide a sympathetic viewpoint, acting as a support for both parent and child. Several interviewees spoke about a step-parent's basic obligation both to back up the biological parent and to promote the child's welfare by acting as a guardian in the absence of that parent:

I mean, quite often I find that the way that I deal with that sort of thing is to do that, let Chris deal with it and then kind of come in later and add my weight to the argument.
(Paula – White, middle class, mother and non-resident step-mother)

I mean we talk about me as being a guardian for Lewis in the sense that hopefully I've got his best interest at heart.
(Mark – White, middle class, step-father and expectant father)

He's very much a background person. But Lewis will ask him for advice on things. And opinions. Quite often when I'm not here, if Lewis needs to get hold of one of us he'll ring Mark at work automatically if he can't get hold of me.
(Lisa – African-Caribbean, middle class, mother)

Material and financial issues

While there were various views about how step-fathers should or should not be involved in discipline and authority issues, there was a more general implicit assumption about how they might take on the role of father-as-provider. Nevertheless, parents' and step-parents' accounts of material and financial commitments to children were complex, and highly gendered. While the male provider role has been undermined to a certain extent by the large numbers of mothers returning to work after the birth of children, the notion of the male breadwinner remains key to understandings of fatherhood. Money issues, in the form of child maintenance and the specifics of household expenditure, were a common focus of discussion for our interviewees, revealing the meaning and symbolism attached to spending money on children. For the most part, financial obligations were associated with fathers and step-fathers, with little reference made to mothers' part in financially providing for children, even though a large number of the mothers in our sample were in paid employment. At times there was an implicit suggestion that financial responsibility constituted fathering itself. Paul (African-Caribbean, working class, step-father and father), for example, explained how he had taken over the role of father, since they had not received maintenance from his step-daughter's biological father:

> I've taken that role on as a father. I didn't ever expect anything from him so it was never an issue. If he did give anything it still wouldn't have been a problem. Because it would help towards her upbringing. But he never has and it's not that I was looking for him to.

A number of mothers described an expectation that their ex-partners would continue to support their children, with many basing this assumption on the moral principle that fathers have an obligation to provide for their children. For several mothers, financial contributions from fathers represented an important acknowledgement of parental responsibility, as well as a material requirement. Lisa, for example, described how she enforced what she saw as her son's right to receive maintenance from his father:

> And I didn't take him to court or anything, I just insisted. I said, 'Well if you don't I will take you to court'. And I knew where he worked so I'd go to this place at payday and get Elliot's money. We agreed a sum and I'd go and collect Elliot's money. It was the principle more than the money. And it was sort of acrimonious for a while. But then after that he saw that I didn't really want anything, I just wanted him to remain a part of Elliot's life.
> (Lisa – African-Caribbean, middle class, mother)

Money and rights

Like Lisa, many interviewees saw regular maintenance as representing an enduring connection between a non-resident father and his children. Financial contributions were also regarded as significant in terms of bestowing entitlements, both as parents and as step-parents. For some mothers there was a fear that money might be seen by non-resident fathers as translating into rights, enabling them to exercise power and control over childcare decisions. Several expressed relief that their children's fathers had not paid regular maintenance, explaining how they preferred not to deal with the 'complications' of an involved father. One mother described her nervousness that her Turkish ex-partner might feel more inclined to try and take her son out of the country if he was contributing financially. Another explained how her ex-partner's failure to pay maintenance, and subsequent fear of the Child Support Agency, led him to agree to his daughter being adopted by her step-father. Similarly, mothers who received little in the way of maintenance from their ex-partners were more confident about dictating terms and conditions of access:

*Well as far as I'm concerned Dino doesn't contribute in any way, financially
or emotionally really, to Eva's upbringing. So we have first refusal. Which
means she will spend it* [Christmas] *with us.*
(Tina – White, middle class, mother)

Many step-fathers also felt that their own financial contributions towards
a step-child's upkeep should entitle them to basic parental rights:

*'Cos if somebody says, 'Right I'm not contributing anything', then OK, or
'I don't want to have anything to do with the children', then can't the
person that has been doing all the financial bits, doing all the love, being
there, you know things like that, can't they have, in inverted commas, a
'Right'?*
(Simon – White, middle class, step-father and expectant father)

Like Simon, most step-fathers were aware of their invisible legal status, in
spite of their practical and financial contribution to parenting. For some this
resulted in a feeling of being undervalued, particularly by step-children who
might place greater significance on receiving presents and occasional treats from
their biological fathers – an issue which could cause deep resentment. The sense
that financially providing for a child on a day-to-day basis entitled a step-father
to certain 'rights' was shared by many parents and step-parents (discussed further
in Chapter 5).

Money as symbolic

While financial maintenance was generally accorded great significance, the issue
of fathers spending money on their children in the form of treats and presents
was interpreted in various ways. Discussion of this topic emerged largely in
response to Vignette 2, a story about a non-resident father who spent
considerable amounts of money on his daughters while the new step-family
struggled to make ends meet. In general, interviewees' responses to this
hypothetical situation ranged from a position which condoned the non-resident
father's actions as an attempt to express care and commitment, to an explicit
condemnation of such an attempt to 'buy love'. In attempting to recognise the
complexity at the heart of this issue, a number of interviewees hovered between
these two perspectives, at times expressing both simultaneously.

In an analysis of the meanings attached to gift giving, David Cheal (1987)
highlights the significance of spending money on others, suggesting that a present
may be seen as better than money as a gift, if it can be shown that the giver
took time to think about the receiver. Many parents and step-parents in our
sample did regard the buying of presents and treats as an important channel
through which a non-resident father could communicate caring and
commitment. This view was based on the notion that the non-resident father
may have limited ways of expressing love, given both the part-time nature of
his relationship with his children and the tendency of fathers to suppress their
feelings. This was often discussed sympathetically by mothers, with the
underlying implication that non-resident fathers inevitably sustain an inferior
relationship with their children compared to the time-rich content of full-time

parenting. For Jessica and Kate, spending money was an effective way for the father in the vignette to demonstrate his feelings and to make up for lost time:

> *I would say to the children that, you know 'That's the way dad shows you how much he loves you, that's the way he does it, but here we show you this way'.*
> (Jessica – White, middle class, mother and resident step-mother)

> *He's clearly making up for the fact that he hasn't got the children living there all the time.*
> (Kate – White, middle class, mother)

The view that non-resident fathers should be allowed to spend money as they liked on their children was largely expressed by mothers who felt treats and presents were symbolic of love. This strikes a chord with Cheal's (1987: 153) claim that gift giving is part of a 'feminised ideology of love'. However, many other mothers also felt that non-resident fathers should be encouraged to spend money on their children in a more responsible way than was featured in the vignette, primarily by consulting the mother about what the child might need. This suggestion was based on the premise that, as the primary caretaker, the mother would be able to ensure that the money is spent in a more appropriate way. It was felt that the father's spending ability could be put to a positive advantage if he would negotiate with the mother to buy more sensible, practical presents.

Some suggested that biological fathers could be seen as a financial resource, providing money and treats when things were tight. Several, like Gina, described how they could negotiate to ensure that money was well spent:

> *I mean he'll ask me 'What shall I get him for his birthday. What shall I get him for Christmas?' Then I say 'Well tell your mum that he needs these'. So I really have got control with what goes on.*
> (Gina – White, working class, mother)

Others described more fraught attempts to exert some control over the non-resident father's present buying practices:

> *I've spoken to him about it rationally. A couple of times saying, you know she's got 15 Barbies. I know it's her one passion but really there are other things in the world. Make her interested in something else ... So it's that sort of thing. It must be very difficult for him. And I do understand that he wants to buy her stuff. Especially as he doesn't speak about feelings well, so it probably is the best way he can show that he does care for her. And I think that's important. But he's also got to be responsible about it. And that's where the problems come in. He's bought really silly shoes. Sort of like a tart rather than an eight-year-old child. Completely ridiculous, completely impractical.*
> (Tina – White, middle class, mother)

As this quote from Tina demonstrates, tensions were often experienced between allowing the non-resident father to spend money in order to express emotional attachment and demonstrate to children that they are loved, and protecting the child (and the step-family) from the consequences of irresponsible spending. According to Cheal (1987), for a present to be successful in communicating its symbolism it must be something the individual wants, knowledge which may not be accessible if the giver has had limited contact with the receiver. By buying things that children ask for, fathers can ensure that they are giving something that is wanted. However, this action may fail to convince their ex-wives/partners that they have given sufficient thought, care and time for their present to effectively symbolise their love.

Money as an inappropriate substitute for love

Other interviewees were less approving of the notion that spending money on children can convey love or sustain an emotional attachment. A range of parents and step-parents interpreted the father's actions in the vignette as a cynical attempt to 'buy' loving relationships with children, as an alternative to engaging in more authentic forms of parenting. This hard-line position was generally underpinned by the notion that love is a special and precious emotion that cannot be bought. The father's behaviour was regarded either as a sad misunderstanding of the authentic nature of responsible emotional caring, or as a deliberate manipulative attempt to subvert the natural path of love through bribery:

> Sounds as if he's trying to buy them.
> (Dawn – White, working class, mother)

> Unfortunately money can be perceived as a tool to gain people's emotional attention, especially children.
> (Pete – White, middle class, step-father)

Although this practice might be viewed as morally wrong and ineffectual, there was some sympathy for what was regarded as a symptom of parental insecurity or even desperation. Mothers often described, with pity, their ex-partners' efforts to make themselves popular, by buying treats and presents, while some step-fathers acknowledged the temptation to try and buy affection. For example, Jackie referred to her ex-husband's misguided efforts to retain his children's love, while Rob confessed that he had himself bought presents in a bid to secure his role as a step-father:

> I think my ex-husband used to buy, he still does really, at mealtimes he used to buy the children exactly what they wanted for tea. Regardless ... he does do things because he feels the children won't love him if he doesn't ... I have actually spoken to my ex-husband about your children always loving you ... and I think as time's gone by he has come to realise that.
> (Jackie – White, middle class, mother)

> He's obviously buying affection ... And I have to confess I do that with Liam a lot. Kate doesn't realise that that's why I'm doing it, but I buy him sweets and things that she gets really annoyed about. And I've never actually told her that I'm actually trying to buy myself into a role.
> (Rob – White, middle class, resident father and step-father)

Generally, however, efforts to buy love were regarded as self-defeating, and though they might capture the children's attention, they would eventually backfire:

> *Eventually after a few years the kids will actually realise that their father is just trying to buy them.*
> (Geoff – White, middle class, step-father and father)

> *It's clichéd I know, but there's much more than money isn't there? And kids see through that.*
> (Sue – White, middle class, half-time resident mother)

Although most interviewees felt that splashing money around in a manipulative attempt to buy children's affections was ill-fated and somewhat pathetic, several people suggested that money could be spent in a more authentic way. Treats and presents were regarded as superficial, but contributions towards day-to-day items such as clothes or shoes were identified as more legitimate demonstrations of parental commitment. This was summed up in the responses of June and Rob to Vignette 2.

> *Perhaps he should give the Mum a bit more. Not buy them so much expensive things and give the Mum a bit more money. Perhaps to help out with clothes and things that they actually need. 'Cos expensive things don't bring love. It's no substitute for even food or things they really need. But I found that happened to me when I was on my own. I couldn't afford to keep buying them things, but they didn't love me any different. And they didn't think 'Oh well Dad's bought us this and took us here and you didn't'. And I think it will wear very thin.*
> (June – White, working class, mother)

> *If he does want to become involved with the care of the children he could contribute much more around the day-to-day. Because it's just as important for a child to have a pair of trainers and jeans and tee shirts than it is to have a model racing car. In fact more important. It's less glamorous and there's less kudos attached to that, but it's more real. It's like having a real parental role.*
> (Rob – White, middle class, father and step-father)

Interviewees highlighting the shallow nature of lavishing money on children often pointed to the 'real' work of responsible parenting as an effective contrast. The significance of spending time, as opposed to money, doing everyday family activities was emphasised as valuable and integral to developing relationships:

> *The thing that you miss out on most if you're not a full-time parent in that situation is that you don't get to do the boring things. I think that's sad really, because I think it's the boring day-to-day things that forge the relationship.*
> (Paula – White, middle class, mother and non-resident step-mother)

> *If he spends time with them, I'm sure that taking them to the park will last longer than a, you know, Cindy doll and you know, things like that.*
> (Simon – White, middle class, step-father and expectant father)

As well as being a poor substitute for time, the spending habits of the father (Mark) in Vignette 2 were also seen as a potential threat to the structure and functioning of the step-family. Some interviewees were concerned that the children would become 'spoilt' and difficult to live with, and felt the father should restrain his spending for the sake of the children. Others focused on the potential difficulties the irresponsible spending could cause for the step-father (Tony), in terms of making him feel inadequate. For many, particularly working-class step-fathers, the link between money and power was seen as problematic, in that it reinforced the influence of the non-resident father, breached step-family boundaries and challenged the legitimacy of the step-father in exercising the rights of a breadwinner:

> It would appear that Mark's trying to destroy the relationship by buying all these things when he knows the new man can't provide.
> (Paul – African-Caribbean, working class, father and step-father)

> By doing what he's doing, he's undermining Tony. Tony's their father figure, and because he can't provide for 'em as much as he would like to provide for 'em, this other one's undermining him, it makes him feel [pause] useless.
> (Trevor – White, working class, non-resident father and step-father)

Again, this concern appeared related to the predominantly working-class view that a step-father's emotional and financial commitment mirrors that of a biological father.

Everyday understandings of public concerns

By exploring parents' and step-parents' accounts of caring for children, maintaining authority and discipline, and negotiating their material and financial obligations, we have shown how the issues of biology and time were crucial in ordering everyday understandings. We have also highlighted how meanings were patterned in relation to gender and social class, in terms of how these themes were experienced and lived. As we discussed in Chapter 3, notions of accountability for children are deeply gendered, and this was clearly reflected in interviewees' discussions of the differential roles and responsibilities accorded to parents and step-parents. However, these gendered views were cross-cut by the highly significant dimension of social class, with differences focusing most visibly around meanings of biology. Most middle-class interviewees stressed the importance of the genetic link between parent and child, constructing it as a distinctive, unique relationship characterised by a natural closeness and commitment. In contrast, working-class interviewees drew on biological analogies to highlight the symbolic rather than objective relevance of heredity, focusing on the potential of social relationships to achieve an equally close bond.

These contrasting views were evident throughout interviewees' discussions of caring, authority and material provision, underlining the significance of biology to their understandings of family life. For middle-class interviewees, the genetic status of a child was perceived as largely determining emotional attachment, appropriate discipline strategies and financial responsibility. For working-class interviewees, time spent with a child was a more significant factor in generating the emotional and practical commitments that constitute parent–child relationships. While middle-class interviewees also emphasised the importance of time in building better step-relationships, they did not see its relevance as rivalling the biological tie.

As well as highlighting the significance of biology and time, many of the issues discussed in this chapter implicate issues of 'fairness'. Notions of authority and financial responsibility were often articulated in terms of what was fair and right, and several working-class step-fathers described their decision to treat step-children as their own as an important moral guideline. In the next chapter we focus in more detail on how understandings of 'fairness' are drawn on to manage family practices within and across households.

Note

1   'Foster parent' was the term Gill herself used, and that was the designation used at the time she was involved in fostering. Since that date there has been a shift in language to that of 'foster-carer' (see Nutt, 2002, for discussion).

Chapter 5

'It's just not fair!' The rights and obligations of 'doing family'

One of the questions we asked everybody in our study concerned whether step-families are different from other families. We discussed the parents' and step-parents' variable responses to this question in Chapter 2. We saw how much our interviewees valued and used the language and imagery of 'family' rather than 'step-family', although they varied as to whether they did indeed regard step-family life as different. These variabilities were strongly patterned by social class, and we considered in Chapter 4 some of the ways in which social class differences might be played out in the everyday concerns of caring, disciplining and providing for, children. We also saw in Chapter 3 how far there were moral underpinnings to our interviewees' discussions, and the centrality of social constructions of Child and Adult in shaping these moral understandings. In this chapter we move on from our discussion of the detail of parenting in Chapter 4, to draw on all these preceding themes together in considering how far our interviewees invoked a guiding theme of 'fairness' in working out the implications of the moral imperative for the everyday practicalities of 'family' living.

The theme of fairness developed out of our inductively based analyses of our interviewees' accounts of their everyday (step-)family lives. Other recent research, on families after divorce and re-partnering, has similarly identified fairness as a significant theme (Allan and Crow, 2001; Lewis, 2001; Smart *et al.*, 2001). Methodologically and theoretically, our discussion entails moving between the concepts used by our interviewees (first-order constructs), and the moral imperative that we as researchers have identified as underpinning these interviews (second-order analysis). 'Fairness' occupies a significant position here, because it sits between these two frameworks of analysis, providing a way of invoking rights and obligations, and giving them substantive applications as a (potential) practical aid to everyday living. Given the vacuum identified by earlier research on step-families concerning the appropriate norms by which to guide (step-)parenting behaviour in re-partnered households (see Chapter 1), does the principle of 'fairness' serve to provide a guideline in working out what to do? And if so, what do people actually mean by it?

The need for some sort of guidance in working out how to 'do' step-family life was a feature of some of our middle-class interviewees' accounts (see Edwards *et al.*, 1999a). Sue (White, middle class, half-weekly resident mother) explicitly raised this in her interview, which occurred just at the point of embarking on a new 'family' project as she and her partner set up home together (although we saw in Chapter 2 how ambivalent she was about this project):

It's really interesting doing it [the research], *just because there are so many aspects of the whole step-parenting thing, I think it's made me think a lot more about things. And just what* in the field *it is and how it's almost like you're wanting a set of guidelines or issues to be thinking about. In fact, if someone could give you a checklist, 'Okay, you're going into a step-parenting situation, these are the areas, these are the norms', you know, 'This is what you're going to stumble across'.*

Elizabeth and Jonathan (White, middle class) had been living together, along with their son, in a part-time step-family situation for several years, when Jonathan's sons from his first marriage came to live with them, creating a full-time step-family. They were both quite explicit about how demanding they had found the situation:

Elizabeth: *I suppose just that it turned out to be a lot more difficult than I'd imagined it to be. And it made me face things in myself that I had no idea were there.*

Such as?

Elizabeth: *Boundless irrationality* [laughs], *capacity for anger* [laughs].

Jonathan: *It was very painful at times ... One had got to the point where one simply had to escape from an impossible situation and yet there was a situation still there that had to be dealt with ... a certain amount of compromise and tension.*

In trying to work out how to deal with such difficulties, the theme of 'being fair' was pervasive in some accounts. But the meanings of fairness could be quite variable between interviewees according to their differing ideas about 'being a family'. The degree to which it was discussed as central, and/or experienced as problematic, varied according to how and where people drew their boundaries of inclusion and exclusion.

In Chapter 2 we saw that people's understandings of 'being a family' invoked ideas of a unit, with external boundaries and internal cohesion. Key issues that people have to grapple with in almost all family units, but which may become more contested after re-partnering with children, are:

- Where do the boundaries lie, and how open or closed can/should they be?
- How do we understand the nature of the different elements that constitute the family unit, with regard to their needs and capacities, rights and obligations?

Since the 'family' unit is meant to serve as a mutual support union with everyone 'doing their bit', the question arises as to how to work out what are 'the bits' that each is expected to contribute, and how the support is expected to flow. In this context, 'fairness' was a theme that some interviewees strongly invoked. For a team effort to be meaningful, there has to be a clear sense of who is a member of that team, in terms of whose needs are to be taken into account, and who may be seen to be obligated to provide for those needs. Everyone involved is supposed to be 'playing their part' and 'pulling together' in such a way that no-one is being 'put upon' unfairly, even though inputs may vary both qualitatively and quantitatively. The team effort is thus expected to work at both a pragmatic level (as a way of life that works) and a moral level (as a way of life that is just and good).

The boundaries issue for re-partnered households potentially raises particular themes around:

- The difficulties that occur because the external boundaries may not always be clearly established and may shift about both in the present and over time.

- Inclusion/marginalisation/exclusion. There is much discussion in our interviews about whether people feel excluded, left out, or are made to feel included. From this it is apparent that the issues involved in both exclusion and inclusion may lead to resentments – implying things are not fair – or jealousy.

- The difficulties that occur if there are internal boundaries within the unit. Inclusion and exclusion tends to refer to just one person being left out, but sometimes there may be alliances of particular individuals within the unit which undermine the cohesiveness of the whole.

For some of our interviewees, the boundaries were drawn around the current household, and fairness was an issue largely set around 'family' members who were co-resident. If biological ties were also seen as largely irrelevant, issues of fairness might not be experienced as especially problematic. For other interviewees, particularly our White, more 'liberal' middle-class interviewees, boundaries were very diffuse and cut across households. In these circumstances, trying to be 'fair' to everyone could consume a great deal of energy. Indeed, some people could be seen to be striving hard within the interview itself to be seen to be 'fair' in their representation of other people's actions and values.

Fairness might be expressed explicitly in terms of use of language, or indirectly in terms of resentments and bad feeling, and it is played out in practical, concrete and symbolic ways in everyday family relationships. Time and money are significant issues within this, as key but limited resources about which people can make choices signifying priorities in their lives and relationships (see Chapter 4). In exercising these choices, people may be seen as more or less responsible, and more or less caring about, and close to, various (potential) family members. Decisions therefore have to be made about how to prioritise relationships in the present, with implications too for investments in the long-term project of family over generations. Indeed, some of the tensions may themselves relate to differences in this time orientation. How far is there an orientation towards the current (present) residential unit or towards the longer-term family project (which carries the potential to forefront biological ties, whether of the non-resident father or the grandparents)? And how far is there space for being fair to adults in their own right, particularly in relation to coupledom? But in order to understand the meaning of 'fairness' for our interviewees, we have to recognise again the distinction between Child and Adult (as discussed in Chapter 3). In this regard it is noteworthy that much of the literature that explores people's understandings of 'fairness' in family lives has largely been concerned with perceptions of fairness around household divisions of labour, and in this context with relationships between adults only (for example, Thompson, 1991; Lerner and Mikula, 1994; John *et al.*, 1995; Sullivan, 1997; Risman and Johnson-Sumerford, 1998).[1]

In understanding the needs and capacities of family (team) members, generation is absolutely crucial (as we go on to elaborate), but individuals are also defined by other key (largely ascribed) characteristics. Gender, biological parenthood, birth order, personality characteristics, individualised histories and chronological age are all dimensions that can shape how your needs may be seen, as well as how your capacities and obligations are defined (see Finch and Mason, 1993, on the ways in which needs and capacities around family obligations are worked out between adults). Children are at the forefront of this team effort in all sorts of ways. Their needs are taken to be paramount, and their obligations are minimal. And since this is so, they are crucial to the definition of the boundaries, and yet may also disrupt those boundaries because their biological ties may not coincide with their residential ties, and their needs may or may not be seen to be in conflict with the ties of coupledom (see Chapter 3).

Being 'fair' to children: rights and inalienable needs

In relation to children, there are two inextricably interlinked meanings to fairness that are apparent. In one aspect, fairness is concerned with what is just for children, and children's rights (to a good childhood). Notions of impartial justice may perhaps be invoked more readily in relation to older children, who may be seen as more mature with regard to the sort of rational and dispassionate reasoning that underpins such ideas. Additionally, however, in relation specifically to children, fairness encapsulates another dimension, which is concerned with what is good for children, with children's needs and what constitutes a good childhood. This aspect may be invoked more readily with younger children. In this regard it is interesting to note the links here with some of the ambiguities that surround the notion of children's rights generally, concerning tensions between protection and assertive citizenship (see Chapter 3).

An example of the intertwining of the two meanings can be seen in the dilemma of Kim (White, working class, upwardly mobile, mother) as to whether to let her partner, Ben, be part of the family and become involved as a parent to her young daughter Rosie, or to keep him at arm's length. Kim feels that she has had an erratic relationship with Ben over the past few years, never knowing whether he is committed to a relationship with her or not. In discussing 'if it's fair to ask him to tell [Rosie] off when she won't take any notice of me', she expresses her worry about what will happen to Rosie if if she draws Ben into parenting, and he then leaves again (discussed in Chapter 3). Here, the 'fairness' of asking Ben to tell Rosie off when she won't take any notice of Kim relates both to whether it is just to encourage an involved relationship in terms of Rosie's right to a stable childhood without a sense of loss, and the 'goodness' of this for Rosie.

The position of a step-father with regard to discipline is also being addressed in this next quote, from Margaret (White, middle class, mother). It highlights not only the subtlety of what is meant by 'fairness', in terms of both 'justness' and also 'goodness for children', but also a number of other issues that we pursue later, including the ways in which adults can earn 'rights' and the importance of children being able to 'see' fairness in operation:

*I think after about six months James felt that he'd got to know them a bit
better and he'd won a right in a sense to be more part of the discipline
structure. At first it was left to me but gradually he's taking over, and I
think that's been good. He's not harsh at all, he's very fair and I think they
can see that.*

When Paul and Karen first decided to marry, Paul (African-Caribbean,
working class, father and step-father) gave a great deal of thought as to what
was good for his teenage step-daughter, Isis, including her right to be informed
of what was happening:

*I don't think she was ever kept in the dark as to our relationship or what
was going to happen. Everyone was up front and nothing was hidden
from her. Because I've got a firm belief that children, no matter how
simple we think they are, they understand a great deal. So it's only fair to
let them know what's happening.*

The next example also highlights the subtle meaning of 'fairness' in relation
to children, and raises the further issue of how being 'fair' to children can
disrupt household boundaries:

*I mean once or twice I've said to Bob, 'Oh it would be so much easier if
there wasn't anybody else, just the six of us, just get on with it, and that
was it. It would be so much easier'. But then that would be unfair, because
Ruth and Nikki wouldn't see Sue, and Joe and Grace wouldn't see Daniel,
so it wouldn't be fair you know.*
(Jessica – White, middle class, mother and half-weekly resident
stepmother)

Part of Jessica's dilemma (above) relates to what she sees as the children's
rights to relationships with their biological parents who live elsewhere.
Disruptions to the external boundaries of the family/household unit may also
raise other issues of fairness to children. Karen (African-Caribbean, working
class, mother) regarded her ex-partner as failing to behave as an Adult, resulting
in unfair treatment of their daughter:

*That's the hardest thing I think about step-parenting. The other party. If
they will play it as an adult it could go quite well. But sometimes they
don't and it really messes up the child. Promises that aren't kept and
things like that. Which are really hurtful. Not just to her, it hurts me as
well.*

Lyn (White, middle class, mother and resident step-mother) expressed
similar difficulties in terms of disruptions from outside the household. She
referred to the need for fairness around children's feelings of being cared about,
here symbolised by money as a gift from outside the household:

*Although you try and be fair at home there are all these outside things.
And of course, we do have a problem because we do try and give them
all the same. And then they come back and, 'Oh, Dad's given us ten
pounds each'. What do we do? They've got an extra ten pounds and the*

'It's just not fair!' The rights and obligations of 'doing family'

109

other two haven't. I say to Martin, 'Oh, it's really unfair, why don't you give them some money and say your sister sent it?'

In the other direction, Gill (White Irish, working class, mother) was thankful that she did not have to mediate such external disruptions, since her daughter's father had never been part of her life, making the relationship with her step-father, Tony, easier:

I think that's maybe why it's easier for Josie to relate to Tony. Because her own father isn't around. If he was, I think that can be very difficult for children. Divided loyalties.

Underlying both meanings of justness and goodness are ideas about children's needs. In terms of justness, a child is seen to have a moral right to have her/his needs fulfilled, in a context of (impartial) equal treatment. Similarly, in terms of goodness, a child should also have her/his needs met in order to have a good childhood. Furthermore, children have rights to a good childhood without incurring any obligations in themselves. They are deserving in the sense of having needs that should be met unconditionally rather than as morally deserving persons: their needs are inalienable (see Chapters 3 and 6).

Children as equal or different

Children of different biological parents living in the same (step-)family household can be seen as needing to be treated fairly in two ways. The first involves the idea that children should be treated as equal and the same, i.e. that children who live in the same household as part of the same 'family' should receive equality of treatment, and none should be favoured:

What we do in this house, is we treat all the children equally. They all have the same. If I go shopping I won't buy one an article of clothing unless I've got them all something. You know, we treat them fairly.
(Lyn – White, middle class, mother and resident step-mother)

The second is the idea that children should be treated as equal but different, i.e. that each child may be understood as having different, perhaps unique, needs that should be met. Fairness from this perspective involves equality in terms of having needs met in ways that may be different but individually appropriate. Karen (African-Caribbean, working class, mother) talked about her oldest daughter 'needing' more attention, now she has a half-brother and two half-sisters:

The only thing that I do find I have to do is take Isis out for a shopping spree, or window shopping I should say. Take her out for the day 'cos she tends to need a bit more attention.

She does?

Yeah, at the moment now. Obviously with all these kids around it feels as if she hasn't got any space for herself.

Jessica (White, middle class, mother and half-weekly resident step-mother) often made this tension around fairness quite explicit in her account:

> Sometimes you can't be fair and treat everybody the same, as well, because you can't because they're all individuals and need different things ... so you can't always be – you have to be fair, but not too fair that you're saying that everybody has the same treatment, 'cos you can't do that.

Jessica also felt it was impossible to ensure the same treatment for everyone when they were moving between different households, and might encounter different expectations and customs in different places:

> and of course Sue [step-daughters' mother] sent the stockings over to them [for Christmas Day] and of course, [my children] didn't have a stocking and I was feeling a bit sort of, oh dear, maybe I should have done stockings.

Other interviewees could feel much the same in terms of children's visits to their non-resident parent's household, say at weekends, with different rules in different households, and different ideas about discipline. Sue (White, middle class, half-weekly resident mother) was unsure what to think about such differences, when her children spend their time equally between her own household and that of their father:

> But then he's got the kids and what sort of example is he setting the children? And what then right do you have to criticise? What are the rules about commenting on each other's behaviour? ... but there's some sort of taboo there isn't there, which wouldn't be there if you were still operating as a couple. And it's all about values, what role models you are offering the kids.

These different ideas about fairness – as equality or difference – can produce tensions with each other in daily (step-)family lives. A good example of this was the discussion of 'treats' by Bob (White, middle class, half-weekly resident father and step-father). Bob had wanted to take his own two children out for a meal separately from his step-children, in order to acknowledge 'as a parent' that they had gone through some difficult times recently. He described a disagreement between himself and his wife, Jessica, over this, moving between the two different ideas about what constitutes 'fairness':

> Jessica was very anti doing that because of, um, separating the two children out from the two pairs of children. Um, and whilst we haven't argued about it strongly, I would still say, 'Look, I should be doing this because this is something –'. Jessica would say, 'Well, we should be acknowledging the four things'. [Her son] had gone through a very difficult phase with the sleeping and then rewarded by a trip to the Science Museum in London by Jessica. So I just feel that it would be doing the same thing for them.

Bob also talked about the difficulties created when Jessica's children's non-resident father, Daniel, gave his children money (as was also the case for Lyn, quoted earlier). This potentially undermined the 'equal and the same' notion of fairness:

> The most difficult thing [Daniel] does is give them lots of money ... we agreed to give all the children one pound a week pocket money, and that's an agreement he was involved in as well. Um, one pound a week sweets money. And if they come back from a weekend [with Daniel] with more, what does that mean? ... In relation to my children, I can't afford to do that, give them that money. Um, or do I give it to them to make things easier?

In this latter instance, though, in Bob's mind there was no notion of Jessica's children having different needs from his own.

Feeling included

Treating children fairly is a demonstration that they are included as members of the 'family' household. To feel included, not excluded, is in itself understood as one of children's needs. Dawn (White, working class, mother) demonstrates this particularly clearly. For her, the important issue seems to be that everyone must feel involved in a 'family' (something she did not experience herself as a child), whether biologically based or not, so that no-one feels 'left out'. Here she is discussing her own children's feelings since the re-marriage of their father, which she feels has been counterbalanced by her own forthcoming marriage to Trevor:

> [The girls] used to go up there [to their father's house with his wife and step-daughter] to stay of a weekend but now they don't. You know, I tried to explain to the two girls that now they're married, they got their own life. I said, 'They know you're happy now, so they don't worry', but I said, 'Your dad's always there for you' ... [the girls] don't feel as if they're getting anything now, they feel pushed out a bit ... They don't worry now they've got Trevor you know, they're quite happy now.

In Dawn's account, the concept of 'fairness' is muted, but for others such issues of inclusion and exclusion sometimes seem to be strongly implicated in ideas of fairness, so that no-one feels undervalued. Elizabeth (White, middle class, mother and resident step-mother) implied something like this when she talked of being horrified by the possibility that her step-sons, Neil and Sam, might have felt they were less important than her own son, Jake:

> When Jake was a few weeks old we were all in the car going over to see my parents, and I was in the back with Jake and Sam, and Sam suddenly said out of the blue, [imitates a pathetic child's voice:] 'Who's the most important person in this car?'
>
> What, with a voice like that?

> *Yes* [laughs], *it was so pathetic, it was awful, it was really awful. Of course,*
> *I tried to say, 'Jake is a baby so he needs a lot more physical looking*
> *after but you're all equally important'. It was very difficult.*

For Elizabeth and her husband Jonathan, such issues of internal divisions became very significant as first Jonathan's eldest son, and later his second son, decided to live with them as teenagers. There then followed several years of severe tension as Elizabeth struggled to deal with their negative behaviour towards Jake, and Jonathan struggled to 'be fair' to everyone. Similarly, for Sarah and Dave (White, working class) internal divisions became intolerable when Dave's daughter came to live with her father, step-mother and step-siblings. While Elizabeth and Jonathan struggled to carry on as a household together, Dave's daughter decided to go back to live with her mother after a year. (Both cases are discussed further below.)

The existence of different surnames can be a very important symbol of such internal divisions, and several interviewees discussed this issue. It was especially significant if the mother changed her name when marrying her new partner, leaving her own children with a different surname, which was felt to be 'unfair'. For Lyn (White, middle class) it was particularly sensitive because she is also a resident step-mother:

> *It does seem a bit unfair* [to my daughter] *that you take on other children*
> *and then you take on their name as well. It does seem unfair. I can*
> *understand how she feels.*

Some interviewees discussed the significance of step-children deciding to change their names to signify that they were all members of one 'family':

> *Because we thought well, it might be easier if they wanted to have* [my
> surname] *... so the boys were quite keen to have the same name as their*
> *mother.*
> (James – White, middle class, step-father)

Isis was Karen's only child from her first relationship, and has half-siblings from Karen's marriage to Paul. Although she still had some contact with her biological father, Isis had decided to change her name and be adopted by her step-father:

> *This is what she wants ... she wants to have the same name as her*
> *brothers and sisters.*
> (Paul – African-Caribbean, working class, step-father and father)

For two of our step-clusters, issues of interracial relationships were involved, which could make it hard to ensure a fully cohesive unit, when wider social structures and expectations put individual step-parents and children into different positions:

*I think it's hard for a young black man to grow up. And I can't understand
those issues that are involved. So I can't really see it from his perspective
so it's difficult for me ... so it's really not up to me to try and give him
advice.*
(Mark – White, middle class, step-father and expectant father)

Fairness between children: whose obligation?

Issues of residence and biology may also be seen to shape adults' obligations to
act fairly towards children and meet their needs in the context of re-partnered
households. Although children have the right to have their needs met, it is not
always clear *who* is obligated to meet those needs. Adults do not necessarily
feel they have an obligation to act fairly towards *all* children involved in a step-
cluster, where those children are not their own biologically (and it can be unfair
if they are forced to do so, see below). In Trevor's interview, unusually, his
(biological) teenage children from previous relationships are largely discounted,
partly because he does in fact describe them as undeserving because of the way
they have treated him,[2] and partly because he defines fatherhood strongly in
social terms. For Trevor, then, fairness is crucial only in the context of your
current social family and household.

Inappropriate inclusion or exclusion of children by parents or step-parents
can be seen as unfair on both children and/or adults, and can raise delicate
issues. One mother talked about her expectation that her son, Andrew, from a
previous relationship should be included in the will of her current partner:

*But then I think I would be resentful if something happened and he wrote
his will and excluded my children. I think I'd be hurt and upset. Especially
Andrew, because he's been there for Andrew. Andrew's been part of his
life since he's been six years old.*

So you've talked about that as well then?

*Yeah. I don't even know if I've got a right to because it's his money. And
it's his children, but I think it would probably upset Andrew. I don't think
Andrew would expect it, because he's always treated Andrew as his
concern. So I don't know.[3]*

In Janet Finch and colleagues' research on English inheritance practices,
they found that the making of wills was generally regarded as very problematic
(Finch *et al.*, 1996). It created tensions between the key principles which people
generally use to underpin decisions about inheritance, i.e. that 'the claims of
the surviving spouse should take priority; children can expect to inherit
eventually; children should be treated equally'(Finch, 1997: 143).

From a different perspective, Chris (White, middle class, father and non-
resident father) talked about the way contact with his son, Laurie, was unfairly
impinged upon by his ex-wife's attitude. She insisted that Laurie came as an
'equal and the same' package with his half-brother Ned, the son she had had
with her new husband:

> *Ned comes quite often and is just included in our family as if he was one of mine ... I'd think, oh, it would be nice to do such and such a thing with Laurie, and would turn up, ring up, and say, 'Oh, we're thinking of taking Laurie to the whatever'. We'd be told, 'Oh well, you'll have to take Ned too'. That was it. We'd have to take Ned.*

In a similar vein, Dino (White, Italian, middle class, non-resident father) felt aggrieved by his ex-partner's expectation that when buying presents for his daughter (Eva), he should spend an equal amount on her half-sister (Jade). From Dino's point of view, Jade does not need to have the same spent on her, and it would be 'pretending' something if he were to do so. He also appears to suggest implicitly that he would be impinging on Jo's (Jade's father) territory if he were to act in this way. (This quote is a bit unclear. English is not Dino's first language and he was quite worked up at the time.)

> *But in another way, like we argued, she's got another daughter and maybe she's going to have another one. And Eva, when she comes to me and we go out and she likes something, it's like I'll buy it for her. I'll buy things even for her sister or her friend. And we had an argument last time with Tina but I think she called up me ... she said, 'You have to treat them, maybe it's a different situation, but to treat Eva and Jade the same way'. 'I do, but it's different. You know Eva is my daughter and Jade is her sister, your daughter. Nothing to do with me.' What I can do of course if I go there I buy a present ... Because she said to me, 'You have to be equal. If you spend £100 for Eva then you have to spend £100 for Jade'. But I told her it was not right ... they don't really need the same thing ... But if I see her sometime and we go out and I feel like she wants something, oh well. I don't pretend I think Jo should be equal. Because you know they live together. I wouldn't pretend. If he does something for his daughter I understand that. Wouldn't go there and say, 'Well Jo, why did you?', you know. I wouldn't want to say that. But if I found out one day he beat my daughter then it might be different. But I wouldn't step in to care more for his daughter. Even if it should be equal.*

It is evident, then, that the absence of clear external boundaries, and the possibility of inappropriate internal boundaries, can raise some difficult and complex issues in being fair to children and meeting their rights and needs.

Being 'fair' to adults: the rights and obligations of (step-) parenthood

'Fairness' is also seen as relevant to adults in the step-family cluster, but here it can be negotiable and contingent: there are circumstances that need to be taken into account. For adults, fairness is associated with rights to something and the justice of a situation, while unfairness refers to a situation in which an adult's rights are unjustly unfulfilled. We have not found a concern with fairness or unfairness in terms of what is 'good' for adults in their own right. Rights here are moral and/or legal, and may sometimes be inextricably bound up with children's needs. In this regard, we find that it is possible for adults to require 'fair' treatment with respect to their own needs, either as individuals or as part of a couple. This only occurs, however, if it is framed in terms of something

'It's just not fair!' The rights and obligations of 'doing family'

115

that is necessary to enable them to parent properly (and see Lawler, 1999, for a similar discussion concerning mothers generally).

The obligations of an adult to a step-child may not be seen as equal to those of a parent to a biological child, and it can be unfair if they are put in the position where this is not recognised – at least in the view of some of our middle-class interviewees. For them, even the passage of time need not lead to equality of obligation between biological and step-parent. Lisa (African-Caribbean, middle class, mother) had a son from a previous relationship, and when he started to be a troublesome teenager, she thought this was unfair on her new partner, Mark:

> It put a lot of strain on our relationship. Because I felt as though Mark doesn't need all this ... why should we put all this on him? It's not his child. He doesn't need this aggro and bother.

Conversely however, a parent, and especially a step-parent, can *acquire* a moral right to something because they have put in recognised effort, and therefore it is only fair, just and deserving that they in turn earn a right to have their needs taken into account. Gina (White, working class, mother) felt that her new partner, Tom, had contributed more than could be expected in his relationship with her son Craig:

> I think Tom does deserve a bit of credit. Because you know, who else would have done what he's done for Craig? I'm quite lucky that I've found somebody who's prepared to be as caring. I mean, there's a lot of chaps who wouldn't take on a child. Or if they did they'd probably push the child out. And Tom doesn't have to do what he does for Craig but he loves Craig. He says he loves him.

It is therefore unfair if a step-parent who has incurred obligations over and above those that are not morally their own (towards non-biological children) does not have this recognised and reciprocated. Nevertheless, if this does not happen, the step-parent may still feel that they have to 'hang on in there' in fairness to the child/ren (since children's needs have to come first), and be unfair to themselves. Furthermore, because fairness to children is inalienable but fairness to adults is contingent, being unfair to a parent or step-parent can be just if it is necessary in order to be fair to a child.

Jessica (White, middle class, mother and half-weekly resident step-mother) provides a good example here. She is co-parenting step-mother to her husband Bob's two children, as well as resident mother to her own two children. Jessica feels that she put in a lot of effort with her step-children for very little acknowledgement from Bob or his ex-partner – an unfairness to her:

> whereas all half-terms normally they're with us, 'cos I'm off [college] and the childcare comes down on me quite a lot.
>
> How do you feel about that?
>
> Better now. I used to be – I felt I was put upon by everybody. But better now ... And that's why I said [to Bob] on the calendar, you write down

there on the calendar when we're having them. 'Cos otherwise the children say to me, 'Are Ruth and Nikki staying tonight?' 'Um, I don't know'. I don't know who I'm cooking for. And it's like a bit – you know, what's happening?

Several of our interviewees discussed similar issues around the contributions made by step-parents to the lives of the children involved, without this being given much recognition. This was especially likely to be seen in terms of step-parents' involvement in the daily lives and activities of the children they live with:

That annoys me sometimes when they're sort of like ... 'Yes, yes, Dad's here, Dad's here', you know ... He himself, as I see it, doesn't give them a lot of time, three hours on a Saturday, and that's it, and sometimes he can't even do that. And sometimes it's, 'I'll stick a video on, here's a bag of sweets and that's it' ... and I've had to deal all week, running around, very rarely does he run them anywhere, I take them to all their football matches, parents' evenings, all that sort of thing.
(Simon – White, middle class, step-father and expectant father)

Trevor (White, working class, step-father and non-resident father) feels that this sort of input by a step-father means that perhaps he should continue with care of the child/ren if anything happened to their mother:

I think they should be left with the parents they've been brought up with, not the one that's been away, and hasn't had all the dealings with 'em, all the rest of it.

Kim (White, working class, upwardly mobile, mother) makes a similar point in relation to her partner, Ben, saying she would be:

horrified that if something happened to me that [my ex] *would have more, much more, legal right to Rosie* [daughter] *than Ben would ... I think that's unfair because biologically or not you can form very strong attachments to a child.*

Financial contributions could be another thorny issue in relation to fairness for adults, as exemplified by this White, middle-class step-cluster which straddled two households. Between Lorna, Pete (her husband), Chris (her ex-husband), and Paula (Chris's wife), there is an underlying tension around what is fair in terms of financial contributions towards the maintenance of Lorna and Chris's children. Pete pays for their maintenance when Chris's income is stretched, but Lorna makes her own decision (against Chris's preference) not to be a working mother, unlike Paula:

Lorna: *Pete really does the money earning around here, and sometimes he gets cross about things ... he saw how he used to live before the kids were around, and how he lives now, you know! And no matter how many kinds of ways you can account for it, there is that vast difference.*

'It's just not fair!' The rights and obligations of 'doing family'

117

Pete:	I think Chris has abdicated a little bit on his responsibilities. He says he's interested but ... And I think, you know, if you've got children you can't just say, 'Well, I haven't got any [money]'. It's not what it's about is it? I mean, what about if I haven't got any? It's like, somehow, 'You can sort it out, it's nothing to do with me, you know. I haven't got any money'.
Chris:	So whenever I would say, 'But I've got no money, I'm poor', Lorna would say, 'But I've got nothing'. And I would say, 'But you and Pete have got money'. And it even got to the stage where I was sort of thinking, well the only way we can deal with this is if I stop work, Paula goes out to work, and I'm going to say I've got nothing.
Paula:	You don't mind giving anybody anything if there's a feeling of reciprocation, that if you need something they'd worry about giving it to you. So there's always that feeling of one-sidedness. They just take. It's only one side.

Money was not the only source of a sense of unfairness in these relationships, however. Paula implied a similar sense of being 'put upon' in relation to childcare as Jessica (quoted above). She talked about an incident where she was expected to have Lorna and Pete's child for the day, along with Chris and Lorna's own child:

> I mean I felt pretty pissed off really ... I'm expected to help out, but I've got my own emotion that I feel annoyed as well ... I just felt imposed upon ... so it's unbalanced I think.

Nevertheless, she felt generally that it was only fair to her step-children if she continued to make an effort:

> I don't know, I wonder if [Chris and I] split up if I would see them again. I'm not sure where I stand on that one ... It would feel strange if I didn't considering I've spent nine years of my life knowing them ... I'm not sure how it is with them. I'm just trying to do my best really! I'm not a very imposing person. I mean I think I could probably impose more, but I'm not very confident about imposing my expectations on them really. I just try to be flexible and, you know, be there if they want.

As is the case for children, there are issues of the demonstration of inclusion and exclusion at stake here in relation to membership of the (step-)family and/ or household (as we saw earlier in relation to Dave). As a part-time step-mother, Paula felt that she and the young son, Jack, she had had with Chris, were unfairly sidelined within the (step-)family cluster as a whole. The issue of birthdays exemplified this exclusion for her. Talking about birthday parties that Chris's ex-wife organised for the children, she said:

> Birthdays, Chris gets invited along. I tag along too and Jack goes too ... I don't think I've ever been personally asked to anything. I mean it's assumed that I'll go too I suppose, but if I didn't go nobody would be

> *bothered! That's how I feel about it. I feel that if I didn't go nobody would say, 'Oh, where's Paula?'*

And of her own son Jack's birthday:

> *I wish that Jack wasn't sidelined so much. And, um, that sort of shows itself in funny ways really. That when it was his birthday nobody remembered it. But that was probably partly because – I don't know – well, no, none of the kids sent him a card or remembered it.*

Graham Allan and Graham Crow (2001) also found step-parents might express feelings of not 'belonging' in similar ways to biologically related household members.

Rob (White, middle class, father and step-father) also discussed how he felt unfairly marginalised in the family, despite his efforts and commitment to his step-son, Liam, as if he was competing for time with his partner, Kate. He explained how, before the birth of their baby together, he tolerated feeling like an outsider in the family for the sake of Liam. He also emphasised the misfit between his substantial contribution as a step-father, and his lack of legal rights:

> *So that bit was definitely harder and needed some adjustment. I mean it works now but it's still there. I had all sorts of odd feelings. I felt rejected. I felt that Kate had to spend a lot of time working with Liam to make him feel safe. So for a long time I felt that this is what had to be. There are good effects of living together but this is one of the things that we have to manage ... I mean, I've devoted time, energy, money and years. Liam's in my will, somewhere along the line he will inherit from me. But you know, I have no formal relationship to him at all. So it does strike me that after 11 years it's a bit of an anomaly.*

Thus, moral fairness to adults is contingent. This contingency can be seen to operate not only in relation to the greater claim of fairness to children, but also in relation to parents' and step-parents' own treatment of those children. Parents and step-parents can earn a moral right and deserve reciprocally fair treatment, whether resident or not with the children. Equally, however, they can also cease to make an effort and therefore forfeit their moral rights. Nevertheless, this can be a delicate issue with regard to biological parents, because it is not only the rights of the adult that are potentially at stake: children's right to a relationship with their father may also be involved, and this is more difficult to override. Thus James (White, middle class, step-father) felt he had to recognise his step-sons' rights to have a loyal relationship with their father who had died:

> *I think I've got to be careful not to, particularly with [the eldest boy], to pretend to be his Dad, 'cos he's obviously got very clear memories of his Dad. And so I need to be sensitive to that.*

Mandy (White, middle class) felt that her own rights as a (non-resident) parent could have been more fully recognised by her ex-husband, particularly in the context of her own primary care responsibility for their earlier years:

I felt sort of marginalised I suppose, when you've had them on your own for ten years, you know ... Sam [younger son] says he'll come and do something and he might come for an hour ... But all I feel is, it would be really nice if Jonathan [his father] sort of said, you know, 'Your mother needs you now'. And I expect if they'd been made more aware when they were younger ... I just feel it would be nice to have some support really, or some involvement with them.

Conversely, while Tina (White, middle class, mother) facilitates her daughter Eva's relationship with her non-resident father, Dino, she feels that his lack of input into Eva's life means that he has forfeited his rights to have his wishes prioritised (see Chapter 4). Similar sentiments were expressed by John (White, middle class, half-weekly resident step-father) towards his partner's children's father, Bob, who shares their care half-time. John feels there are limits as to how far he is willing to accommodate differences of opinion:

I think that only extends to a certain amount because, you know, he was the one who left them in the first place. You know, if he'd wanted to bring up children himself then he shouldn't have walked out.

Bob, for his part, feels that his own input into his children's lives is considerable, and states that he would 'be very angry if anybody said that [I am an absent father]'. He contrasts his own fathering involvement with the involvement of his step-children's father:

He only has them once for 24 hours basically once a fortnight, so the involvement there is minimal.

Consequently, Bob finds it difficult that he can only be a 'father figure' to his step-children and cannot 'step into being a father', despite his daily involvement in their lives.

While these interviewees weighed up the respective rights each parent or parent substitute might have earned or lost, others felt that biological fathers could lose their rights completely. Thus Paul (African-Caribbean, working class, step-father and father) emphasised the irresponsibility of his step-daughter's father, describing his drunkenness, empty promises and erratic visits. According to Paul, this failure to meet obligations of fatherhood warrants the decision made by himself and his wife to file for adoption. Again, though, he is careful to construct this decision around the imperative of children's needs:

Because what I don't want is cutting her off totally and then she turns round and accuses me of not allowing her to know her father. So she's had all the opportunities, and he's had all the opportunities to come and see her. Which he didn't take. He's missed most of her birthdays or whatever. So it was hard when she asked, 'Why didn't he come round?' Even though you're thinking, 'Am I not being a good Dad, why are you still asking?'. But I didn't make it an issue. But as far as the father's concerned, we've filed for adoption, I thought 'Is this where things will get serious?' But it didn't ... And it's something she wanted. I'd have loved to have done it earlier, but I wouldn't do it unless she wanted it. And it's now come to a head that this is what she wants.

Similarly, Ben (White, working class, upwardly mobile, step-father) suggested that his step-daughter's father had 'given up his fatherly rights' because of his long-term absence. Sheena (White, Irish, working class, upwardly mobile, mother) felt that her own children's father had behaved so badly that 'he had no rights as far as I was concerned, all he was was sperm'.

Legally, then, a resident or non-resident parent may have rights in relation to their biological children, but these are not seen as inalienable. A parent can morally forfeit their legal rights if they do not behave in a deserving fashion, with the implication that it is only just that they should lose them. It is unfair for a parent to abdicate their obligations with no consequent loss of rights. Furthermore, if a parent acts unfairly in this way, then it can be fair if the other parent or step-parent acts unfairly towards them.

Being fair to adults: the rights and obligations of (step-) grandparenthood

The position and relevance of grandparents is also apparent in various ways in these sorts of equations. Like biological parents, grandparents may be seen to have 'rights' by virtue of their biological link, and investment in the long-term project of 'family' over generations. Similarly, children may be seen to have rights to a relationship with their grandparents. In turn, grandparents can be at risk of losing their rights to their grandchildren, and also may be seen to have obligations to treat all grandchildren and step-grandchildren equitably.

This last issue was explicitly raised in Vignette 3 (see Appendix), which drew different responses in line with people's variable views on the significance of biology and the right to assert the needs of the main family unit to pursue equity regardless of biology. Thus Paul (African-Caribbean, working class, step-father and father) discussed how his parents' relationship with his step-daughter was fine until he had his own child with his wife, Karen:

> *I think up until* [our first child] *was born, everything was fine and there wasn't a problem. But then after he was born it was like he got all the attention. And for a while* [my step-daughter] *felt kind of left out as if she was like a stand-in until the real one came along.*

Karen (African-Caribbean, working class, mother) herself also discussed some of these difficulties, and suggested it is up to the parents to tell the grandparents to deal equitably with the children:

> *What parents have to deal with is children's rivalry. And it is unpleasant ... and grandparents will stay that way unless they basically are shown that it's not on. It is not acceptable to do that ... and it's not really fair on the children.*

In contrast, Margaret (White, middle class, mother) discussed the rights of her children's paternal grandfather to see and be valued by them. This was a sensitive issue because the death of their father (his son) also undermined his own family project over generations:

> *And I mean obviously we try to see an awful lot of the grandfather, partly because he's on his own and partly just the situation, we don't want him to feel left out. In fact, we've made more of an effort to see him, so much so that I've, you know, actually neglected the others really.*

This relationship was also seen as in need of careful attention because Margaret's sons had changed their surname to that of their step-father:

> *I just desperately didn't want to hurt him* [the paternal grandfather] *you see, 'cos he was still alive ... I said to him that it won't affect the relationship at all, 'They're still your grandchildren and always will be'.*

Simon (White, middle class) was a step-father expecting his first child with his wife, Catherine. He described tensions in his relationship with his mother-in-law, who he feels regards him as an intruder into the family relationships with her grandchildren:

> *Because, you know, Catherine's worked and you know,* [her mother's] *been there, she's always had quite an influence on the kids, I mean, again, I'm not trying to come straight in and upset the apple cart, but you know, from time to time I sometimes feel that she tries to undermine me.*

Simon also feels some concern about whether or not his own child will receive equal treatment:

> *All I hope is that there's no preferences if you see what I mean, with our baby coming up. I'm hoping it's gonna, you know, like, bring us all even closer together.*

Lyn (White, middle class, mother and resident step-mother) implies that practicalities may in the end make it almost impossible for grandparents to treat all their (step-)grandchildren equitably. For example, her husband's parents wanted to take his children to stay with them in the USA:

> *And I suppose you can't expect them to have four children. I suppose you can only take it so far. You can only do so much to treat them fairly.*

Where exactly lines of fairness can and should be drawn in such situations can be a source of disagreement. Sarah (White, working class, mother and non-resident step-mother) felt that her partner's parents only made a futile gesture towards her children from previous relationships, in comparison with their own grandchild, Leanne:

> *This Easter, Leanne doesn't live with us now, they bought her clothes, Easter eggs, shoes. They sent up an envelope with £5 in it for my kids, which was fine, but Leanne as well. So she had to have all that and then even what my kids had. I'd sooner they didn't send anything. I mean, if they don't want to accept my kids, that's fine, that's okay. But it's this token, you know. Like, 'We're making an effort'. 'Don't bother, because you're not.' It's either one or the other. You either do it wholeheartedly, or not at all. Don't play about with kids' lives and their emotions. It's not fair.*

Conversely, Sue (White, middle class, half-weekly resident mother) felt that the input of several sets of (step-)grandparents was difficult to incorporate, with potentially two sets of step-grandparents as well as two sets of grandparents wanting to be involved in her children's lives now that she had re-partnered. In this situation, access to grandchildren and input into their lives was seen as a bonus for grandparents rather than an obligation for them to deal with everyone fairly:

> And then there would be John's Mum and Dad, who are sort of like eager to get in there, another set of grandchildren to take on. And Katie and Nicki have not really responded to it ... but you know, they're there. They are there in the background and expect to be acknowledged as grandparents ... there's a bit of competition going on at grandparent level.

Achieving and demonstrating fairness

In working out how to 'be fair' across the family unit as a whole, there are issues about who is to take responsibility for its achievement, and whether or not everyone accepts that it has been achieved. Kathryn Backett (1982) discusses issues of fairness between adults/parents in a situation where middle-class couples subscribed to an ideal of fairness regardless of gender, alongside an ideal of equally involved parenthood. She raises the question of *who* is seen to be responsible for maintaining 'fairness', and our interviews suggest that it is the resident biological mother who is supposed to fulfil this role. This of course raises queries about the position of resident step-mothers (discussed in Chapter 1). In the present study, we interviewed four women who were currently, or had previously been, in the position of being the primary or half-time carer for their partners' children from a previous relationship, while also having their own biological children living with them. One of these situations had not been sustained – that of Sarah and Dave, a White, working-class couple. Dave's daughter had returned to live with her mother. Two instances appeared to be experienced as quite stable and manageable, with both step-parents and biological parents taking some responsibility for monitoring fairness (Lyn and Martin, and Jessica and Bob, both White, middle-class couples). The fourth household (Elizabeth and Jonathan, a White middle-class couple) was sustained, but apparently at a considerable cost to the adults involved.

In the case of Elizabeth and Jonathan, a comparison of the interviews with each of them, as well as with Jonathan's first wife Mandy, points to the possibility that no-one had quite taken responsibility and authority for ensuring fairness. The issues were experienced as particularly fraught after Jonathan's teenage sons came to live with him, Elizabeth and their son, Jake. The older boys' behaviour to Jake was seen by all parties to be highly rejecting and difficult to cope with. Elizabeth suggests this may have been the result of their feeling neglected by herself and Jonathan, with a young child of their own alongside financial pressures. Looking back, Elizabeth wonders whether she should have more actively mediated the relationships involved:

> *I think maybe I, you know, was more important to them than I realised at that stage, and I should have been working a lot harder to give them [her step-sons] more attention as well. I mean that's quite possible. And I kind of thought at the time, well, I should really be doing something with the boys or making sure that Jonathan is, or something, rather than just sort of leaving everybody to their own devices.*

This pattern of relationships led to internal divisions within the household/ family, such that at one point Jonathan believed that Elizabeth was seriously considering moving out with Jake. Nevertheless, it is clear that at times Elizabeth did indeed act as a mediator of various relationships. For example, she tried to mediate between Jonathan and Mandy to solve the problem of the boys' homework when they used to visit at weekends, with the underlying assumption that she should be guided by what was best for the children. Yet both she and Mandy appeared to feel the situation was unfair to her. Thus Mandy explicitly discussed the burden that she felt was unfairly put on Elizabeth by Jonathan's attitude, and also described how she felt Jonathan should have mediated her own relationship with her sons as a non-resident parent (as quoted earlier):

> *I think [the boys] were always quite ... resentful of Jake and resentful of Elizabeth. I mean they certainly didn't make her life any easier, and of course Jonathan was never there to sort of, you know, sort them out. A lot has fallen on Elizabeth which shouldn't have fallen on her ... but also if Elizabeth says something they don't [pause] they resent, or have in the past I think. There's an element of resentment there. And it's very difficult for her, she shouldn't have to be in that position, you know, Jonathan should have been there and sorted them out. And they weren't very respectful, I don't think, of Elizabeth, but then she was expected to do things that she shouldn't have had to do without their father being there really ... I mean I think she's been a brick really ... But I still think she allows herself to be 'put on' you know, as we all do, but in that situation I think she should have had more back-up there.*

Elizabeth's own views are more muted but she did describe herself as trying to mediate relationships in ways she found almost impossible, with all members of the household competing for Jonathan's time and attention:

> *It was weekends that were worst if we were all expecting to have time with Jonathan. And it drove him round the bend, because when he was here he was having to divide up his time, certain amount of time with Neil, certain amount of time with Sam. Because they always wanted to do different things anyway, and then a certain amount of time with me and Jake.*

In her interview, Elizabeth appeared to be striving to present everyone's point of view 'fairly', but in response to one of the vignettes she was more explicit about her own position:

> *I actually feel that that's quite important, that the new partner shouldn't actually have too much responsibility, because it puts a relationship on a different basis and puts too much strain on it. You know, I really feel*

*that it might have been different if I hadn't had ... I'm sure he thinks I'm
blaming him for – which in a way I suppose I am by saying, you know, I
felt I needed more support and it wasn't there.*

Jonathan himself described how he felt like Solomon, in an impossible
situation, with strong underlying feelings of wanting to run away, and 'waiting
for the bad times to pass':

*Life seems to have been one huge long period of coping rather than
enjoying life ... all the logistical problems of coping with everybody's
different needs. It still makes it difficult to see what the hell's in it for us
... we had Jake and Elizabeth on one side, and Neil and Sam on the other
side. There was a period of feeling that it was trying to get oil and water
to mix, and that I was having to be the, you know, Solomon and
judgement over the whole damn thing and trying to stop people falling
apart or being violently rude to each other ... [Elizabeth and I] were both
working quite long hours, and always coming home to vast amounts of
tension, and having to surmount to, a balancing act between it all and
feeling that neither side felt I was being fair.*

Did that make you feel like not coming home?

*Yup. There were times when it was easier to stay in the office and work.
We got over it.*

Elizabeth worried that Jonathan felt let down because she did not become
a surrogate mother (although Jonathan himself says that he did not expect this
of her):

*I think Jonathan actually wanted me to be more of a surrogate mother
probably, because he was so angry with Mandy probably.*

She discussed how differently she feels the relationship is with her own
biological child, because she finds it much easier to understand him, but she
may also have found it easier to be angry with Jake than with her step-sons
(and see Chapters 2 and on other discussions about anger in biological and
step-relationships):

*I still think I was a lot harder on Jake over some things. And Jake certainly
feels that ... I actually do expect higher standards of behaviour in some
ways from Jake ... But of course that's not how Neil and Sam see it, they
think I'm being much harder on them than on Jake. And probably I am in
relation to different things ... It's so difficult being even-handed, and I'm
sure Jonathan thinks I've always sided with Jake against Neil and Sam
as well. He really thinks he's been through it on his own, which is awful.*

A second important issue in Backett's (1982) study arose from the way in
which the parents involved subscribed to the ideal of 'fairness' but were faced
with a situation (of early parenthood) in which it was clear that equity could
not be achieved by any straightforward similarities of roles or activities. Backett
identifies a number of ways in which her interviewees strove to maintain their
belief that things were 'fair' despite the inequities of the situation. This parallels

'It's just not fair!' The rights and obligations of 'doing family'

125

Andrea Doucet's (1995) discussion of 'sharing' household work and care. She argues that the significant thing is not for people to be all doing the same things, but for people to be seen to be 'pulling together' and each doing their part according to their own capacities and needs (see Chapter 2). Backett discusses the use of 'temporary' and 'disapproved expedients', which are a way of recognising that it is impossible to actually maintain fairness fully in everyday lives. Nevertheless, she found that it was regarded as wrong to be *knowingly* unfair (resonating with some of our discussion of moral tales in Chapter 3).

In line with this, a further aspect of the negotiation and contestation of 'fairness' in (step-)family lives concerns its visible demonstration to all concerned, since fairness must be *seen* to be occurring. This can involve extensive discussions and persuasions at time, to help children 'see' what is 'really' going on in terms of the contributions made by various adults to the making of the family. Indeed, when some adults (particularly step-fathers) voice resentment about their part in the (step-)family picture, it tends to be expressed not so much in terms of being asked to contribute more than their fair share, but in terms of a resentment that this contribution is undervalued or even totally obscured:

> *Me and Eva were in the car and talking and she mentioned that she gets all this stuff and* [her Dad] *buys her everything. I just went mad because I just pointed out to her the reality of the situation is such that it just isn't so.*
> (Jo – White, middle class, resident step-father and father)

Demonstrating 'fairness' may relate to the significance of time and money (discussed in Chapter 4), because these are *visible* symbols of being fair. It also underscores the emphasis that may be put on explaining things to children, so that they will then be able to appreciate that fairness is operating:

> *It really annoys me, because they can't see that* [their father's] *treating them like shit. Sheena's made this point to them several times when they complain about not having enough money ... the problem is actually with the lads recognising it ... and we said, 'That's what we spend in a year on each of you, how much does your father spend in a year on each of you?'*
> (Geoff – White, working class, upwardly mobile, step-father and father)

Treatment *appearing* to be fair is important, even if underlying feelings around biological relationships are felt to be inevitable, or 'natural' as Allan and Crow (2001) term it. Catherine (White, middle class, mother) has three children from her first marriage, and is now expecting a child with her husband, Simon, who will be the first grandchild for his parents. She discussed possible inequities of feelings on the part of her parents-in-law, which she anticipates could arise after the arrival of the baby:

> *I know there's going to be some favouritism because there will have to be, but if it becomes evident, I will say something to them. I've told him he's got to treat them all the same ... I've always said that if he has one* [of his own], *he's got to treat them all the same, 'cos I will. I know it's impossible, but you've got to say that.*

Similarly, Gill (White, Irish, working class, mother) commented in response to our vignette about tensions with grandparents:

> I mean you can't make people love children. But I would definitely object to presents being bought for some children and not. They don't have to be the same, but just something.

One of the step-fathers interviewed had previous experience of living in a step-family. He found that an appearance of fairness was shattered after the death of his mother, when the will 'disowned' his adopted step-daughter:

> [My mother] professed to accept her, but in fact didn't ... [My step-daughter] hasn't seen that will and I shall never show her.[4]

Conclusion

While fairness and equity were seen as relevant values by almost everyone in our study, this could be emphasised to varying degrees and framed in different ways, with variable sets of people added in to the equation. For some, what is crucial is for everyone to feel included and valued, with or without a concern for fairness. For others, it is equitable treatment that is stressed as the key issue in being fair. Contrasts also occur in terms of how biological ties are understood (see Chapter 4). Where biological differences of parentage are seen as having little relevance, the emphasis is on fairness within the current social family and household. In contrast, where the implications of biological difference are seen as inevitable, such sources of difference between children must be controlled and mitigated by adults. This can take a great deal of thought, emotional management and keeping up appearances. Sometimes it can be achieved by an idea of different-but-equal forms of relationship (despite unclear boundaries). What is then at stake is similarity of treatment within the relevant family relationships, such that the children involved should feel they all are equally important regardless of parentage. Nevertheless, some parents and step-parents expressed strong feelings of being torn in different directions, trying to equal out the varying obligations of biological parenthood and co-resident, social parenthood. (Children's own agency could be significant here too, as we saw in Chapter 3.)

Understandings of fairness in doing family are therefore subject to considerable variation. Furthermore, while fairness may be posed in ways that highlight complexity and difference for step-family relationships, it may also be framed in ways that emphasise the continuities between step-families and other family types. 'Family' does not happen naturally and inevitably, and fairness may be a significant theme in its social construction in contemporary British lives, whatever the household formation.

Across all the discussions, however, being fair to children is understood differently from being fair to adults. Being fair to children involves more, in the terms of meeting their needs as well as acknowledging their rights, and it takes priority over being fair to adults. Fairness is thus a concept that is fundamentally shaped by the categories of Child and Adult. While the concern to demonstrate

'It's just not fair!' The rights and obligations of 'doing family'

127

that standards of fairness are being met resonates with ideas about impartial justice, which require not only that justice is done but that it is seen to be done, it is not clear that it can be seen as strictly equivalent. We turn to such issues in our final chapter.

Notes

1 It is noteworthy that the collection edited by Melvin Lerner and Gerold Mikula (1994) includes only one chapter out of 14 that is concerned with the presence of children.

2 This does not necessarily undercut the argument we make in Chapter 6, that a dependent child cannot be placed as undeserving within a moral tale, since Trevor is discussing teenage children, who are moving from Child to Adult status.

3 This quote has not been fully attributed as we felt it could be a sensitive issue between the mother, her son and her partner.

4 This quote is left unattributed because of its sensitive nature.

Chapter 6

Conclusions: difference, morality and democracy in (step-)families

This book has been concerned with how biological parents and step-parents make sense of parenting and family, both within and between households, and within the wider social context. At the start of the book we posed several questions about the nature of step-family life and its relationship to family life generally in contemporary society, concerning whether or not step-families were different from 'ordinary' families, and what this might mean. In the chapters that followed, our discussions of the lives and understandings of the people we interviewed who were involved in 'step-clusters' all threw light on these questions. Their accounts of their life histories and significant events, and of family, couple and parenting relationships are all unique. Each has its own complexity and particularity. Nevertheless, as will also have been clear from the preceding chapters, there have been some pervasive cross-cutting themes around gender, generation and social class in how these parents and step-parents, and in a few cases their children, produced meaningful realities and formulated the social world in the narrative 'tales' that they told us. In this final chapter, we review and explore these issues further. In particular, we want to draw out some of the key theoretical implications from the evidence that we have presented about how people themselves can understand their family lives under changing circumstances.

How can we understand step-family lives?

Underlying the questions we have raised about whether or not step-families are the same as, or different from, other families, are deeper issues. These relate to the nature of research enquiries that seek to provide answers to such concerns in the reflexive enterprise of social science. We began to address this point in Chapter 1, when we discussed how the statistical presentation of trends in family forms and household types can be emphasised in different ways to construct particular arguments about the state of contemporary family life, and noted how statistical categories such as 'step-', 'nuclear', 'lone-parent' families are administratively defined and then regarded as socially significant and understood as 'different' from one another. Chapter 1 also began to raise issues, which were further noted in later chapters, about how the category 'step-family' may be used to explain every aspect of the experiences of people involved in them. This may obscure the possibility that the experiences at issue are reflections or extensions of deep-rooted gender divisions or other tensions within (heterosexual) families more widely. Just as lone motherhood can be a focus for broader public concerns about gender relations (see Song and Edwards, 1997; Duncan and Edwards, 1999), step-families may be constituted as a categorical site for playing out more general worries about the nature of family life, coupledom and parent–child relations in contemporary society.

In writing this book, we have also been mindful of how we understand and write about step-family lives, conceptually and linguistically. This is especially important where the research endeavour seeks to retain research participants' perspectives in exploring and making 'public' the 'private', domestic and intimate aspects of people's lives. In researching family lives, we are constantly moving between, and potentially reframing, forms of understanding that may differ between public and private ways of being (Edwards and Ribbens, 1998). We have thus been acutely aware that we are involved in the social construction and production of 'knowledge' about step-family life, and that it is all too easy to import and apply uncritically theories, concepts and discourses which have been developed in relation to people's activities in – and which have purchase within – the public sphere. This is an issue that we will return to later in this chapter, when we discuss how the language of public individualised citizenship and democracy has become a feature of academic discussion of family life generally, eclipsing more private, socially located languages of morality and connection, especially around children.

The fact that a key concern of this book has been the 'moral tales' of the interviewees who took part in our research has also meant that we have had to think carefully about how we portray their accounts. This focus on moral responsibility arose from our inductive analysis of recurring preoccupations and images in our interviewees' narratives of parenting and step-parenting under changing family circumstances. Asking people to talk about their family relationships places them in double jeopardy in terms of their moral adequacy and interactional competence (Jordan et al., 1994). Further, while all parenting is morally charged, divorce or separation, subsequent re-partnering and the raising of children in step-families, in particular have generated concern. As we discussed in Chapter 1, being brought up by their (married and resident) biological parents is widely regarded as best for children, and step-family life is seen to engender particular stresses and difficulties, and even the abuse of children. Thus, parents who are seen as placing their children at potential risk through their re-partnering or non-residence are in a morally questionable situation, and may have their moral identities especially at stake.

In writing about morality around our interviewees' family lives, then, we have been particularly concerned to make clear that we do not wish to be heard ourselves as moralising and evaluating our interviewees' lives in these terms (as we attempted to convey in introducing our discussion in Chapter 3). We do, of course, have to recognise that, as individuals, we did inevitably react to some of the things people told us, and that we found some people's accounts more morally acceptable than others. We also recognise that some of the issues involved in discussing step-family life, especially around the care of children, are so deeply imbued with moral overtones that it is very difficult for us to address these matters at all without being regarded as making moral statements, whatever our own intentions. Nevertheless, in presenting our analysis, we have sought to try to understand what people were saying to us on their own terms (Gubrium et al., 1994).

We are clear, however, that taking a non-judgemental stance is not the same as adopting a detached, 'objective' position. We are firmly taking up a value-imbued position, arising out of personal, intellectual and political commitments to make visible people's understandings and experiences of their family lives. Family members' own perspectives and everyday experiences are often marginalised. We hope that our work can help not only to bring these views onto the academic and policy agendas, but to reformulate and reshape those agendas.

(Step-)family life: parents' and step-parents' perspectives

So, what have been the main conclusions that we can draw from our exploration of our interviewees' understandings and experiences of step-family life?

In Chapter 1 we began our review of the wider discourses around step-family life with an overview of Jacqueline Burgoyne and David Clark's (1984) classic sociological study of British step-families. We noted their findings that the majority of their interviewees drew on and were committed to 'ordinary' nuclear family norms as the being best environment for bringing up children. We wondered, given recent arguments about the individualisation and democratisation of contemporary family life, whether people in step-families on the cusp of the twenty-first century would still be making families by drawing on similar images to those used in the late 1970s? It appears that they are. In Chapter 2 we saw that – despite their own experiences of family change and the fact they were grappling with 'making families' that might not map neatly onto household structures – our interviewees still held strongly to ideas of family as a unit involving togetherness and commitment, and which was dependable and long lasting. Furthermore, they preferred to think of themselves as a family, rather than a step-family. In contrast to recent theorising of contemporary family life as involving contingent 'pure relationships' and the emergence of 'elective affinities', these parents and step-parents still adhered to notions of family as being about ties that bind, and were attempting to build a – supposedly superseded – 'community of need' (issues that we will return to later in this chapter). Our interviewees' 'family practices' were framed by a set of long-standing ideas about the nature of family life, rather than around negotiating fluidity and diversity. We also saw, in Chapter 3, that gender – as (step-)mother or (step-)father – is implicated in how our interviewees understood their particular contribution to doing and being 'family'.

We had also wondered whether Burgoyne and Clark's (1984) finding that their step-couples did not put much emphasis on romance and coupledom would still hold in the light of claims that romantic love is now the individualised centre of contemporary couple relationships. Certainly, as we discussed in Chapter 3, this was more of a feature of our interviewees' narratives. Nevertheless, they either posed their coupledom as a foundation for making family or, if they perceived a conflict with family life and parenting, subordinated romantic love to the needs of family life and children. Rather than individual happiness in a couple relationship being pursued at the expense of responsibilities towards children, the parents and step-parents asserted and took for granted that children took priority.

Our discussion in Chapter 4 of the meanings that our interviewees attached to caring, authority and material provision in parenting further confirmed notions of family as involving commitments and the investment of time towards creating solidarity, in that these were all issues that the parents and step-parents tackled in their attempts to make enduring families. They formed a framework for family living that involved unquestioned and unremarkable assumptions about responsibilities for and towards children even under changing circumstances. Indeed, as we had already seen in Chapter 3, rather than expressing a sense of contingent and chosen obligations, children were associated with a moral imperative that parents and step-parents should take responsibility for children in their care and seek to put their needs first. This was echoed in Chapter 5's exploration of 'fairness' as a variable but significant theme by which many interviewees tried to work out how to make families under changing circumstances. Within this overall theme, however, what is just and good for children is prioritised over what is felt to be fair (just) for adults.

Nevertheless, our interviewees' stress on family as ties of obligation and commitment, and their rejection of the term step-family as a descriptor of their situation, did not necessarily mean that their understandings were all the same or that they saw step-families in general as the same as other families. Here, social class enters the picture (as it did for Burgoyne and Clark, 1984, with their minority of 'progressive' step-couples largely being middle class – although Burgoyne and Clark themselves did not pursue this aspect of their data). As we saw in Chapters 2 and 4, middle-class parents and step-parents regarded biology as important in parent–child relationships. In contrast, working-class parents and step-parents asserted that biology was largely irrelevant to parenting relationships and that it could be harmful to see relationships within step-families as different from other family relationships.

This strong social class difference in our interviewees' understandings of how to make a (step-)family is one aspect of deep-rooted social divisions evident in our data, leading us to question the extent to which individualisation and fluidity have taken hold in contemporary society in relation to how people understand their (heterosexual) family lives. It also raises issues around how far step-families are, in fact, different from other families. The gendered images of moral responsibility in (step-)parenting evident in Chapters 3 and 5 reflect widespread gender divisions in parenting roles within British families generally. Creative and plural lifestyle possibilities were not much in evidence in our step-families.

As we saw in Chapter 1, gender is recognised as an issue in step-parenting, and the literature often points to major differences between step-fathers' and step-mothers' understandings and experiences of step-parenting. Social class, however, has received very little attention as an issue, particularly in recent years. It seems that the concern with individualisation in sociological theory may well be a feature in this.

The marginalisation of working-class understandings

The relationship between social class and perspectives on parenting does not seem to have received much attention in discussions of dis/continuity in contemporary family life, and some argue that there has been a general decline in academic theorising about social class (for example, Crompton, 1993; Skeggs, 1997; Lawler 2000). According to Beverley Skeggs (1997), there has been a 'retreat' from addressing social class across a range of academic sites, belying its previous status as a central explanatory concept.

Some attribute this retreat to the difficulty in operationalising social class. Alongside varying theoretical perspectives, there is no universal agreement over what constitutes a definitive measurement of class. Various classification scales have been devised, placing emphasis on different indicators. Feminist writers in particular have pointed out the exclusion of women from traditional class analysis, and have challenged accounts of class that are overly concerned with measurement and focus exclusively on social production and economics, drawing instead on theories that foreground culture, subjectivity and practice (for example Reay, 1997; Skeggs, 1997; Lawler, 2000). Some historical analysis is also concerned with class as a process of human relationships over time, rather than as a structure or category (for example Thompson, 1981). (Our own multidimensional operationalisation is noted in Chapter 1.)

For others, however, the rise in individualisation is regarded as having made social class obsolete in social explanation. Major economic and cultural shifts since the Second World War, it is argued, have transformed the social landscape. For example, it has been suggested that the decline in the manufacturing base has eradicated traditional working-class communities and resulted in the demise of social class as a significant social indicator (Gorz, 1982). It is claimed that while previous class divisions were characterised by more identifiable, uniform patterns of lifestyle, values and expectations, contemporary experiences are now more fragmented and less predictable (Payne, 2000). Ulrich Beck (1992, 2002a) argues that old class identifications and ties have been replaced by individualised lifestyles in which people choose amongst various identities and allegiances as part of a more pervasive struggle to negotiate risk and uncertainty. While Beck does not argue that social divisions and inequalities have disappeared – indeed he sees them as growing – he suggests that inequality now has a 'non-class character'. It is likely to be experienced at the personal level and increasingly understood in terms of personal responsibility. Walkerdine (1996) and Skeggs (1997) discuss how a working-class identity is seen as an individually stigmatising position in the face of discourses around social mobility.

Many feminist, as well as more traditional social class theorists, however, have emphasised the consistency of social differentiation within the context of social change (for examples of the latter see Goldthorpe and Marshal, 1992; Evans and Mills, 1999; Scott, 2000). Rosemary Crompton (1993) attributes the reluctance to use class as an explanatory concept to the 'new individualism' characterising postmodern theorising, where class is argued to conceal a multiplicity of positionings in terms of race/ethnicity, gender and sexuality, with an emphasis on the plurality of difference. As Skeggs (1997) notes, however, the concept of difference is often used as a replacement for the concept of inequality and social divisions. Diane Reay (1998) sees the consequence of a more general cultural shift from collective to individual as the tendency to take social inequalities for granted, while Skeggs feels that middle-class academics have little incentive to explain or theorise a phenomenon that, for them, has become completely invisible: 'To think that class does not matter is only a prerogative of those unaffected by the deprivations and exclusions it produces' (1997: 7).

As we have seen at various points throughout this book, class has been a key feature in how parents and step-parents understand parenting and family life within and across households. While the numbers in our study are small, the patterns in our interviews are striking and consistent. Furthermore, our finding that our working-class interviewees were more concerned with parenting as social practice within the (step-)family, in contrast to our middle-class interviewees' emphasis on biological parenthood across households, finds resonance with other in-depth studies of step-family life in other national contexts. Didier Le Gall and Claude Martin's (1997) research on French step-clusters identifies two attitudes towards parenting and family life – 'replacement' and 'continuity' – according to whether their interviewees were, in their terms, 'disadvantaged' or 'more fortunate' (thus in our view, they are concerned with social class). 'Disadvantaged' (working-class) parents and step-parents were concerned with 'replacement', focusing on a 'relatively traditional concept of family ... [in which] the couple think of themselves as forming a family and the presence of children immediately gives substance to this. Couple and family are one' (Le Gall and Martin, 1997: 186). The new family unit erases or replaces the previous one. In contrast, their 'more fortunate' (middle-class) interviewees were concerned with 'continuity', where 'the family continues to exist in spite of separation' (1997: 190). The children involved move between households, and step-fathers find difficulty in modelling a fathering role and thus occupy a precarious position.

Similarly, research on Swedish step-clusters carried out by Margareta Bäck-Wiklund, Maren Bak and Kristina Larsson Sjöberg (see Edwards et al., 2000) shows that working-class step-fathers emphasise achieved social relations, seeing step-fathering as mirroring and conflating with fathering practices, while middle-class step-fathers emphasise ascribed biological ties, understanding step-fathering as a disengaged practice, such that it largely does not equate with fathering at all (Edwards et al., 2000). Paralleling this is the evidence that we mentioned in Chapter 1 concerning working-class non-resident fathers being more likely to curtail contact and/or 'step' aside when the mother of their child/ren re-partners. This is found in different national contexts (for Britain, see Simpson et al., 1993, and Maclean and Eekelaar, 1997; for France, Le Gall and Martin, 1997; for Australia, Henman and Mitchell, 2001).

The question then arises as to why such a class difference in family practices occurs. The interplay between economic and material circumstances and culture over time may well be an issue here. A middle-class emphasis on the significance of biological ties may reflect a wider culturally and historically inscribed concern with legitimacy and inheritance. As Leonore Davidoff and colleagues (1999) point out, notions of biological parentage and the replications of genes have tended to be promoted through the concept of lines of descent, with principles of genealogy playing a traditional role in establishing enduring claims of political and economic privilege. Heredity has occupied a historically significant role in, in this case English, middle-class culture, understood in terms of the replication of social worth, respectability, intellect and other personal traits and characteristics (Rose, 1989). The transmission of property and inheritance involved control of women's sexuality through the respectable, stable nuclear family structure resulting in legitimate heirs. This route has now become untenable with increasing rates of divorce, separation and lone motherhood. Offsetting a pervasive sense of risk and uncertainty in social life, the development of genetic 'hard scientific knowledge' appears certain and irrevocable: 'Genetic relations have thus come to stand for the naturalness of biological kinship' (Strathern, 1992a: 72). The creation of certainty through the construction of a link between biology and emotion in parent–child relations, replacing the certainty of procreative (patriarchal) links between men and women in material inheritance, may thus be relatively new.

A comparison of our work with Jacqueline Burgoyne and David Clark's (1984) findings shows that, within step-families, the middle-class emphasis on biological parenthood as emotionally irreplaceable and non-replicable seems to be relatively new. Burgoyne and Clark's study contained little evidence that parents and step-parents regarded a step-parent as unable to act or feel in the same way as a biological parent. It may be that contemporary middle classes construct biological parenthood as something solid, natural, enduring and stable in a context of increasing feelings of societal change and uncertainty. If, as Ulrich Beck and Elisabeth Beck-Gernsheim (1995) have argued, children are perceived as 'an anchor' in the context of a diverse and precarious society, biological status may be seen by middle-class people as embodying and cementing permanency and control in the face of the loss of other stabilities of middle-class life. 'Nature' has become the keystone of a 'reality' that is placed beyond social construction (Strathern, 1992a).

In contrast, working-class families have long been subject to social conditions of risk and uncertainty. Valerie Walkerdine and Helen Lucey (1989) give a moving account of the material hardships, lack of power and constant life insecurity of their own and other working-class childhoods, and their effects on their understandings of the social world. Further, an emphasis on social parenting may make good sense in a world where men may be in a poor position to provide well for their families in stable households, and women have less chance of earning a decent income in their own right. Men who are prepared to act as provider and father to children are more significant and pertinent than biological fatherhood. Moreover, where resources are limited, stretching them across families/households, rather than concentrating them in the current family/ household, can be difficult and self-defeating.

Anthropological discussions of family and kinship reveal the diversity of cultural understandings of the nature of biological reproduction and parenting, and whether and how they are considered to be linked (for example, Riviere, 1985; Shore, 1992; Strathern, 1992a, 1992b). As we showed in Chapter 1, in Britain working-class understandings of the value of social parenting, however, are increasingly marginalised and subordinated in legal and policy terms in favour of the middle-class emphasis on biological ties (and in other national contexts too – see Agell, 1993; Wardle, 1993; Funder, 1998). Indeed, in many respects, it appears that the discourse concerning the primacy of biological ties between parent and child is seeking to shift people's opinions and understandings in a particular direction. Other writers (Finch, 1989; Maclean and Eekelaar,

1997; Lewis, 2001) have suggested that there are considerable difficulties in Government attempts to intervene effectively in personal relationships in ways that are too far removed from people's own understandings of those relationships, and that changes in family law to impose biological parents' obligations have not arisen out of public demands. Rather, they are the result of 'top-down', narrow political and professional concerns, driven by the demands of particular sections of the middle class, especially via pressure groups (Smart, 1997), and Government economic considerations. They are a prescriptive attempt to impose a recently emergent middle-class normative order.

Indeed, there is the irony that policies that have been developed to deal with one aspect of fluid contemporary change (divorce, non-traditional families, etc.) are not entirely 'progressive'. Rather, in large part, they rely on more conservative (biological) notions of parenthood in seeking to reproduce a revised traditionally ascribed notion of parenting. Yet, in their turn, ideas about fluidity and negotiation in family relationships can marginalise and subordinate still other aspects of the understandings of the parents and step-parents who took part in our study. In this vein, we now turn to consider the implications of our findings for theorising the nature of contemporary family life, morality and intimacy.

Generation, gender and morality

Much recent sociological attention has been paid to the changing nature of contemporary morality, but little to the ways in which dependent children might reframe the arguments being put forward in these debates. Our own analysis has identified a moral imperative that adults must take responsibility for children in their care and therefore must seek to put the needs of children first. This moral view was adhered to, mainly to a greater but sometimes to a lesser extent, by all the parents and step-parents in our study. We have argued that this moral imperative fundamentally arises from the ways in which we have constructed the relational social categories of Adult and Child in contemporary societies. We have also shown the ways in which gender is a significant feature of this moral imperative, requiring different responsibilities for children from (step-) mothers and (step-)fathers. There were also greater possibilities available to men than to women in terms of bypassing responsibility and accountability for children's needs without sacrificing moral identity.

The significance of the fundamental nature of the categories of Adult and Child and their links to moral responsibility is evident if we compare and contrast our work with Janet Finch and Jennifer Mason's (1993) influential study of obligations to adult kin. They argued strongly that family responsibilities are negotiated in context rather than being defined in terms of ascribed duties, and identified several implicit guidelines that people use in order to work out whether or not they had a responsibility to help their adult kin. Two of their key guidelines – reciprocity and deservingness – illustrate the way that care of dependent children fundamentally reshapes notions of moral responsibility.

Reciprocity concerns the need for a balance to be struck in helping others. Finch and Mason show how the adults in their study strove for a balance of dependence and independence. If there is no balance, and too much one-way help, they argue that there is a risk of compromising or undermining the recipient's adult status. That is, the recipient becomes symbolically turned into a dependent child who is not responsible for her- or himself, but is taken responsibility for. Indeed, as Jenny Hockey and Allison James (1993) have discussed, this is how we understand dependence in modern society – as child-like. In relation to the step-families who form the focus of this book, however, there is no such weighing up of reciprocity, precisely because our adult interviewees are considering dependent children.

Deservingness concerns whether or not someone should be helped. Finch and Mason (1993) show that if someone is perceived as not deserving help, this can be used as a reason for not taking responsibility for assisting them – they are considered morally unworthy. Again, it is crucially important that they are considering adult kin relations when they make this argument. For our adult interviewees, it was not acceptable to position the dependent children in their care as morally unworthy, to say that they were not responsible for their children because the children did not deserve it and should take responsibility for themselves.

Nevertheless, there are some similarities between our own and Finch and Mason's work, again revealing the fundamental nature of the Adult/Child distinction for moral responsibility and identity. Finch and Mason show that, between adult kin, if reciprocity and deservingness are established, an inability, rather than an unwillingness, to help constitutes an acceptable justification for not helping. People want and strive to have what Finch and Mason call their 'excuses' accepted as legitimate and to present their actions in a good light. Our own work has found that some of our parents and step-parents could adhere to the moral imperative of meeting the needs of dependent children, but show that they themselves were not in a position to do so. One of the ways they were able to 'bypass' (our preferred term) adult moral responsibility was by taking the position of Child rather than Adult. They did not place themselves as morally unworthy because they showed that they would have taken moral responsibility if they could – it was just that they were not as good at it as somebody else, or did not know what to do, or did not have enough experience, or that things happened over which they had no control or choice. It was far easier for fathers and step-fathers in our study to do this – to tell an amoral tale – than it was for the mothers and step-mothers. Finch and Mason similarly found that women can have more difficulty in getting certain positions accepted as legitimate excuses than men.

This brings us to issues concerning the nature of morality in contemporary society, and whether or not our interviewees could have told us an immoral tale. As we saw in Chapter 3, there was the basis for another moral tale, another set of responsibilities that some of our interviewees prioritised in their account: a duty towards the self. Where it occurred, this individualistic discourse was invoked most strongly by men. We do not see this as gender specific in any essentialist way, but rather related to the socially gendered nature of (step-) parenting and daily responsibility for children in contemporary society.

Carol Smart and Bren Neale (1999), however, find rather more evidence of an ethic of care of self, in the form of issues concerning space, independence and becoming your 'own person', amongst the divorced mothers that they interviewed. They also argue that some divorced parents saw their (even quite young) children as having an independent moral and emotional life. The issues involved for people in 'breaking' a family (as in divorce) and 'making' a family (as with step-families) are quite different. It may be that, going through what can be the draining process of divorce, some parents may pose their children as Adults, and thus not requiring the exercise of responsibility. Indeed, Smart and Neale observe that in follow-up interviews a year later, their interviewees could define this earlier symbolic positioning of their children as co-Adults as having been misplaced. Furthermore, regarding children as independent beings who can exercise moral awareness and agency is not the same as placing them as Adults who must exercise moral responsibility through choice and be held to account for meeting needs, as we argued in Chapter 3 in relation to Smart and Neale's further study with Amanda Wade (Smart *et al.*, 2001) on children after divorce or separation. It is also clear that the 'project of the self' that Smart and Neale identify in their mothers who retained the main care of children was in the context of establishing themselves as new or different persons in relation to their ex-spouses rather than in relation to their children.

The gendered nature of the invocation of an individualistic discourse has resonance with writings about the content of morality and the nature of contemporary society by (mainly male) social theorists. For example, an ethic of care of the self is conceptualised by Michel Foucault (1986a, 1986b) in terms of how we think about ourselves in everyday life. He argued that it is one of a number of ethical discourses that circulate independently of us, and on which we can draw to produce and govern ourselves to be 'good' people. He poses this ethic of care of self as a resistory alternative to dominant pastoral and disciplinary governance discourses. A similar style of ethic is also a feature of Zygmunt Bauman's (1992) discussion of contemporary moral responsibility and his equation of 'being with and for the Other', i.e. being an autonomous empathetic being alongside another autonomous being. Like Foucault, he poses this ethic as an alternative, this time to the abstract principles of modernism – issues to which we return below. An ethic of care of the self also underlies Anthony Giddens' (1992) conception of the role of intimacy in modernist society, in a reflexive project of the self, and in his model of confluent love and pure relationships as the ethical guideline for lifestyle politics. Ulrich Beck and Elisabeth Beck-Gernsheim (1995) similarly outline a process of individualisation focusing on self in late modernity. As we noted in Chapter 1, however, they point out that it is this very focus on self that pushes people into seeking closeness and identification in relationships with others, which can include focusing on children as 'an anchor for one's life' (Beck and Beck-Gernsheim, 1995: 73).

Feminist writers such as Carol Smart (1997), Selma Sevenhuijsen (1998) and Lynn Jamieson (1998) have highlighted some of the difficulties with this theorising about the ethic of care of self, in that it views the self as the only knowable thing, is about an unconnected subject, or is about relationships between peers or equals. Few of these 'ethic of self' theorists fully address relationships with, and care of, dependent children. In fact Sevenhuijsen goes further, to say that they tend to equate care and dependence with domination, 'echo[ing] a (male) urge to suppress our dependence on the mother' (1998: 18). Nevertheless, where some feminists who are theorising and researching the nature of morality and contemporary family change do agree with these authors, is in their conception of the nature of morality in the post- or high modern, as opposed to the modernist, society. Bauman (1992) in particular argues that the demise of foundationalism and moral absolutes has not brought us into a moral vacuum. Rather, it has offered us the possibility of becoming truly modern, of exercising agency based on recognition of ambiguity, dilemmas and responsibility. Moral norms are not fixed but are subject to dispute, interpretation and negotiation in social – and for feminists, relational – contexts. To be moral in contemporary society does not mean to be good in the sense of unthinkingly adhering to abstract imperatives, but to actively and reflexively exercise choice with responsibility. This seems quite a middle-class picture of life, and it may also be rather ethnocentric (for example, see the discussion of the Bangladeshi couple in our sample in Chapter 3).

Sevenhuijsen (1998) similarly contrasts the morality of modernity with that of postmodernity, arguing that modernity is about moralism, rather than morality, with its emphasis on restrictive and absolute value judgements and rules stating what should or should not be done. Modernity continuously aims at legislating moral truths and attempts to 'educate' those who are constructed as 'not yet moral'. Certainly, recent Government prescriptions about parenting responsibilities and duties for homework and bedtimes, and legislation for parenting classes for those with 'disorderly' children, chime with this – even when framed in the language of 'support' rather than coercion, as in the Home Office (1998) document *Supporting Families*. Sevenhuijsen argues that such prescriptive political attempts to impose rules, and indeed increased public debate about morality, arise precisely because in the postmodern condition people take part in a variety of social practices and in a plurality of lifestyles and moral orientations, in which the fundamental postmodern question is not 'What should I do or not do?' (as in modernity), but 'How should I deal with this?'

Certainly Finch and Mason's (1993) work on kin obligations and Smart and Neale's (1998) on divorced parents fits within this postmodern ethical framework. It is negotiation that is the operative word here. Both sets of authors agree that there is no clear consensus about rules – no clear abstract moral imperative about what to do in the family situations they address. It is negotiation in context that is, in fact, the norm. This is why they each produce sets of guidelines that their interviewees implicitly used in how to work out what to do (some of which we have just discussed in relation to Finch and Mason). Thus both sets of authors identify their interviewees as moral beings, as demonstrating morality, because they formulate and reflect upon dilemmas: 'What makes people moral agents is ... whether they reflect upon the decisions they take and weigh up the consequences of their actions' (Smart and Neale, 1998: 114). Indeed, each notes that they could find no cases in their data where people wanted to be seen as wilfully avoiding responsibility for, respectively, kin or the effects of divorce on children. In our sample we too did not find any immoral tales of parenting or step-parenting in any account as a whole from our interviewees.

This then raises the question of why this should be. There may be several explanations here. One may be that people who would tell an immoral tale do not take part in research – we simply do not get to hear their stories. We are not, however, inferring that people's refusal to take part in our research was because they would be unable to present a moral tale about their behaviour (as we saw in Chapter 1, it could reflect uneasy relationships within the step-cluster). Another issue may be that, within the conception of the postmodern (adult and child) subject demonstrating morality through reflecting on dilemmas, the in-depth interview in itself produces this demonstration. We in fact invite people to be reflexive and justify themselves and their actions when we interview them. This research method production of morality would apply to our own study, to Finch and Mason's (1993), and also the various studies by Smart and colleagues (Smart and Neale, 1998; Smart *et al.*, 2000).

Yet another explanation, which we favour on the basis of our evidence, is that – in the case of parenting and step-parenting – people cannot sustain an immoral tale in their constructions of their actions, although they may tell an amoral one. Any immorality is in the eye of the beholder or ear of the listener only. In Chapter 3 we identified two ethics of care operating in people's tales: a dominant one for dependent children, and a less common one for self. These did not exist equally side by side, however. There was, in fact, a clear abstract and non-negotiable moral norm: that adults should seek to take responsibility for children in their care and put their needs first. There was not much in the way of ambiguity here. Where the two ethics of care came into contact with each other, then the ethic of care of self became an unsustainable, immoral stance. People could not weave them together equally in one narrative and still present themselves as a morally responsible adult (parent) in their own terms. Where the ethic of care of self formed the major moral theme in a few of our interviewees' accounts (as we detailed in Chapter 3), this was not posed immediately alongside the ethic of care of dependent children, so that these men (they were mainly men) did not place themselves as telling an immoral tale in their own terms or in how they expected us to hear them (see our discussion of researcher as audience in Chapter 1).

Our analysis of the tales of the parents and step-parents we interviewed thus throws light on the issue of what it is to be moral in contemporary society, because we and our interviewees are explicitly considering the care of dependent children. We have shown the significance of dependent children to the sustenance of morally adequate identities, with the cross-referencing social categories of Adult and Child as fundamental to this process. Our interviewees held themselves morally accountable for children in their care, simultaneously constructing those children as outside moral agency. This led to an ascribed and non-negotiable moral imperative to seek to put children's needs first. While there may be choices and dilemmas for people about how they substantively exercise the responsibility for children in their care and exactly how they put children's needs first (as we saw in Chapters 4 and 5), it is clear that the practical content of the moral imperative is in fact deeply gendered and patterned by social class. People may feel that they are unable to exercise this responsibility, and there may be (gendered) bypass routes available to them, but this means that they are implying that they would exercise it if they could. Whatever the variations, these parents and step-parents did not have a choice or dilemma as to whether or not to place the children in their care as in need of their adult responsibility. Furthermore, our interviewees were unable to espouse an ethic of care for dependent children alongside a choice or dilemma of putting care of self first, and still retain a moral position. They could only avoid posing a choice between the ethics by stressing the ethic of care of self in isolation or, if they did pose their situation as a choice or dilemma, they did not do so from the position of retaining main care of the children involved. These are particularly difficult steps for a woman to take.

Thus, we have reached a similar conclusion to that of Jamieson (1998) in her extensive review of the literature about the nature of intimacy in modern society, though our arguments are more circumscribed as they concern (step-) parenting relationships with dependent children rather than intimate relationships as a broad category. Like Jamieson, we are doubtful that our interviewees are in fact postmodern moral subjects who are exercising agency based on recognition of ambiguity and dilemmas, and negotiating their responsibilities within a plurality of social practices and moral orientations. When it comes to parenting and step-parenting, the categories of Adult and Child seem to be constructed in such a way that, to a large extent, we still appear to be living in a modernist, morally absolute, society. The moral imperative that children's needs take precedence may be one of the few remaining unquestionable moral assertions.

If our interviewees do not seem to be postmodern moral subjects, they do not seem to be living in post-familial families either, as we have already discussed. Both parents and step-parents, particularly the women, held a far more connective and relational view of their lives, especially in relation to their obligations to children. This has consequences for how we conceptualise relationships between family members, given the turn to envisaging these as democratic, which we will elaborate in a while. The ethic of care of self is premised on the view of an autonomous self-directing bounded subject (Nutt, 2002). Similarly, the language of 'democratic families' links to notions of individualisation, rights and justice – very 'public-world' concepts. This raises the question of how far such concepts are applicable to the ways in which parents and step-parents understand making families.

Fairness, justice and care

As we have noted at various points throughout this book, recent theorising about contemporary family life is focused on individualisation and democratisation. Elisabeth Beck-Gernsheim, for example, has argued that people are increasingly forced into charting their biographies and making their own decisions, including about the issue of 'fairness' in families:

> *The character of everyday family life is gradually changing: people used to be able to rely upon well-functioning rules and models, but now an ever greater number of decisions are having to be taken. More and more things must be negotiated, planned, personally brought about. And not least in importance is the way in which questions of resource distribution, of fairness between members of the family, have come to the fore.*
> (Beck-Gernsheim, 1998: 59)

It is just this issue that we have considered in some depth in this book – the notion of 'fairness' as guiding our interviewees' discussions about 'making families' in terms of parenting and step-parenting within and across households. But contrary to Beck-Gernsheim's assertion of a lack of 'well-functioning rules', we have shown how the practice of fairness relates strongly to the moral imperative adhered to by our interviewees, that of seeking to put children's needs first. Within this, the meaning of fairness was variable, with fairness (as justice and goodness) for children taking precedence over fairness (as justice) for the adults involved. But we have also seen that in both cases fairness was often concerned with inclusion – that the people concerned should feel they had a place within and were part of a family, rather than being marginalised from it, so that they would feel valued and fundamentally connected. It was not necessarily about an abstract distributive justice, as implied in Beck-Gernsheim's quote, but a particularistic connective justice.

Notions of 'fairness' seem to be part of a particularly family-based set of understandings and language around goodness and inclusion, even perhaps a 'childish' one ('It's not fair!'), although they may also carry overtones of a more publicly based political and legal language around rights and justice. Liberal public concepts of rights and justice concern issues of legal and political equality between individuals. These are abstract, rational, generalised, universal and formalised principles of autonomy, obligation and entitlement. Thus individuals are understood as citizens, who are disembodied and always equivalent (unless they are disqualified from such Adult status as Children, or as mad or bad). In this understanding, justice has been contrasted by some feminist writers and others as being a publicly based concept, a term that is in some tension with an ethic of care rooted in more connected, particularised, concrete and informal, private ways of being. Others, however, see care and justice as interrelated, even to the extent that the justice is subsumed into care.

Justice was certainly not a word that our interviewees, whether parents, step-parents or children, used about their family relationships (as we saw in Chapter 5). This may be because individuals are understood very differently in the team effort of family lives, as people fundamentally located by ascribed characteristics of gender, age/generation, birth order and biological parenthood, as well as particular personal histories and characteristics. So what we find instead is a language of fairness, obligations and neediness. In relation to children, fairness incorporates ideas about both rights and what is good. For both adults and children, fairness can also be discussed in the context of notions of inclusion and belonging.

Sara Ruddick (1996) has argued that ethics of justice and care cannot be subsumed under each other and cannot be integrated. In her view, justice depends on a notion of the individual as a detached being rather than a relational being, and so it cannot take account of close identifications such as that between parent and child. It poses individuals as defined by their possession of similar characteristics, whereas family members are fundamentally defined by their differences (the generation and gender differences that we have identified). Thus ideas about justice and equality are difficult to apply in families, which are concerned with the care of those who cannot be equal. It is not possible really to apply the justice 'test' of whether the rational and self-interested individual would consent to the situation where family obligations are based at least partially on the particular characteristics of the relationships involved themselves. Nevertheless, Ruddick also argues that justice as well as care should apply to the whole moral domain, i.e. to both family and public life. In particular, she feels that a strong case can be made for wanting to apply the language of justice and rights to aspects of exploitation and domination in family relationships.

David Wong (1996) also argues that justice does have a particular place in conceptualising family life. He contends that there are underlying notions of justice at stake (in terms akin to fairness) in understandings of reciprocity in family relationships. This would certainly seem to resonate with ideas that it is not fair if one family member is unreasonably 'put upon' (as we saw in Chapter 5 in the resentments expressed by some parents and step-parents). Wong does recognise the particularity of how things are worked out in family relationships, and for this reason he suggests that liberal justice can only be a partial perspective on families, but equally for this reason, notions of justice may also be important for theorising families through providing a 'critical distance'. Feminist theorists have also put forward a variety of similar reasons for the necessity of regarding concepts of justice and care as complementary, and the need for them to be integrated in thinking about social life generally (see review in Porter, 1999: 16–18).

In contrast, Selma Sevenhuijsen (1998) has gone further, to argue for reformulating the conception of justice so that it is no longer opposed to or separate from, and thus does not require reconciling with, an ethic of care. Feminist criticisms of justice from care perspectives, she says, have been directed towards a specific variety: that of the liberal, rational, distributive model of justice. In her view, discussion about the compatibility of care and justice can usefully be freed from these parameters. There is a need to have concepts of justice that are not framed exclusively in distributive, sameness and universal terms, but which take into account situations and consequences, especially experiences and interpretations of quality of life. Thus Sevenhuijsen fundamentally reframes justice to see it as a process rather than rules, a process involving an ethics of care in a situated way based on values of reconciliation, reciprocity, diversity and responsibility, and with an awareness of power. Justice does not stand alone but is simultaneously incorporated into, and informed by, care. This comes much closer to our interviewees' own use of notions of fairness, in two ways. Firstly, it encompasses the parents' and step-parents' concerns with a just fairness as particularistic and connective, especially in the concern with inclusion. Secondly, it is clearly relevant to our discussion (in Chapter 5) of who should take responsibility for fairness. An ethics of care is also about responsibilities (what is the fair course of action, who should take fair action, whose needs for fairness should be met) rather than rights (to fairness and to have needs met).

Sevenhuijsen is largely concerned with bringing a more 'privately' generated ethics of care into the framework of understandings that guide public policy and law. Our own discussion has started from a consideration of public languages and concepts being applied to family lives in ways that may be inappropriate, partial and misleading. We continue this concern in our discussion of an issue that is closely related to debates about justice and care: the democratisation of family life. What are the gains and losses of viewing family life through this lens?

Democratic families or communal families?

The idea of contemporary family life as democratic concerns its characterisation by values of autonomy, equality and communication. This has elements both of describing current practice and/or its inevitability as a future mode of family practice, and actually prescribing that practice. Either way, though, there are crucial questions about the appropriateness of the concept of democracy as a way of understanding what is going on, or should be going on, in families.

Ulrich Beck and Elisabeth Beck-Gernsheim, both separately and together (Beck and Beck-Gernsheim, 1995, 2002; Beck, 1997; Beck-Gernsheim, 1998), see individualisation as producing an emergent democratisation of contemporary family life. In an article that focuses on 'children' (although he is really discussing young people, who are at the point of leaving 'childhood' behind), Beck (1997: 156) argues that 'the spirit of democracy' as a core dynamism of modernity means that children/young people are individualising themselves, actively designing their own lives 'behind the walls of private life' (1997: 162). Families, however, are not yet truly democratic because children/young people and adults currently do not fully understand, and communicate about, one another's lifestyles:

> In a very central sense, it is not quite possible (yet?) to speak of a 'democratisation of the family'. The old authority structures may indeed be damaged, and certainly their paint is scuffed; negotiation is becoming the dominant pattern, as a demand ... however, the elements of dialogue, of a virtual exchange of roles, of listening and taking responsibility for one another remain under-developed.
> (Beck, 1997: 165–6)

Anthony Giddens (1998: 93) makes the staggering assertion that 'There is only one story to tell about the family today, and that is of democracy'. He too poses individualisation, in the form of pure relationships, as 'the structural source' of 'a democratic personal order' (1992: 188), including in relation to parent–child relationships. In doing this he draws explicitly on conceptualisations of democracy in the public sphere. Indeed, Giddens' (1998) conception of post-divorce family relationships for children is focused around individualised rights and obligations, with biological parents as 'equal rights holders' who have responsibilities of protection and care for their children. His notion of democratic family life in general centralises the provision of open debate involving mediation, negotiation and the reaching of compromises:

> Can a relationship between a parent and young child be democratic? It can, and should be, in exactly the same sense as is true of a democratic political order. It is a right of the child, in other words, to be treated as a putative equal of the adult. Actions which cannot be negotiated directly with a child, because he or she is too young to grasp what is entailed, should be capable of counterfactual justification. The presumption is that agreement could be reached and trust sustained, if the child were sufficiently autonomous to be able to deploy arguments on an equal basis to the adult.
> (Giddens, 1998: 191–2)

Smart and colleagues focus explicitly on children after divorce to argue for a democratisation of family life. They consider that the process of divorce or separation of their parents may mean that children begin to 'think for themselves' and want more say in matters that affect them:

> The cultural phenomenon of divorce has focused attention on children in such a way that post-divorce parent–child relationships can no longer be taken for granted in the way that relationships in cohabiting families may still be. The very fact that these relationships have been problematized means that there is a cultural space available in which change, reflection and redefinition can occur … These changes represent different ways of raising children as citizens of the family, allowing them to take certain responsibilities and gain experience of participation and decision-making.
> (Smart et al., 2001: 113, 172)

Smart and colleagues put forward the notion of a 'moral conversation' in the context of post-divorce childhood, whereby all those with a 'stake' in a family, including children, can participate in the discussion of difficult issues, with the other parties involved listening to them and placing value on what they say. To further this, they state that there is a need to challenge parents' views of their children and to engage in 'cultural campaigns' to achieve a 'cultural shift in parenting practices', because it is parents who must assume the responsibility of engaging in 'asymmetrical reciprocity' with their children.

As we indicated earlier, we believe that there are some critical problems in conceptualising family life, and in particular relations between parents and children, through the lens of a concept that is drawn from notions of individualised citizenship rooted in the public sphere. These centre around the inherent social class bias of the historically and culturally situated concept of 'democracy', and its dependence on an individualised notion of public personhood, as we elaborate below. Giddens' idea of biological parents as 'equal rights holders' in relation to children after divorce, for example, has been subject to the criticism that it completely sidesteps concrete relational care (Sevenhuijsen, 2000). But more than this, it also particularly cuts across the understandings of working-class parents and step-parents in our sample, that the ability to forge close emotional (step-)parent–child relationships is not dependent inherently on biology but on actively created, sustained commitment, such that children do not necessarily need both their biological parents involved in their lives, and a step-parent can be just as much of a parent.

There are also dangers of marginalising and pathologising working-class families generally in the premise that 'democracy means discussion' (Giddens, 1992: 186). Smart and colleagues (2001: 113) are careful to warn that 'how family democracy manifests itself can vary greatly', and they cannot provide a blueprint for it. They are also clear that children can voice their views but that they are not, and should not be treated as if they were, adults within the 'moral conversations' that they advocate, i.e. they retain the categories of Adult and Child (see also Smart et al., 1999). Nevertheless, their notion of moral conversation implies negotiative talk. These sorts of ideas are very likely to chime with the understandings of middle-class, particularly White 'liberal', people, and to ride roughshod over the life experiences and practices of working-class and minority ethnic parents. Social and economic class differences mean that for Black and working-class families, it can be either inappropriate to focus on children as a self-project or difficult to maximise a space for this (e.g. Phoenix, 1987; Dahlberg, 1996; Reynolds, 1998). Valerie Walkerdine and Helen Lucey (1989: 72), for example, pose mothers' childrearing as 'a central guarantor of the possibility of a liberal democracy' in that 'the family' is crucial to socialisation into notions of personal regulation that are compatible with liberal capitalism (see also Rose, 1989). But, they say that this is differentially regulated for middle- and working-class mothers and children. They argue that middle-class mothers' childrearing is concerned with avoiding overt regulation, conflict, power battles and insensitive sanctions. Middle-class mothers debate with their children, all opinions are given equal status and all have a voice; they encourage 'intellectualisation' of feelings and self-regulation. In contrast, working-class mothers' childrearing is often regarded as authoritarian and contrasted unfavourably with democratic approaches. They make power and conflict visible and painful. They do not entertain debate with their children.

Walkerdine and Lucey regard class differences in employment and living conditions as the base for this distinction, as we noted earlier in this chapter. Middle-class mothers can intellectualise and maintain the illusion of equal status and free will because middle-class professional employment and life conditions give them greater control over their lives. Working-class people, however, are subject to the constant reminder that they need to work for money rather than satisfaction, that life is insecure and they have little power. Walkerdine and Lucey, moreover, argue that 'democratic childrearing' is an illusion and a fantasy. Power and conflict are not dispersed or eliminated, they are suppressed 'beneath reasonableness lie the passions' (1989: 103). Walkerdine and Lucey's highlighting of more deep-rooted social structures as a feature of childrearing also points us towards the national context in which calls for the 'democratic family' are being put forward. In Britain, parenting is a privatised, individualised responsibility, and there is little discussion of the wider structures that can support or constrain particular family practices.

Skeggs (1997) has drawn on her own research on working-class women, and Marilyn Strathern's work (1992a) discussing how individuality is a property of the English White non-working class, to argue that her respondents' subjectivity was focused on duty and obligation through relationships rather than autonomous independence. She argues that '[Working class women's] subjectivity is not part of a discourse of individualism; rather, it is part of a discourse of dialogism and connection ... The project of the self is a western, bourgeois project' (Skeggs, 1997: 163–4). Skeggs' highlighting of an alternative, more relational, view of self brings us to our next concern about importing notions of democracy to understand contemporary family life, which goes beyond social class: the notion of 'the individual as the basic unit of democracy' (Beck, 2002b: 208) cuts across the findings of this research.

Beck-Gernsheim argues that step-families are an example of 'elective family relationships' – the emergence in modernity of family links that are no longer a matter of destiny and obligation, but one of choice and personal inclination. Generally, she contends that:

Whereas, in pre-industrial society, the family was mainly a community of need held together by an obligation of solidarity, the logic of individually designed lives has come increasingly to the fore in the contemporary world. The family is becoming more of an elective relationship, an association of individual persons, who each bring to it their own interests, experiences and plans and who are each subjected to different controls, risks and constraints.
(Beck-Gernsheim, 1998: 67)

Such a portrayal of step-family life sits uneasily alongside the research that we have reported in this book. It seems to equate changes in form with changes in content. It is certainly possible to argue that forms have changed: a previous family/household is likely to have ended, and people in step-families are often living in complex situations within and across households. The content of their lives, however, is a different matter. We have seen how people still strive to create cohesive family units, focused around commitment, and how people strive for a fairness between members that relates to feelings of inclusion, not just distribution. We have seen how children are not regarded as subject to elective affinity, but that the meeting of their needs is regarded as a moral imperative. We have seen how couple relationships are either subsumed as part of the family project or are subordinated to prioritising children's needs, and how fairness to children overrides fairness to adults. In short, apart from a few cases (mainly men), our interviewees largely emphasised relationships and connection in their accounts, rather than a primary perspective based on the contained self. Indeed, a key implication arising from our research is that the people seem to regard the (step-)families they are living in more as 'communities of need', with children at the centre, than as 'elective' relationships.

June Jordan (1993) draws attention to the way that our deepest sense of our being is continuously formed in connection with others and is inexplicably tied to relational movements. She points to the ways in which dominant theoretical language constantly tends to take us back towards abstraction, emphasising separateness. Specifically here, for us, the notion of 'democratic families' remains a fundamentally 'public' concept that is being imported into the 'private' sphere in ways that can misrepresent people's family lives and misshape our understandings of those lives. The notion implies direct exchanges of benefits within a democratic system. In contrast, the notion of a communal system is concerned with exchanging benefits in response to needs or as part of demonstrating a general concern for the other people involved. A specific debt or obligation to return a comparable benefit is not necessarily created. In this way, communal relationships are not just long-term exchange relationships; indeed they are not regarded as an exchange. Rather, they provide security and fulfilment and a sense of connection (Clark and Mills, 1993; Clark and Chrisman, 1994). Adults' care for young children is thus a clear example of a communal rather than a democratic relationship, since our data has shown that the parents and step-parents see themselves – as Adults – as having a moral obligation to meet the needs of children in their care without them – as Child(ren) – being required or expected to reciprocate. This does not deny the possibility of children being able to express their views, but – as Smart and colleagues (1999, 2001) attempt to argue – places this in a broader, and for our interviewees, more significant, context of generational relational connection.

Concluding remarks

In this final chapter, we have not attempted to draw out any explicit family policy conclusions that we see as arising from our work (as others might expect us to). Our arguments here are not concerned with saying that step-family life should be conducted in any particular way, or that one way is better than another. Such a stance is fraught with difficulties.

Indeed, continued contact with several of the families involved in our study has revealed that some we might have pointed to as 'success stories' have since experienced severe difficulties, with some step-parenting couples separating, while others whose attempts at making a (step-)family may have appeared doomed are still flourishing at the time of writing. Our concern has been to listen to what people have to say about how they bring up children within and across households, and within the wider social context. It is in this light that we have questioned notions of individualisation and democratisation as fully representing either what is occurring in family life or as necessarily what should be occurring. On the basis of our data, these are not the best way of understanding how people experience living in step-families – or indeed families more generally.

Beck has contended that in the face of individualisation, many sociological concepts are 'zombie categories' – they are 'dead and still alive' (2002b: 203). He specifically singles out 'the family' and 'social class' as exemplars. Their form exists but their content has changed so much and is so open that the category no longer bears much relationship to people's lived realities (i.e. this argument is very similar to, though rather more colourful than, Giddens' (1999) notion of 'shell institutions'). This, of course, seems to presume that 'the family' as a category with a fixed and taken-for-granted content existed before the posited rise of individualisation, rather than having to be actively created and interpreted in everyday life – an issue that is contentious in itself (see, for example, Gubrium and Holstein, 1990). Moreover, and in further contrast, while we would accept that family forms may be said to have changed (in which respect we have been discussing step-families), we would contend that the content of what people seek to create and adhere to when they are 'making families' remains less flexible, even under changing circumstances, and indeed is remarkably socially patterned by supposedly zombie categories. We began this book with the contention that looking at step-families can tell us something significant about family life and parenting generally. Despite the fact that step-families may be seen as in the vanguard of family change and the shift towards individualised democratic families, our work has shown that key and long-standing issues of gender, generation and social class still act as powerful mediators of meaning in how people understand and experience their (step-)family lives. They are very much alive in the here and now, rather than being living dead.

Our conclusions about the meaning of family life in contemporary society, we believe, pose some challenge to the views of many social theorists concerned with familial change, precisely because our work has been centrally concerned with adults caring for dependent children in parenting relationships. Once children are included in the picture, it changes fundamentally because children cannot merely be tacked onto, or reframed in terms of, understandings about adult relationships. Ideas about children's needs have major ramifications for adults, carrying inescapable consequences for how parents and step-parents understand their lives and relationships. Indeed, they have major consequences for sociology as an enterprise. Our own picture of 'making families' in contemporary society thus looks quite different and has, we believe, important theoretical consequences for a sociology concerned with family life.

Appendix

We reproduce here the full text of the six vignettes that formed a structured part of the interview guides. They are introduced in Chapter 1, as part of the outline of the study's methodology. The analysis of the responses to these vignettes is incorporated at appropriate points in Chapters 2–5.

Vignette 1

Angela's marriage has ended and she and her two daughters, aged four and two, have gone to live with Angela's new partner, Patrick. Angela works an evening shift and leaves the children in the care of Patrick. Patrick seems pleased to have a ready-made family, and has taken on their financial support without resentment, buying them toys and making the garden safe for them. But he is stricter with the children than Angela, and the children know that they disagree over discipline. One evening Angela comes back from work to find her older daughter, Samantha, still awake. She has a red mark on her leg and says that Patrick hit her.

- What should Angela do? Why?
- Have you ever been in a situation like this one? What happened?

Vignette 2

Ann has lived with Tony for the past two years, with her two daughters aged nine and seven from a previous relationship. Tony has recently been made redundant and, although Ann has a part-time job, money is very tight. The children's father, Mark, has regular contact with them, and often takes them out and buys them expensive toys and clothes. Tony feels that Mark is splashing money around to show him up as not such a good father, while Ann feels that the girls are getting spoilt and are becoming too demanding at home. Ann briefly mentioned to Mark that he was spending too much on them, but he says they are his daughters and he should be able to provide them with the extra treats he'd buy them if they lived with him anyway.

- What should they do? Why?
- Have you ever been in a situation like this one? What happened?

Vignette 3

Pauline and Dave have been married for two years and have recently had a baby. Pauline's three children from a previous relationship also live with them, and Dave's two children from his previous marriage come to stay with them every other weekend and during the holidays. Dave's mum and dad live nearby.

When Dave's children come to stay, they come to see their grandchildren, often bringing them presents and sometimes taking them out for the day. They also dote on their new grandchild. Pauline is becoming increasingly upset that Dave's parents are not prepared to act as grandparents to her children from her previous relationship in the same way as they do to the baby and Dave's children. She feels her own children should also have some presents and be taken out for the day. Dave says his parents are too old to cope with so many children at once, and that in time he's sure they'll come to see themselves as full grandparents to her children too. Pauline says that if they haven't learnt to love her children after two years, she doesn't think they ever will.

- What should they do? Why?

- Have you ever been in a situation like this one? What happened?

Vignette 4

Jan and Paul have three children – Katie aged 14, Nola aged four and Tom aged two. Nola and Tom are Jan and Paul's children, but Katie is from Jan's previous marriage. Paul has been involved in bringing up Katie since she was three years old without any problems, but now Jan and Paul are finding Katie quite difficult. She stays out later than the time set for her to come home, and won't help in the house. Paul gets really cross with her and they argue all the time, with Katie shouting that he is not her real father and so she doesn't have to take any notice of him. One day they receive a phone call from a social worker. Katie has gone to social services and complained that Paul is trying to turn her out of the house. The social worker wants to call round to see Jan and Paul, and have a talk with them.

- What should they do? Why?

- Have you ever been in a situation like this one? What happened?

Vignette 5

Andrew and Joan have been living together for two years, with Joan's two children from her first marriage and Andrew's daughter from his first marriage. Andrew and Joan both work full time because of financial pressures, and Joan also has elderly parents living nearby who need an eye kept on them. Once a month, Joan's children go to stay with their father for the weekend, leaving her and Andrew on their own with Andrew's daughter, Ruth. Joan looks forward to time alone with Andrew, but he seems to spend much of the weekend on Ruth's various sporting activities, and Joan is becoming upset and resentful. She feels that Andrew runs around after Ruth and won't refuse her anything. Andrew feels he doesn't have much opportunity to give Ruth the individual attention and support he thinks she needs.

- What should they do? Why?

- Have you ever been in a situation like this one? What happened?

Vignette 6

Sandra's marriage broke up when her son was three, and her ex-husband left them. Sandra and her son, Simon, went to live with her parents for five years, until Simon was eight. When Sandra remarried, they went to live nearby with her new husband Melvin. Melvin has never got on well with Simon, and admits he feels jealous of him. Sandra and Melvin have recently had a new baby of their own. Simon, now aged ten, has become increasingly difficult since the birth of the baby and has started wetting the bed at night, as well as becoming very defiant. Sandra and Melvin are rowing over Simon. Sandra is bewildered by Simon's behaviour, and Melvin wants Simon to go and live with his grandparents to give the baby a chance of a happy family life.

- What should they do? Why?
- Have you ever been in a situation like this one? What happened?

References

Adams, B.N. (1999) 'Cross-cultural and U.S. kinship', in M. Sussman, S. Steinmetz and G. Peterson (eds) *Handbook of Marriage and the Family*, Dordrecht: Kluwer Academic Publishers

Adoption Law Review (1992) Review of Adoption Law: Report to Ministers of an Interdepartmental Working Group, Consultative document, London: Department of Health

Agell, A. (1993) 'Step-parenthood and biological parenthood: competition or co-operation?', in J. Eekelaar and P. Sarcevic (eds) *Parenthood in Modern Society*, Dordrecht: Kluwer Academic Publishers

Aleksander, T. (1995) *His, Hers and Theirs: A Financial Handbook for Stepfamilies*, London: STEPFAMILY Publications

Allan, G. and Crow, G. (2001) *Families, Households and Society*, London: Palgrave

Allan, G., Crow, G. and Hawker, S. (1999) *Step-families and the Construction of Kinship*, Final report to the Economic and Social Research Council, Southampton: University of Southampton

Ambert, A.-M. (1986) 'Being a stepparent: live-in and visiting stepchildren', *Journal of Marriage and the Family*, 48, pp. 795–804

Apthekar, B. (1989) *Tapestries of Life: Women's Work, Women's Consciousness and the Meaning of Daily Experience*, Amherst: University of Massachusetts Press

Archard, D. (1993) *Children, Rights and Childhood*, London: Routledge

Atkinson, C. (1986) *Step-parenting: Understanding the Emotional Problems and Stresses*, Wellingborough: Thorsons

Backett, K. (1982) *Mothers and Fathers: A Study of the Development and Negotiation of Parental Behaviour*, London: Macmillan

Backett, K. (1987) 'The negotiation of fatherhood', in C. Lewis and M. O'Brien (eds) *Reassessing Fatherhood*, London: Sage

Batchelor, J., Dimmock, B. and Smith, D. (1994) *Understanding Stepfamilies: What Can be Learned From Callers to the STEPFAMILY Telephone Counselling Service*, London: STEPFAMILY Publications

Bauman, Z. (1992) *Postmodern Ethics*, Oxford: Blackwell

Bauman, Z. (2000) *Liquid Modernity*, Cambridge: Polity Press

Baxter, L., Braithwaite, D. and Nicholson, J. (1999) 'Turning points and the development of blended families', *Journal of Social and Personal Relationships*, 16, pp. 291–313

Beck, U. (1992) *Risk Society: Towards A New Modernity*, London: Sage

Beck, U. (1997) 'Democratization of the family', *Childhood*, 4:2, pp. 151–68

Beck, U. (2002a) 'Preface', in U. Beck and E. Beck-Gernsheim *Individualisation*, London: Sage

Beck, U. (2002b) 'Zombie categories: interview with Ulrich Beck', in U. Beck and E. Beck-Gernsheim *Individualisation*, London: Sage

Beck, U. and Beck-Gernsheim, E. (1995) *The Normal Chaos of Love*, Cambridge: Polity Press

Beck, U. and Beck-Gernsheim, E. (2002) *Individualisation*, London: Sage

Beck-Gernsheim, E. (1998) 'On the way to a post-familial family: from a community of need to elective affinities', *Theory, Culture and Society*, 15:3–4, pp. 53–70

Becker, G. (1981) A *Treatise on the Family*, Cambridge, Mass.: Harvard University Press

Becker, G. (1996) *Accounting for Tastes*, Cambridge, Mass.: Harvard University Press

Beishon, S., Modood, T. and Virdee, S. (1998) *Ethnic Minority Families*, Bristol: Policy Studies Institute

Berger, G. and Berger, P. (1983) *The War Over the Family*, London: Hutchinson

Bernardes, J. (1985) 'Do we really know what "the family" is?', in P. Close and R. Collins (eds) *Family and Economy*, London: Macmillan

Bernardes, J. (1987) '"Doing things with words": Sociology and "Family Policy" debates', *Sociological Review*, 35:4, pp. 679–702

Bernardes, J. (1997) *Family Studies: An Introduction*, London: Routledge

Bertaux, D. and Delcroix, C. (1992) 'Where have all the daddies gone?', in U. Björnberg (ed.) *European Parents in the 1990s: Contradictions and Comparisons*, London: Transactions

Boh, K. (1989) 'European family life patterns – a reappraisal', in K. Boh, M. Back, C. Clason, M. Pankratova, J. Qvortrup, G.B. Sgritta and K. Waerness (eds) *Changing Patterns of European Family Life*, London: Routledge

Booth, A. and Dunn, J. (eds) (1994*) Stepfamilies: Who Benefits? Who Does Not?*, Hove: Lawrence Erlbaum Associates

Bornat, J., Dimmock, B., Jones, D. and Peace, S. (1999a) 'Generational ties in the "new" family: changing contexts for traditional obligations', in E.B. Silva and C. Smart (eds) *The New Family?*, London: Sage

Bornat, J., Dimmock, B., Jones, D. and Peace, S. (1999b) 'The impact of family change on older people: the case of stepfamilies', in S. McRae (ed.) *Changing Britain: Families and Household in the 1990s*, Oxford: Oxford University Press

Boyden J. (1990) 'Childhood and the policy makers: a comparative perspective on the globalisation of childhood', in A. James and A. Prout (eds) *Constructing and Reconstructing Childhood: Contemporary Issues in the Sociological Study of Childhood*, Lewes: Falmer

Bradshaw, J., Stimson, C., Skinner, C. and Williams, J. (1999) *Absent Fathers?*, London: Routledge

Brannen, J. (1988) 'The study of sensitive subjects', *Sociological Review*, 38:3, pp. 552–63

Brannen, J., Dodd, K., Oakley, A. and Storey, P. (1994) *Young People, Health and Family Life*, Buckingham: Open University Press

Brannen, J., Heptinstall, E. and Bhopal, K. (2000) *Connecting Children: Care and Family Life in Later Childhood*, London: RoutledgeFalmer

Bunting, M. (2001) 'Gene genie', *Guardian*, Monday 2 July

Burghes, L., Clarke, L. and Cronin, N. (1997) *Fathers and Fatherhood in Britain*, London: Family Policy Studies Centre

Burgoyne, J. (1987) 'Stepfamilies and contemporary family values', *Concern*, 61, pp. 3–4

Burgoyne, J. and Clark, D. (1982) 'From father to stepfather', in L. McKee and M. O'Brien (eds) *The Father Figure*, London: Tavistock

Burgoyne, J. and Clark, D. (1984) *Making A Go Of It: A Study of Stepfamilies in Sheffield*, London: Routledge and Kegan Paul

Burman, E. (1994) *Deconstructing Developmental Psychology*, London: Routledge

Burnett, J. (1991) *To and Fro Children: A Guide to Successful Parenting After Divorce*, London: Thorsons

Cahill, S. (1990) 'Childhood and public life: reaffirming biographical divisions', *Social Problems*, 37:3, pp. 390–402

Cahill, S. (1998) 'Toward a sociology of the person', *Sociological Theory*, 16:2, pp. 13–48

Chamberlayne, P., Bornat, J. and Wengraf, T. (eds) (2000) *The Turn to Biographical Methods in Social Science: Comparative Issues and Examples*, London: Routledge

Cheal, D. (1987) 'Showing them you love them: gift giving and the dialectic of intimacy', *Sociological Review*, 35:1, pp. 150–69

Cheal, D. (1991) *Family and the State of Theory*, Hemel Hempstead: Harvester Wheatsheaf

Cheal, D. (1993) 'Unity and difference in postmodern families', *Journal of Family Issues*, 14:1, pp. 5–19

Clark, M.S. and Chrisman, K. (1994) 'Resource allocation in intimate relationships: trying to make sense of a confusing literature', in M.J. Lerner and G. Mikula (eds) *Entitlement and the Affectional Bond: Justice in Close Relationships*, New York: Plenum Press

Clark, M.S. and Mills, J. (1993) 'The difference between communal and exchange relationships: what it is and is not', *Personality and Social Psychology Bulletin*, 19:6, pp. 684–91

Clarke, L. and Roberts, C. (2002) 'Policy and rhetoric: the growing interest in fathers and grandparents in Britain', in A. Carling, S. Duncan and R. Edwards (eds) *Analysing Families: Morality and Rationality in Policy and Practice*, London: RoutledgeFalmer

Coleman, M. and Ganong, L. (1995) 'Family reconfiguring following divorce', in S. Duck and J. Woods (eds) *Confronting Relationship Challenges*, Thousand Oaks, Calif.: Sage

Collier, J., Rosaldo, M.Z. and Yanagisako, S. (1982) 'Is there a family? New anthropological views', in B. Thorne and M. Yalom (eds) *Rethinking the Family: Some Feminist Questions,* New York: Longman

Cornwell, J. (1985) *Hard-Earned Lives*, London: Tavistock

Crompton, R. (1993) *Class and Stratification: An Introduction to Current Debates*, Cambridge: Polity Press

Crow, G. (2002a) 'Families, morality, rationality and social change', in A. Carling, S. Duncan and R. Edwards (eds) *Analysing Families: Morality and Rationality in Policy and Practice*, London: RoutledgeFalmer

Crow, G. (2002b) *Social Solidarities: Theories, Identities and Social Change*, Buckingham: Open University Press

Dahlberg, G. (1996) 'Negotiating modern childrearing in family life in Sweden', in J. Brannen and R. Edwards (eds) *Perspectives on Parenting and Childhood: Looking Back and Moving Forward*, London: South Bank University/ESRC/Institute of Education

Dalley, G. (1996) *Ideologies of Caring: Rethinking Community and Collectivism*, Basingstoke: Macmillan

Daly, M. and Wilson, M. (1998) *The Truth About Cinderella: A Darwinian View of Parental Love*, London: Weidenfeld and Nicolson

David, M., Edwards, R., Hughes, M. and Ribbens, J. (1993) *Mothers and Education: Inside Out? Exploring Family-Education Policy and Experience*, Basingstoke: Macmillan

Davidoff, L., Doolittle, M., Fink, J. and Holden, K. (1999) *The Family Story: Blood, Contract and Intimacy*, Harlow: Pearson

Davies, J. (ed.) (1993) *The Family: Is It Just Another Lifestyle Choice?*, Choice in Welfare No. 15, London: Institute of Economic Affairs Health and Welfare Unit

Dennis, N. and Erdos, G. (1993) *Families Without Fatherhood*, London: Institute for Economic Affairs Health and Welfare Unit

Denzin, N. (1987) 'Postmodern children', *Society*, 24:3, pp. 32–36

Doucet, A. (1995) 'Gender equality and gender differences in household work and parenting', *Women's Studies International Forum*, 18:3, pp. 271–84

Duncan, S. and Edwards, R. (1999) *Lone Mothers, Paid Work and Gendered Moral Rationalities*, Basingstoke: Macmillan

Duncombe, J. and Marsden, D. (1993) 'Love and intimacy', *Sociology*, 27:2, pp. 221–42

Dunne, G. (1997) *Lesbian Lifestyles: Women's Work and the Politics of Sexuality*, Basingstoke: Macmillan

Edwards, R. (1993) *Mature Women Students: Separating or Connecting Family and Education*, London: Taylor and Francis

Edwards, R. (1999) 'Step-fathering: policy and everyday experience', Paper presented to Department of Sociology and Social Policy seminar, Southampton University, 2 November

Edwards, R. and Ribbens, J. (1998) 'Living on the edges: public knowledge, private lives, personal experience', in J. Ribbens and R. Edwards (eds) *Feminist Dilemmas in Qualitative Research: Public Knowledge and Private Lives*, London: Sage

Edwards, R., Bäck-Wiklund, M., Bak, M. and Ribbens McCarthy, J. (2000) 'Step-fathering: comparing policy and everyday experience in Britain and Sweden', Paper presented to the Social Policy Association annual conference, University of Surrey, Roehampton, 19 July

Edwards, R., Gillies, V. and Ribbens McCarthy, J. (1999a) 'Biological parents and social families: legal discourses and everyday understandings of the position of step-parents', *International Journal of Law, Policy and the Family*, 13, pp. 78–105

Edwards, R., Ribbens, J. with Gillies, V. (1999b) 'Shifting boundaries and power in the research process: the example of researching "step-families"', in J. Seymour and P. Bagguley (eds) *Relating Intimacies: Power and Resistance*, Basingstoke: Macmillan

Ennew, J. (1986) *The Sexual Exploitation of Children*, Cambridge: Polity Press

Ermisch, J. and Francesconi, M. (2000) 'Patterns of household and family formation', in R. Berthoud and J. Gershuny (eds) *Seven Years in the Lives of British Families: Evidence From the British Household Panel Survey*, Abingdon: Policy Press

Evans, G. and Mills, C. (1999) 'Are there classes in post-communist societies? A new approach to identifying class structure', *Sociology*, 33:1, pp. 23–46

Fast, I. and Cain, A.C. (1966) 'The stepparent role: potential for disturbances in family functioning', *American Journal of Orthopsychiatry*, 36, pp. 485–91

Ferri, E. (1984) *Stepchildren: A National Study*, Windsor: NFER-Nelson

Ferri, E. and Smith, K. (1996) *Parenting in the 1990s*, London: Family Policy Studies Centre

Ferri, E. and Smith, K. (1998) *Step-parenting in the 1990s*, London: Family Policy Studies Centre

Finch, J. (1987) 'The vignette technique in survey research', *Sociology*, 21:1, pp. 105–14

Finch, J. (1989) *Family Obligations and Social Change*, Cambridge: Polity Press

Finch, J. (1997) 'Individuality and adaptability in English kinship', in M. Gullestad and M. Segalen (eds) *Family and Kinship in Europe*, London: Pinter

Finch, J. and Mason, J. (1993) *Negotiating Family Responsibilities*, London: Routledge

Finch, J., Mason, J., Hayes, L., Wallis, L. and Masson, J. (1996) *Wills, Inheritance and Families*, Oxford: Oxford University Press

Foucault, M. (1986a) *The Care of the Self: The History of Sexuality*, London: Penguin

Foucault, M. (1986b) 'On the genealogy of ethics: an overview of work in progress', in P. Rabinow (ed.) *The Foucault Reader*, New York: Pantheon

Fox, R. (1967) *Kinship and Marriage*, Baltimore: Penguin

Fox Harding, L. (1996) *Family, State and Social Policy*, Basingstoke: Macmillan

Funder, K. (1998) 'The Australian Family Law Reform Act 1995 and public attitudes to parental responsibility', *International Journal of Law, Policy and the Family*, 12, pp. 47–61

Furstenburg, F. (1988) 'Good dads – bad dads: two faces of fatherhood', in A. Cherlin (ed.) *The Changing American Family and Public Policy*, Washington D.C.: Urban Institute Press

Giddens, A. (1991) *Modernity and Self-Identity*, Cambridge: Polity Press

Giddens, A. (1992) *The Transformation of Intimacy: Sexuality, Love and Eroticism in Modern Societies*, Cambridge: Polity Press

Giddens, A. (1998) *The Third Way: The Renewal of Social Democracy*, Cambridge: Polity Press

Giddens, A. (1999) *Runaway World: How Globalisation is Reshaping Our Lives*, London: Profile

Giles-Sims, J. (1984) 'The stepparent role: expectations, behaviour and sanctions', *Journal of Family Issues*, 5, pp. 116–30

Gillies, V., Holland, J. and Ribbens McCarthy, J. (2002) 'Past, present, future: time and the meaning of change in the family', in G. Crow (ed.) *Time and the Lifecourse: Age, Generation and Social Change*, London: Palgrave

Gillies, V., Ribbens McCarthy, J., Holland, J. (2001) *'Pulling Together, Pulling Apart': The Family Lives of Young People*, London: Joseph Rowntree Foundation / Family Policy Studies Centre

Gillis, J.R. (2000) 'Marginalization of fatherhood in western countries', Childhood 7:2, pp. 225–38

Glenn, E., Chang, G. and Forcey, L.R. (eds) (1994) *Mothering: Ideology, Experience and Agency*, New York: Routledge

Goffman, E. (1971) *Relations in Public: Microstudies of the Public Order*, London: Allen Lane

Goldthorpe, J. and Marshall, G. (1992) 'The promising future of class analysis: a response to recent critiques', *Sociology*, 26:3, pp. 381–400

Goode, W. (1963) *World Revolution and Family Patterns*, New York: Free Press

Gorell Barnes, G., Thompson, P., Daniel, G. and Burchardt, N. (1998) *Growing Up in Stepfamilies*, Oxford: Clarendon Press

Gorz, A. (1982) *Farewell to the Working Class: An Essay of Post Industrial Socialism*, London: Pluto Press

Goulbourne, H. and Chamberlain, M. (1998) *Living Arrangements, Family Structures and Social Change of Caribbeans in Britain*, ESRC End of Award Report, L315253009, Swindon: ESRC

Graham, H. (1982) 'Coping: or how mothers are seen but not heard', in S. Friedman and E. Sarah (eds) *Women, Health and Healing*, London: Tavistock

Gubrium, J.F. and Holstein, J.A. (1990) *What is Family?*, London: Mayfield

Gubrium, J., Holstein, J. and Buckholdt, D. (1994) *Constructing the Life Course*, Dix Hill, N.Y.: General Hall

Hallden, G. (1991) 'The child as project and the child as being: parents' ideas as frames of reference', *Children and Society*, 5:4, pp. 334–46

Hammersley, M. and Atkinson, P. (1995) *Ethnography: Principles in Practice*, London: Routledge

Haskey, J. (1994) 'Stepfamilies and stepchildren in Great Britain', *Population Trends*, 76, pp. 17–28

Haskey, J. (1997) 'Children who experience divorce in their family', *Population Trends*, 87, pp. 5–10

Haskey, J. (1999) 'Cohabitation and marital histories of adults in Great Britain', *Population Trends*, 91, pp. 5–14

Hayman, S. (1994) *Other People's Children*, London: National Stepfamily Association

Heath, S. and Dale, A. (1994) 'Household and family formation in Great Britain: an ethnic dimension', *Population Trends*, 77, pp. 5–13

Heatherington, E.M. and Jodl, K.M. (1994) 'Stepfamilies as settings for child development', in A. Booth and J. Dunn (eds) *Stepfamilies: Who Benefits? Who Does Not?*, Hove: Lawrence Erlbaum Associates

Hendrick, H. (1997a) *Children, Childhood and English Society 1880–1990*, Cambridge: Cambridge University Press

Hendrick, H. (1997b) 'Constructions and reconstructions of British childhood: an interpretive survey, 1800 to the present', in A. James and A. Prout (eds) *Constructing and Reconstructing Childhood: Contemporary Issues in the Sociological Study of Childhood*, Lewes: Falmer

Hendrick, J. (2001) 'Children's rights', Unpublished lecture given as part of the MA in Family Research, Oxford Brookes University

Hendry, J. (1999) 'Rethinking marriage and kinship', Unpublished lecture given as part of the MA in Family Research, Oxford Brookes University

Henman, P. and Mitchell, K. (2001) 'Estimating the cost of contact for non-resident parents: a budget standards approach', *Journal of Social Policy*, 30:3, pp. 495–520

Hockey, J. and James, A. (1993) *Growing Up and Growing Old: Ageing and Dependency in the Life Course*, London: Sage

Hodder, E. (1989) *Stepfamilies Talking*, London: Macdonald

Holland, J. Gillies, V. and Ribbens McCarthy, J. (1999) 'Living on the edge: accounts of young people leaving childhood behind', Paper presented at the European Sociological Association, Amsterdam, September

Holland, J., Thomson, R., Henderson, S., McGrellis, S. and Sharpe, S. (2000) 'Catching on, wising up and learning from your mistakes: young people's accounts of moral development', *International Journal of Children's Rights*, 8, pp. 271–94

Holstein, J.A. and Gubrium, J.F. (1995) *The Active Interview*, Qualitative Research Methods 37, London: Sage

Home Office (1998) *Supporting Families: A Consultation Document*, London: The Stationery Office

Hughes, C. (1991) *Stepparents: Wicked or Wonderful? An Indepth Study of Stepparenthood*, Aldershot: Avebury

Hughes, C. (1993) *Step-parents, Step-children: Step by Step*, London: Kyle and Cathie

Hutson, S. and Jenkins, R. (1989) *Taking the Strain: Families, Unemployment and Transition*, Buckingham: Open University Press

Ishii-Kuntz, M. and Coltrane, S. (1992) 'Remarriage, stepparenting and household labor', *Journal of Family Issues*, 13:2, pp. 215–33

James, A., Jenks, C. and Prout, A. (1998) *Theorizing Childhood*, Cambridge: Polity Press

Jamieson, L. (1998) *Intimacy: Personal Relationships in Modern Societies*, Cambridge: Polity Press

Jenks, C. (1996a) *Childhood*, Routledge: London

Jenks, C. (1996b) 'The postmodern child', in J. Brannen and M. O'Brien (eds) *Children in Families*, Lewes: Falmer

Jensen, A.-M. (2001) 'Property, power and prestige – the feminisation of childhood', in M. du Bois-Reymond, H. Sünker and H.H. Krüger (eds) *Childhood in Europe: Approaches, Trends, Findings*, New York: Peter Lang

John, D., Shelton, B.A. and Luschen, K. (1995) 'Race, ethnicity and perceptions of fairness', *Journal of Family Issues*, 16:3, pp. 357–79

Jordan, B., Redley, M. and James, S. (1994) *Putting the Family First: Identities, Decisions and Citizenship*, London: UCL Press

Jordan, J. (1993) 'The relational self: a model of women's development', in K. Schreurs, L. Woertman and J. van MensVerhulst (eds) *Daughtering and Mothering: Female Subjectivity Reanalysed*, London: Routledge

Kilkelly, U. (2001a) *The Human Rights Act 1998 and Children: Part 1*, Highlight No.182, London: National Children's Bureau

Kilkelly, U. (2001b) *The Human Rights Act 1998 and Children: Part 2*, Highlight No.183, London: National Children's Bureau

Kitzinger, J. (1990) 'Who are you kidding? Children, power and the struggle against sexual abuse', in A. James and A. Prout (eds) *Constructing and Reconstructing Childhood: Contemporary Issues in the Sociological Study of Childhood*, Lewes: Falmer

Kruk, E. (1993) *Divorce and Disengagement: Patterns of Fatherhood Within and Beyond Marriage*, Halifax, Novia Scotia: Fernwood Publishing

Langford, W., Lewis, C., Solomon, Y. and Warin, J. (2001) *Family Understandings: Closeness, Authority and Independence in Families with Teenagers*, London: Family Policy Studies Centre

Lareau, A. (2000) 'Social class and the daily lives of children: a study from the United States', *Childhood*, 7:2(May), pp. 155–71

Lawler, S. (1999) 'Children need but mothers only want: the power of "needs talk" in the constitution of childhood', in J. Seymour and P. Bagguley (eds) *Relating Intimacies: Power and Resistance*, Basingstoke: Macmillan

Lawler, S. (2000) *Mothering the Self: Mothers, Daughters, Subjects*, London: Routledge

Le Gall, D. and Martin, C. (1997) 'Fashioning a new family tie: step-parents and step-grandparents', in M. Gullestad and M. Segalen (eds) *Family and Kinship in Europe*, London: Pinter

Lee, G.R. (1999) 'Comparative perspectives', in M. Sussman, S. Steinmetz and G. Peterson (eds) *Handbook of Marriage and the Family*, Dordrecht: Kluwer Academic Publishers

Lerner, M.J. and Mikula, G. (eds) (1994) *Entitlement and the Affectional Bond: Justice in Close Relationships*, New York: Plenum Press

Lewis, C. (2000) *A Man's Place in the Home: Fathers and Families in the UK*, York: Joseph Rowntree Foundation

Lewis, J. (2001) *The End of Marriage? Individualism and Intimate Relations*, Cheltenham: Edward Elgar

Lupton, D. and Barclay, L. (1997) *Constructing Fatherhood, Discourses and Experiences*, London: Sage

Lynott, P.P. and Logue, B.J. (1993) 'The "hurried child": the myth of lost childhood in contemporary American society', *Sociological Forum*, 8:3, pp. 471–91

Maclean, M. and Eekelaar, J. (1997) *The Parental Obligation: A Study of Parenthood Across Households*, Oxford: Hart Publishing

McRae, S. (1999) 'Introduction: family and household change in Britain', in S. McRae (ed.) *Changing Britain: Families and Households in the 1990s*, Oxford: Oxford University Press

Marsiglio, W. (1992) 'Stepfathers with minor children living at home', *Journal of Family Issues*, 13, pp. 195–214

Marsiglio, W. (1993) 'Contemporary scholarship on fatherhood: culture, identity and conduct', *Journal of Family Issues*, 14:4, pp. 484–509

Mauthner, N. (1994) 'Postnatal depression: a relational perspective', Unpublished PhD dissertation, University of Cambridge

Mead, M. (1970) 'Anomalies in American post-divorce relationships', in P. Bohannan (ed.) *Divorce and After*, New York: Anchor Books

Miller, T. (2000) 'Negotiation and narration: an exploration of first-time motherhood', Unpublished PhD thesis, University of Warwick

Morgan, D.H.J. (1975) *Social Theory and The Family*, London: Routledge and Kegan Paul

Morgan, D.H.J. (1985) *The Family, Politics and Social Theory,* London: Routledge and Kegan Paul

Morgan, D.H.J. (1996) *Family Connections: An Introduction to Family Studies*, Cambridge: Polity Press

Morgan, D.H.J. (1998) 'Gender practices and fathering practices', Paper presented at the Women and Gender Research Forum, Oxford Brookes University, 2 March

Morgan, D.H.J. (1999) 'Risk and family practices: accounting for change and fluidity in family life', in E.B. Silva and C. Smart (eds) *The New Family?*, London: Sage

Morrow, G.(1998) *Understanding Families: Children's Perspectives*, London: National Children's Bureau

Moss, P., Dillon, J. and Statham, J. (2000) 'The "child in need" and "the rich child": discourses, constructions and practice', *Critical Social Policy*, 20:2, pp. 233–54

Murray, C. (1990) *The Emerging British Underclass*, London: Institute of Economic Affairs

National Stepfamily Association (1995) *Learning to Step Together: Building and Strengthening Stepfamilies*, E. De'Ath (ed.), London: Nuffield Press

Neale, B., Wade, A. and Smart, C. (1998) *'I just get on with it': Children's Experiences of Family Life Following Parental Separation or Divorce*, Leeds: Centre for Research on Family, Kinship and Childhood, University of Leeds

Needham, R. (ed.) (1971) *Rethinking Kinship and Marriage,* London: Tavistock

Nemenyi, M. (1992) 'The social representation of stepfamilies', in U. Björnberg (ed.) *European Parents in the 1990s: Contradictions and Comparisons*, London: Transactions

New, C. and David, M. (1985) *For the Children's Sake: Making Childcare More Than Women's Business*, Harmondsworth: Penguin

Nutt, L. (2002) 'Foster-carers' perspectives: the dilemmas of loving the bureaucratized child', Unpublished PhD thesis, Oxford Brookes University

Office of National Statistics (1998) *Social Focus on Families*, London: The Stationery Office

Osborne, A.F. and Morris, T.C. (1979) 'The rationale for a composite index of social class and its evaluation', *British Journal of Sociology*, 30, pp. 39–60

Papernow, P. (1993) *Becoming a Stepfamily: Patterns of Development in Remarried Families*, San Francisco: Jossey Bass

Parsons, T. and Bales, R.F. (1955) *Family, Socialization and Interaction Process*, New York: Free Press

Payne, G. (2000) 'An introduction to social divisions', in G. Payne (ed.) *Social Divisions*, Basingstoke: Macmillan

Phillips, M. (1999) *The Sex Change Society: Feminised Britain and Neutered Male*, London: The Social Market Foundation

Phoenix, A. (1987) 'Theories of gender and black families', in G. Weiner and M. Arnot (eds) *Gender Under Scrutiny: New Inquiries in Education*, London: Hutchinson

Pilcher J. (1995) *Age and Generation in Modern Britain*, Oxford: Oxford University Press

Porter, E. (1999) *Feminist Perspectives on Ethics*, Harlow: Pearson Education

Rapp, R. (1982) 'Family and class in contemporary America: notes towards an understanding of "ideology"', in B. Thorne and M. Yalom (eds) *Rethinking the Family: Some Feminist Questions*, New York: Longman

Rawls A. (1987) 'The interaction order sui generis: Goffman's contribution to social theory', *Sociological Theory*, 5: pp. 136–49

Reay, D. (1997) 'Feminist theory, habitus and social class: disrupting notions of classlessness', *Women's Studies International Forum*, 20, pp. 225–33

Reay, D. (1998) *Class Work: Mothers' Involvement in Their Children's Primary Schooling*, London: UCL Press

Reynolds, T. (1998) 'African-Caribbean mothering: reconstructing a "new" identity', Unpublished PhD thesis, South Bank University

Reynolds, T. (2002) 'Re-analysing the Black family', in A. Carling, S. Duncan and R. Edwards (eds) *Analysing Families: Morality and Rationality in Policy and Practice*, London: RoutledgeFalmer

Ribbens, J. (1990) 'Accounting for our children: differing perspectives on "family life" in middle income households', Unpublished PhD thesis, CNAA/South Bank Polytechnic

Ribbens, J. (1994) *Mothers and Their Children: A Feminist Sociology of Childrearing*, London: Sage

Ribbens McCarthy, J. and Edwards, R. (2001) 'Illuminating meanings of "the private" in sociological thought: a response to Joe Bailey', *Sociology*, 35:3, pp. 765–77

Ribbens McCarthy, J. and Edwards, R. (2002) 'The individual in public and private: the significance of mothers and children', in A. Carling, S. Duncan and R. Edwards (eds) *Analysing Families: Morality and Rationality in Policy and Practice*, London: RoutledgeFalmer

Ribbens McCarthy, J., Edwards, R. and Gillies, V. (2000) *Parenting and Step-Parenting: Contemporary Moral Tales*, Centre for Family and Household Research Occasional Paper 4, Oxford: Oxford Brookes University

Richards, L. (1990) *Nobody's Home: Dreams and Realities in a New Suburb*, Melbourne: Oxford University Press

Richards, M. (1999) 'The interests of children at divorce', in G. Allan (ed.) *The Sociology of the Family: A Reader*, Oxford: Blackwell

Risman, B. and Johnson-Sumerford, D. (1998) 'Doing it fairly: a study of postgender marriages', *Journal of Marriage and the Family*, 60(Feb), pp. 23–40

Riviere, P. (1985) 'Unscrambling parenthood: the Warnock report', *Anthropology Today*, 1:4, pp. 2–7

Robertson, A.F. (1991) *Beyond the Family: The Social Organisation of Human Reproduction*, Cambridge: Polity Press

Robertson Elliot, R. (1996) *Gender, Family and Society*, Basingstoke: Macmillan

Robinson, M. and Smith, D. (1993) *Step by Step*, Hemel Hempstead: Harvester Wheatsheaf

Rodgers, B. and Pryor, J. (1998) *Divorce and Separation: The Outcomes for Children*, York: Joseph Rowntree Foundation

Rose, N. (1989) *Governing the Soul: The Shaping of the Private Self*, London: Routledge

Ruddick, S. (1996) *Maternal Thinking: Towards a Politics of Peace*, Boston: Beacon Press

Scott, J. (1997) 'Changing households in Britain: do families still matter?', *Sociological Review*, 45:4, pp. 590–620

Scott, J. (2000) 'Class and stratification', in G. Payne (ed.) *Social Divisions*, Basingstoke: Macmillan

Scott, S., Jackson, S. and Backett-Milburn, K. (1998), 'Swings and roundabouts: risk anxiety and the everyday worlds of children', *Sociology*, 32:4, pp. 689–706

Sevenhuijsen, S. (1998) *Citizenship and the Ethics of Care: Feminist Considerations on Justice, Morality and Politics*, London: Routledge

Sevenhuijsen, S. (2000) 'Caring in the third way: the relation between obligation, responsibility and care in Third Way discourse', *Critical Social Policy*, 20:1, pp. 5–37

Shore, C. (1992) 'Virgin births and sterile debates: anthropology and the new reproductive technologies', *Current Anthropology*, 33:3, pp. 295–301

Shotter, J. (1993) 'Psychology and citizenship: identity and belonging', in B.S. Turner (ed.) *Citizenship and Social Theory*, London: Sage

Silva, E.B. and Smart, C. (1999) 'The "new" practices and politics of family life', in E.B. Silva and C. Smart (eds) *The New Family?*, London: Sage

Simpson, B. (1998) *Changing Families: An Ethnographic Approach to Divorce and Separation*, Oxford: Berg

Simpson, B., Corlyon, J., McCarthy, P. and Walker, J. (1993) *Post-Divorce Fatherhood: A Study*, Family and Community Dispute Research Centre Working Paper, Newcastle: University of Newcastle

Simpson, B., Walker, J. and McCarthy, P. (1995) *Being There: Fathers After Divorce*, Newcastle: Relate Centre for Family Studies

Skeggs, B. (1997) *Formations of Class and Gender*, Routledge: London

Smart, C. (1991) 'The legal and moral ordering of child custody', *Journal of Law and Society*, 18:4, pp. 485–500

Smart, C. (1997) 'Wishful thinking and harmful tinkering? Sociological reflections on family policy', *Journal of Social Policy*, 26:3, pp. 301–22

Smart, C. (1999) 'The "new" parenthood: fathers and mothers after divorce', in E.B. Silva and C. Smart (eds) *The New Family?*, London: Sage

Smart, C. and Neale, B. (1999) *Family Fragments?*, Cambridge: Polity Press

Smart, C., Neale, B. and Wade, A. (1999) 'Objects of concern? – children and divorce', *Child and Family Law Quarterly*, 11:4, pp. 365–76

Smart, C., Neale, B. and Wade, A. (2001) *The Changing Experience of Childhood*, Cambridge: Polity Press

Smith, D. (1990) *Stepmothering*, Hemel Hempstead: Harvester Wheatsheaf

Song, M. and Edwards, R. (1997) 'Comment: raising questions about perspectives on Black lone motherhood', *Journal of Social Policy*, 26:2, pp. 233–44

Stacey, J. (1990) *Brave New Families*, New York: Basic Books

Stacey, J. (1992) 'Backward toward the postmodern family: reflections on gender, kinship and class in the Silicon valley', in B. Thorne and M. Yalom (eds) *Rethinking the Family: Some Feminist Questions*, 2nd edn, Boston: Northeastern University Press

Stern, P. (1978) *Stepfather Families: Integration Around Child Discipline*, New York: McGraw Hill

Strathern, M. (1992a) *After Nature: English Kinship in the Late Twentieth Century*, Cambridge: Cambridge University Press

Strathern, M. (1992b) *Reproducing the Future: Anthropology, Kinship and the New Reproductive Technologies*, Manchester: Manchester University Press

Sullivan, O. (1997) 'The division of housework among "remarried" couples', *Journal of Family Issues*, 18:2, pp. 205–23

Sweeting, H. (2001) 'Our family, whose perspective? An investigation of children's family life and health', *Journal of Adolescence*, 24:2, pp. 229–50

Thompson, E.P. (1981) *The Making of the English Working Class*, Harmondsworth: Penguin

Thompson, L. (1991) 'Family work: women's sense of fairness', *Journal of Family Issues*, 12:2, pp. 181–96

Tosh, J. (1996) 'Authority and nurture in middle-class fatherhood: the case of early and mid-Victorian England', *Gender and History*, 8:10, pp. 48–64

Trollope, J. (1998) *Other People's Children*. London: Black Swan

Tronto, J. (1989) 'Women and caring: what can feminists learn about morality from caring?', in A. Jaggar and S. Bordo (eds) *Gender/Body/Knowledge: Feminist Reconstructions of Being and Knowing*, New Brunswick: Rutgers University Press

Van Every, J. (1991–92) 'Who is the Family? The assumptions of British social policy', *Critical Social Policy*, 11:3(33), pp. 62–75

Visher, E. and Visher, J. (1979) *Stepfamilies: A Guide to Working With Stepparents and Stepchildren*, New York: Brunner/Mazel

Visher, J. (1984) 'Seven myths about stepfamilies', *Medical Aspects of Human Sexuality*, 18:1, pp. 52–80

Walker, M.U. (1997) 'Picking up pieces: lives, stories and integrity', in D.T. Meyers (ed.) *Feminists Rethink the Self*, Oxford: Westview Press

Walkerdine, V. (1996) 'Working Class Women: Psychological and Social Aspects of Survival', in S. Wilkinson (ed.) *Feminist Social Psychologies: International Perspectives*, Buckingham: Open University Press

Walkerdine, V. and Lucey, H. (1989) *Democracy in the Kitchen: Regulating Mothers and Socialising Daughters*, London: Virago

Walkover, B.C. (1992) 'The family as an overwrought object of desire', in G.C. Rosenwald and R. Ochberg (eds) *Storied Lives: The Cultural Politics of Self-Understanding*, New Haven: Yale University Press

Wallman, S. (1978) 'The boundaries of "race": processes of ethnicity in England', *Man*, 13:2, pp. 200–17

Wardle, L.D. (1993) 'The evolving rights and duties of step-parents: making new rules for new families', in J. Eekelaar and P. Sarcevic (eds) *Parenthood in Modern Society*, Dordrecht: Kluwer Academic Publishers

Warin, J., Solomon, Y., Lewis, C. and Langford, W. (1999) *Fathers, Work and Family Life*, London: Joseph Rowntree Foundation/Family Policy Studies Centre

Weeks, J., Donovan, C. and Heaphy, B. (2001) *Same Sex Intimacies: Families of Choice and Other Life Experiments*, London: Routledge

White, R., Carr, P. and Lowe, N. (1990) *A Guide To the Children Act 1989*, London: Butterworths

Wong, D.B. (1996) 'On care and justice within the family', in N.E. Snow (ed.) *In the Company of Others: Perspectives on Community, Family and Culture*, Lanham, Md.: Rowman and Littlefield

Woodhead, M. (1990) 'Psychology and the cultural construction of children's needs', in A. James and A. Prout (eds) *Constructing and Reconstructing Childhood: Contemporary Issues in the Sociological Study of Childhood*, Brighton: Falmer

Index